Rescued by...
DOS

Kris Jamsa

a division of Kris Jamsa Software, Inc.

Rescued by Word for Windows

Published by
Jamsa Press
2821 High Sail Ct.
Las Vegas, NV 89117
U.S.A.

For information about the translation or distribution of any Jamsa Press book, please write to Jamsa Press at the address listed above.

Rescued by DOS

Copyright 1993 by Jamsa Press. All right reserved. Except as permitted under the Copyright Act of 1976, no part of this publication may be reproduced or distributed in any format or by any means, or stored in a database or retrieval system, without the prior written permission of Jamsa Press.

Printed in the United States of America.
98765432

ISBN 0-9635851-6-9

Publisher
Debbie Jamsa

Copy Editor
Paul Medoff

Composition
Phil Schmauder

Cover Design
Jeff Wolfley & Associates

Layout Design
Discovery Computing

Technical Editor
Phil Schmauder

Illustrator
Phil Schmauder

Indexer
Ken Cope

Photography
O'Gara/Bissell

This book identifies product names and services known to be trademarks or registered trademarks of their respective companies. They are used throughout this book in an editorial fashion only. In addition, terms suspected of being trademarks or service marks have been appropriately capitalized. Jamsa Press cannot attest to the accuracy of this information. Use of a term in this book should not be regarded as affecting the validity of any trademark or service mark.

The information and material contained in this book are provided "as is," without warranty of any kind, express or implied, including without limitation any warranty concerning the accuracy, adequacy, or completeness of such information or material or the results to be obtained from using such information or material. Neither Jamsa Press nor the author shall be responsible for any claims attributable to errors, omissions, or other inaccuracies in the information or material contained in this book, and in no event shall Jamsa Press or the author be liable for direct, indirect, special, incidental, or consequential damages arising out of the use of such information or material.

This publication is designed to provide accurate and authoritative information in regard to the subject matter covered. It is sold with the understanding that the publisher is not engaged in rendering professional service or endorsing particular products or services. If legal advice or other expert assistance is required, the services of a competent professional should be sought.

Table of Contents

Section One - Getting Started with DOS ... 1
- Lesson 1 - What is DOS? ... 2
- Lesson 2 - Turning Your System On and Off ... 7
- Lesson 3 - Executing DOS Commands and Running Other Programs ... 11
- Lesson 4 - Learning Basic Troubleshooting Techniques ... 15

Section Two - Understanding and Working with Files ... 20
- Lesson 5 - Working with Files ... 21
- Lesson 6 - Fundamental File Operations ... 26
- Lesson 7 - Working with Groups of Files ... 30
- Lesson 8 - Working with Files on Other Drives ... 34

Section Three - Understanding Directories ... 39
- Lesson 9 - Organizing Your Files Using Directories ... 40
- Lesson 10 - Creating and Traversing Directories ... 45
- Lesson 11 - Working with Files and Directories ... 54
- Lesson 12 - Advanced Directory-Manipulation Commands ... 57
- Lesson 13 - Defining a Command Path ... 60

Section Four - DOS Batch Files ... 64
- Lesson 14 - Getting Started with DOS Batch Files ... 65
- Lesson 15 - Controlling Batch File Messages ... 69
- Lesson 16 - Common Batch Commands ... 73
- Lesson 17 - Using Batch Parameters ... 77
- Lesson 18 - Decision-Making Batch Files ... 81
- Lesson 19 - Automatically Executing Commands in AUTOEXEC.BAT ... 88

Section Five - Getting to Know Your Hardware ... 92
- Lesson 20 - Common PC Hardware ... 93
- Lesson 21 - Using Your Keyboard ... 97
- Lesson 22 - Using Your Monitor ... 101
- Lesson 23 - Working with a Mouse ... 104
- Lesson 24 - Working with a Printer ... 107
- Lesson 25 - Understanding Computer Ports ... 111
- Lesson 26 - Storing Information on Disks ... 115
- Lesson 27 - Working with a Floppy Disk ... 118
- Lesson 28 - Working with a Hard Disk ... 124

Section Six - Customizing DOS with CONFIG.SYS 128
- Lesson 29 - Understanding CONFIG.SYS 129
- Lesson 30 - Common CONFIG.SYS Settings 133
- Lesson 31 - Working with Device Drivers 138
- Lesson 32 - Controlling CONFIG.SYS Processing 141

Section Seven - Taking Advantage of the PC's Memory 144
- Lesson 33 - Understanding PC Memory 145
- Lesson 34 - Understanding the PC's Memory Types 149
- Lesson 35 - Using Extended Memory 154
- Lesson 36 - Using the High Memory Area 158
- Lesson 37 - Using Expanded Memory 162
- Lesson 38 - Using Upper Memory 165
- Lesson 39 - Configuring Your Memory Use with MemMaker 170

Section Eight - Using the DOS Shell 173
- Lesson 40 - Getting Started with the DOS Shell 174
- Lesson 41 - Working with Files and Directories 178
- Lesson 42 - Running Programs Within the Shell 183
- Lesson 43 - Using the Task List 187

Section Nine - Backing Up Your Files 189
- Lesson 44 - Understanding Disk Backups 190
- Lesson 45 - Performing Full Disk Backup 194
- Lesson 46 - Performing an Incremental Backup 198
- Lesson 47 - Restoring Files from Your Backup Disks 201
- Lesson 48 - Creating a Backup Policy 205

Section Ten - Preventing Disaster and Improving System Performance 208
- Lesson 49 - Detecting Computer Viruses 209
- Lesson 50 - Undeleting a Deleted File 213
- Lesson 51 - Unformatting a Disk 217
- Lesson 52 - Using SCANDISK to Examine Your Disk's Health 221
- Lesson 53 - Correcting Fragmented Files 224
- Lesson 54 - Improving System Performance with SMARTDRV 228

Section Eleven - Increasing Your Disk Capacity 233
- Lesson 55 - Understanding the DBLSPACE Command 234
- Lesson 56 - Installing DBLSPACE on Your Hard Disk 237
- Lesson 57 - Removing DBLSPACE to Decompress a Drive 240
- Lesson 58 - DBLSPACE and Floppy Disks 243

Section One

GETTING STARTED WITH DOS

When you first turn on your computer's power, a special program named DOS, the Disk Operating System, is the first to run. DOS in turn, lets you run other programs, store information on disk, and use hardware devices such as your printer. Over 100 million PCs currently run DOS! In this section you will learn how to start your computer and, in turn, DOS. After your computer starts, you will learn how to execute your first DOS commands!

Lesson 1 What is DOS?

Lesson 2 Turning Your System On and Off

Lesson 3 Executing DOS Commands and Running Other Programs

Lesson 4 Learning Basic Troubleshooting Techniques

Lesson 1

What is DOS?

Each time you turn on your PC, a special program called the operation system runs. The operating system, in turn, lets you run other programs, such as your word processor or spreadsheet. DOS is the PC (IBM-compatible) operating system. Over 120 million PCs currently run DOS! Whether you use your computer to run accounting software, Microsoft Windows, or even computer games, the first program your computer will run is DOS. This lesson examines DOS, your computer's *disk operating system*. By the time you finish this lesson you will understand

- What is DOS and what DOS does for you
- Why you need to understand DOS, even if you normally run Windows
- The difference between different DOS versions
- What DOS normally looks like to the user

DOS: YOUR COMPUTER'S DISK OPERATING SYSTEM

Software (computer programs) is simply files that contain instructions your computer performs to accomplish a specific task. Your computer's operating system is nothing more than a special software program that oversees your computer's operation. In general, the operating system is your computer's boss, overseeing which programs can run and how information is stored on your disks.

DOS is an acronym for Disk Operating System. Since 1981, DOS has become the most widely-used software program of all time. Almost every PC sold today ships with DOS preinstalled. No matter how you use your computer, you need to understand several key DOS commands and concepts.

STARTING (BOOTING) DOS

Each time you turn on your computer, DOS will automatically start. You won't have to anything special except turn on your computer's power. Many users refer to the process of starting as *booting* DOS. Should someone tell you to "boot your system" or to "boot DOS," they are telling you to turn on your computer. DOS, like all software programs, resides on your computer's disk. Before your computer can run a program, the program must reside in your computer's memory. When you first turn on your PC's power, your PC automatically loads DOS into your computer's memory, as shown in Figure 1.1.

1: What is DOS?

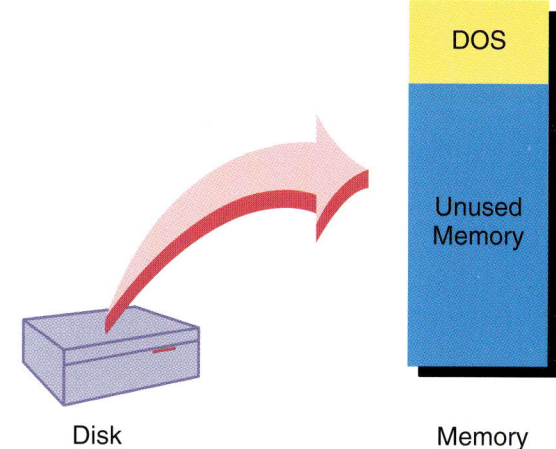

Figure 1.1 *Your computer loads DOS from disk into memory.*

After DOS resides in your computer's memory, DOS will let you run other program and store and retrieve information using files that reside on your disk.

DOS LETS YOU RUN OTHER PROGRAMS

DOS lets you run other programs, such as your word processor or even a video game. When you run a program, DOS loads the program from disk into your computer's memory, as shown in Figure 1.2.

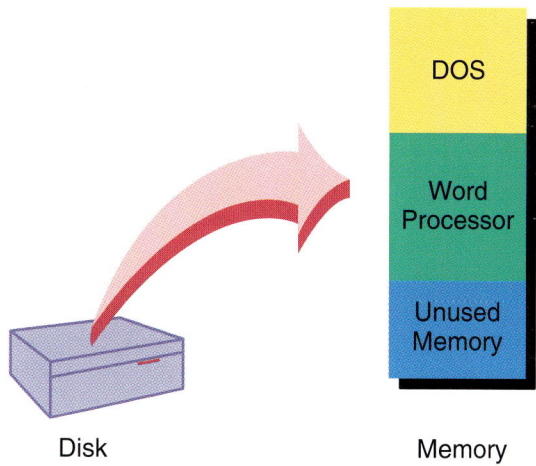

Figure 1.2 *DOS loads the programs you run from disk into memory.*

DOS only lets you run one program at a time. Thus, if you are using your word processor and you need information stored in your spreadsheet, you must first end your word processing program. Next, you must direct DOS to load your spreadsheet program into your computer's memory so the program can run.

Each program you run in DOS will have a unique name. To run the program, you will normally type in the program's name at the *DOS prompt* and press ENTER. The DOS prompt is a set of characters DOS displays when it is waiting for you to type in a command. Normally, the DOS prompt contains characters similar to those shown here:

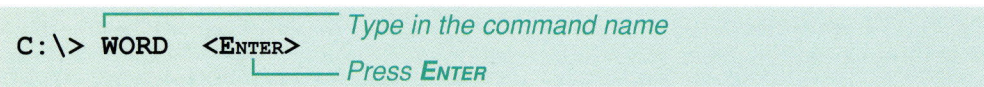

Assuming, for example, you want to run a word processor named Word, you would type **WORD** at the DOS prompt and press ENTER, as shown here:

Most of the examples presented throughout this book show you how to execute commands at the DOS prompt. However, as you will learn in Lesson 40, DOS also provides a menu-driven interface called the DOS Shell. Using the Shell, you can run programs by selecting different menu options. Figure 1.3 illustrates the DOS Shell user interface. A *user interface* is nothing more than a fancy name for the way your programs appear on the screen and steps you must perform to use them.

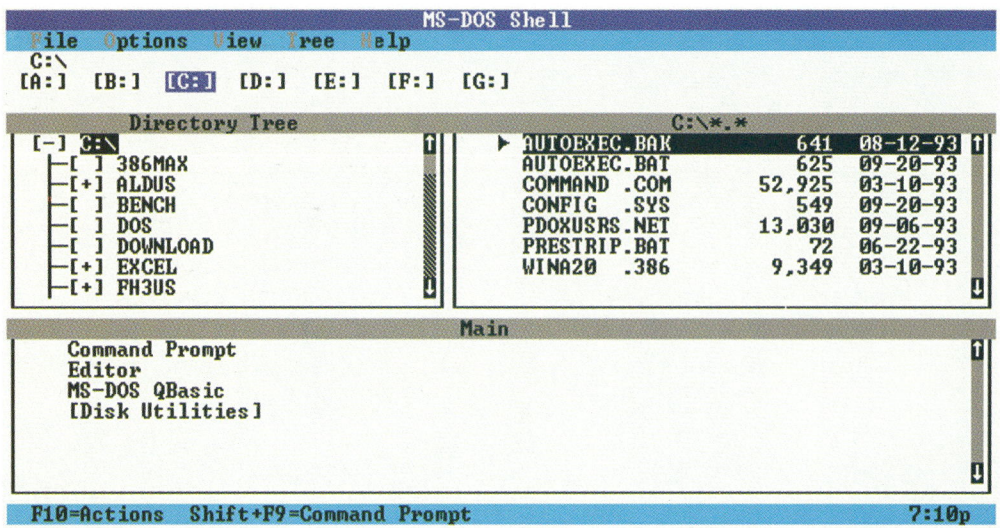

Figure 1.3 The DOS Shell user interface.

1: What is DOS?

WHY WINDOWS USERS NEED TO UNDERSTAND DOS

Over the past two years, Microsoft Windows has become one of fastest growing software programs. As Figure 1.4 shows, Windows replaces the DOS commands you type with easy-to-remember pictures, called *icons*, that you aim at with your computer's mouse.

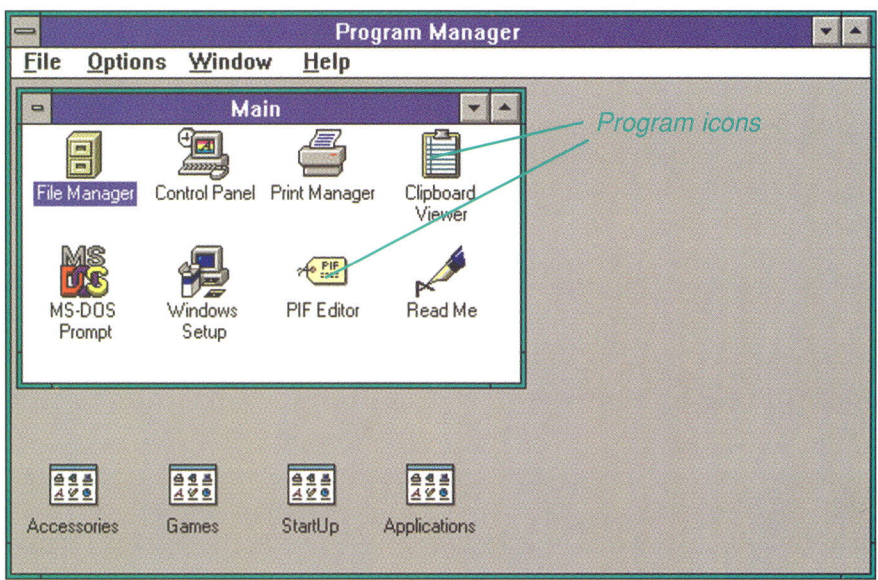

Figure 1.4 Microsoft Windows replaces keyboard commands with graphical icons.

By clicking your mouse on one of the icons, you can quickly run a program within Windows. In addition, you can run two or more programs at the same time from within Windows. Because of its ease of use, Windows has become very popular. Because Windows lets you run programs, you may be wondering why you need DOS. Windows, like DOS, is a software program—the only way you can run Windows is to first run DOS, which, as you have read is a special software loaded into memory by your computer. In addition to letting you run programs, DOS lets you store information on disk. When you use Windows to run programs, Windows uses DOS to help it store your files on disk. Thus, Windows is dependent on DOS. If you are not yet using Windows, you should try it. Most users find it very easy to use. For information on how to get started with Windows, turn to the book *Rescued by Windows*, Jamsa Press, 1993.

HOW ONE DOS VERSION DIFFERS FROM ANOTHER

DOS version 1.0 was originally released in 1981. As new capabilities were added to DOS, the version numbers changed to 1.1, 1.25, and 2.0, and so on through its current version of 6.2. DOS version numbers consist of two parts. As new features are added to DOS and new versions are released, you can use the first and second version numbers to determine the degree of change in new

Rescued by DOS

version. The first number (the 6 in 6.2), is the *major version number*. When the changes to DOS are significant, the DOS developers increment the major version number. For example, DOS 5.0 became 6.0. When the changes are minor, possibly containing fixes to errors in the previous version or only one or two new utilities, the developers increment the *minor version number* (after the decimal point). DOS 6.0, for example, might become 6.1.

Recently, Microsoft and IBM have both released versions of DOS. The IBM version is normally used on IBM-specific machines. The Microsoft version, on the other hand, is used by most PC compatibles. Early in 1993, Microsoft released version 6.0. Later in 93, IBM released its own version of DOS and named it 6.1. The IBM version was very similar to that of DOS 6.0 with some changes to key disk and memory management utilities. Several months later, Microsoft released an upgrade to its previous version 6.0, calling its new version 6.2. In general, versions 6.0, 6.1, and 6.2 are all very similar. If you did not look closely, you would have difficulty determining which version you are using—the features and capabilities are very similar.

In Lesson 55 you will learn that DOS 6 and later provides a special program named DBLSPACE, which lets you double the storage capacity of your disks. DOS version 6.0 was the first version to introduce the DBLSPACE command. Unfortunately, the program encountered errors that caused users to lose the information stored on their disk. The DBLSPACE command provided with version 6.2 corrects these errors. If you are not yet using version 6.2 but you are running DBLSPACE, you should upgrade to DOS 6.2 as soon as possible.

WHAT YOU NEED TO KNOW

In Lesson 2 you will learn how to start your computer and hence, DOS. Before you continue with Lesson 2, make sure that you have learned the following:

- ☑ DOS is the PC operating system. Over 120 million computers currently run DOS. When you turn on your computer's power, your computer will load DOS from disk into your computer's memory. The process of starting DOS is often referred to as booting DOS.

- ☑ Before a program can run, the program must reside in your computer's memory. When you run a program, DOS will load the program from disk into memory. DOS lets you run one only program at a time.

- ☑ To run a program in DOS, you normally type in the program's name at the DOS prompt and press ENTER. The DOS prompt is a unique set of characters such as **C:\>** that DOS displays when it is waiting for you to type in a command.

- ☑ Even if you run all your programs from within Windows, you must still run DOS first. Windows, like all programs must be loaded from disk into memory by DOS and uses DOS to store files on disk.

2: Turning Your System On and Off

Lesson 2

Turning Your System On and Off

You have learned that when your turn on your computer, DOS is the first program that runs. In this lesson you will learn how to start your computer and DOS. You will also learn the operations your computer performs each time your system starts and when it's OK to turn off your PC's power. By the time you end this lesson you will understand how to

- Start your computer, and hence DOS
- Recognize common programs that DOS runs automatically when you start your system
- Know when it is safe to turn off your computer's power

TURNING ON YOUR SYSTEM POWER

Your computer's system unit, monitor, and printer each have their own on and off switches. When you start your computer, you can turn on the power of these devices in any order. When you first turn on your computer's power, your computer will start testing its own internal components. This test, called the *power-on self-test* helps your computer determine if any of its electronic components have been damaged. As your computer performs this test, it will display a count of your computer's working memory on your screen:

```
1024 Kb
```

If the computer's self-test is successful, you might hear one beep. Next, you might hear your computer's disk drive as your computer reads DOS from disk into your computer's memory. If your computer does not successfully start, turn to Lesson 4, which discusses several troubleshooting steps you can perform to determine the cause of the error. To start your system, remove any floppy disks that might currently be in a floppy drive and then turn on your computer's power.

LEARNING TO RECOGNIZE DOS

As you will learn in Lesson 19, DOS lets you specify one or more programs that automatically run each time your system starts. Thus, the programs that run when you turn on your computer might differ, depending on the person who set up your system. This section covers several of the most common possibilities.

Rescued by DOS

DOS Starts Displaying the System Prompt

In many cases, DOS will start without first running any programs. Instead, DOS will display letters similar to the following:

```
C:\>
```

The characters **C:\>** are called the *DOS prompt*. DOS displays its prompt each time it is ready for you to type in a command. For now, press the ENTER key several times. DOS will continually display its prompt, waiting for you to issue a command:

```
C:\>   <ENTER>

C:\>   <ENTER>

C:\>
```

Should your system display the DOS prompt, you are ready to continue your reading with the section titled "Running DOS Commands."

> #### Understanding the DOS Prompt
>
> As you learned in Lesson 1, DOS lets you run programs such as your word processor or spreadsheet. In addition, DOS provides several built-in commands. To let you know that it is ready for you to issue a command, DOS displays a special prompt, such as the characters **C:\>**. To run a program, you simply type the program's name at the DOS prompt and press ENTER. When the program ends, DOS will redisplay its prompt, waiting for you to issue another command.

DOS Starts the DOS Shell

Figure 2.1 illustrates a special program called the DOS Shell. As you will learn in Lesson 40, the DOS Shell lets you run programs, copy files, and perform other common operations with easy-to-use menus. This type of program is called a *graphical interface*.

If DOS displays this Shell, press the **F3** function key to end the Shell program. DOS will then display its prompt, as previously discussed.

2: Turning Your System On and Off

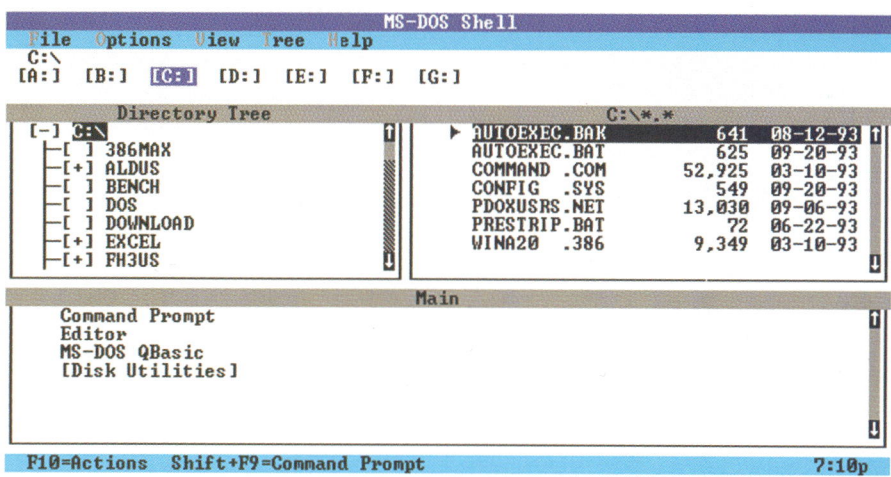

Figure 2.1 The DOS Shell.

DOS STARTS THE WINDOWS PROGRAM

Figure 2.2 illustrates Microsoft Windows, a very popular software program that replaces difficult commands with easy-to-use pictures. To run a program within Windows, you aim your mouse pointer at a picture that corresponds to the program and you click the mouse select button. In addition, Windows makes the operations you normally perform from the DOS prompt available as menu options.

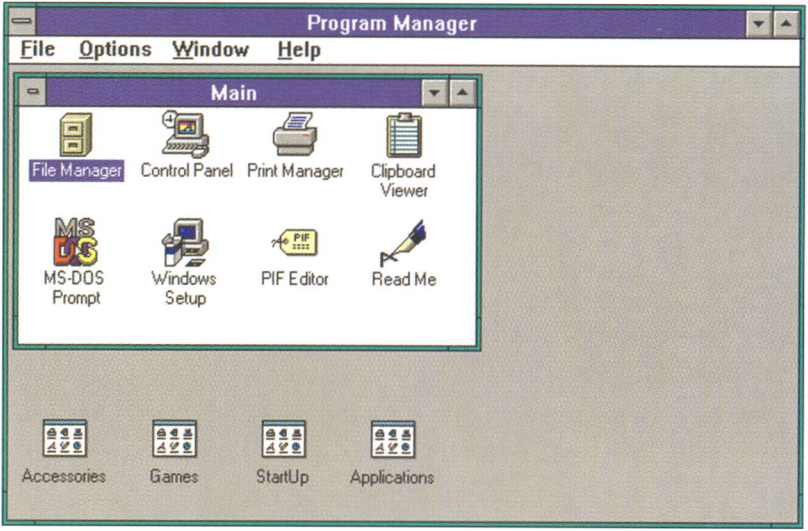

Figure 2.2 The Windows graphical interface.

9

Rescued by DOS

To end the Windows program, hold down the key labeled ALT and, while holding it down, press the F4 function key. Windows will display a box on your screen asking you if you want to end the Windows session. Press ENTER to select the OK option. Windows will end, and DOS will display its system prompt, waiting for you to type in your next command.

DOS Runs a Different Program

A *shell program* is a program that lets you run other programs by selecting the program from a menu of options. Should your computer automatically run a shell program other than the DOS Shell, end the program to the DOS prompt. Many such shell programs provide an Exit menu option. Those that don't might let you press a specific function key to end the program. Examine your screen for an indication of the key you need to press to exit the program. When the program ends, DOS will display its prompt, waiting for you to issue your next command.

Turning Off Your Computer

As a rule, you should only turn off your computer when DOS is displaying its system prompt. Do not turn off your computer while a program is running. Doing so can damage your disk or the files your disk contains. Always end the current program and return to the DOS prompt before you turn off your computer. When DOS is displaying its prompt, it is OK to turn off your system.

> ### Never Turn Off Your Computer When a Program Is Running
>
> When you have finished working with your computer, always end the current program, returning to the DOS prompt before you turn off your computer. If you turn off your computer while another program is running, you risk damaging your disk and the files your disk contains. When the DOS prompt is displayed, it is safe to turn off your computer.

What You Need to Know

Lesson 3 discusses how to run DOS commands and other programs. Before you continue with Lesson 3, make sure that you have learned the following:

- ☑ When you first turn on your computer's power, your computer runs its power-on self-test. During the self-test, you computer examines its internal electronic components, displaying on the screen the amount of working memory the PC contains.

- ☑ If the self-test is successful, your computer will start DOS. Depending on the individual who installed DOS on your system, DOS might display its prompt, or DOS might run another program, such as the DOS Shell or Microsoft Windows.

- ☑ Never turn off your computer's power while a program other than DOS is running. Doing so risks damage to your disk and the files it contains.

Lesson 3

Executing DOS Commands and Running Other Programs

To perform useful work, your computer must run software (programs). Your software might be a word processor that lets you create memos or letters, a spreadsheet program with which you track your company's budget, or even a DOS command itself. As you have learned, DOS lets you run programs. To run a program, you type in the program's name at the DOS prompt and press ENTER. When the program ends, DOS will redisplay its prompt and will wait for you to type your next command. This lesson examines the steps you will perform to run your software. By the time you finish this lesson you will understand how to

- Execute DOS commands at the DOS prompt
- Run software programs such as your word processor
- Read and understand DOS error messages that relate to program execution

UNDERSTANDING SOFTWARE

Software, or computer programs, is simply a list of instructions the computer performs to accomplish a specific task. Software ranges from business programs to computer games. Regardless of the program's purpose, software is nothing more than a list of instructions, similar to those you might find in a cookbook. In the case of the software, however, the computer, not the cook, performs each instruction. Think of your software as having two names—the one on the box, such as WordPerfect, and one that you will type to run the software. The name that you type is normally an abbreviation of the software's box name. In the case of the WordPerfect word processor, for example, you type **WP** to run the program. Likewise, for Microsoft Windows, you would type **WIN**. Table 3.1 lists several popular software programs (their box name) and the name you type to run the program.

Program	Command to Run the Program
Crosstalk	CCM
Lotus 1-2-3	123
Microsoft Windows	WIN
Microsoft Word	WORD
Quicken	Q
WordPerfect	WP
XTree Gold	XTGOLD

Table 3.1 Software box names and command names.

Rescued by DOS

Programs use these abbreviated names for two reasons. First, the shorter name reduces the amount of typing you must perform to run the program. Second, as you will learn later, in Lesson 5, DOS restricts the number of characters in a filename to eight characters—you won't encounter program names that are longer than eight characters.

As you read in Lesson 2, DOS will display error messages on your screen that explain why a specific operation could not be performed. Assume, for example, that you want to run your WordPerfect word processor and you type **WordPerfect** at the DOS prompt. DOS will display the **Bad command or file name** error message, as shown here:

```
C:\> WordPerfect   <ENTER>
Bad command or file name
```

In this case, the error message tells you that your command is bad. The correct command you should have typed is **WP**, the command name. By taking time to read and understand the error message, you can now refer to your software documentation to determine the correct command.

Understanding Program Names

To execute a program, you type the program's name at the DOS prompt. The program name might not match the product name that appears on your software box. Instead, most programs use an abbreviated name. The documentation that accompanies your program will always provide you with the abbreviated name.

Software Resides on Your Computer's Disk

Before you can run a software program, the program must reside on your disk. When you purchase a software program, the box will normally contain a set of floppy disks that you install on your hard disk. Normally, within the box that contained the software you fill find step-by-step instructions you must follow to install the software on to your hard disk. After the program is installed, you can type the program's command name at the DOS prompt to run it. DOS in turn, will read the program from your disk into your computer's memory. A program must reside in your computer's memory before it can run. If you try to run a program that has not yet been installed on your disk, DOS will be unable to find the software. As a result, DOS will display the **Bad command or file name** message previously shown. Thus, if you know the command to start Microsoft Windows is **WIN** and each time you type the command DOS displays the **Bad command or file name** message, the software might not yet be installed on your system.

Also, as you will learn in Lesson 9, DOS lets you divide your disk into directories, to improve the organization of files on your disk. Conceptually, directories are similar to drawers and folders in a filing cabinet. Using directories, you can organize related information. In some cases, users will try

3: Executing DOS Commands and Running Other Programs

to run a program that is stored in a different directory and DOS will display the **Bad command or file name** message. In such cases, the problem is not that the software is not installed on your disk, but rather, that DOS cannot find it. In Lesson 10 you will learn how to move from one directory to another. Likewise, in Lesson 13 you will learn ways to tell DOS how to find your commonly used commands without your having to move into the different directories.

> *RUNNING COMPUTER PROGRAMS*
>
> Before your computer can execute a program, the program must reside in your computer's electronic memory. When you type in a program's command name at the DOS prompt, DOS will load the program from disk into memory. After the program ends, DOS will redisplay its prompt. When you run a second program, DOS will then load that program into memory.

TRYING OUT A FEW DOS COMMANDS

You have learned that, after DOS starts, it will normally display a command prompt such as **C:\>**. To execute a command, you type the command's name at the prompt and press ENTER. For example, in Lesson 2 you typed the **CLS** (clear screen) command, which erases your screen's current contents:

```
C:\> CLS   <ENTER>
```

Next, the DOS **DATE** command lets you display or change the current date. To use the DATE command, type **DATE** at the DOS prompt and press ENTER:

```
C:\> DATE   <ENTER>
```

The DATE command will display what it thinks to be the current date and will prompt you for a new date, as shown here:

```
Current date is Tue 11-16-1993
Enter new date (mm-dd-yy):
```

If the date displayed is correct, you can press ENTER to leave the date unchanged. The DATE command will then end, and DOS will redisplay its prompt. However, if the date is not correct, type in the correct date in the form mm-dd-yy. For example, to type in the date December 25, 1993, you would type **12-25-93**. When you press ENTER, the DATE command will update your computer's date, and the program will end.

13

Rescued by DOS

In a similar way, the DOS **TIME** command lets you display and change the current time. To use the TIME command, type **TIME** at the DOS prompt and press ENTER:

```
C:\> TIME    <ENTER>
```

The TIME command will display what it thinks to be the current time and will prompt you for a new time as shown here:

```
Current time is  8:56:49.84a
Enter new time:
```

As before, if the time displayed is correct, press ENTER to end the TIME command. If the time is not correct, you can type in the current time using a 24-hour (military) format or by typing the time followed by an A (for AM) or a P (for PM). For example, to set the time to 1:45 PM, you type **13:45** or **1:45P**. When you press ENTER, the TIME command will update your computer's current time.

Note: *The TIME command lets you specify hours, minutes, seconds, and even hundredths of a second. You must specify hour and minutes. If you don't specify seconds or hundredths of seconds, TIME will use the value 0 for each.*

What You Need to Know

In Lesson 4 you will learn several steps you can perform to troubleshoot problems when your computer starts, as well as problems when you run different commands. Before you continue with Lesson 4, make sure that you have learned the following:

- ☑ Software, or programs, is a list of instructions that tell the computer how to accomplish a specific task. Your software may be a word processor, spreadsheet, or even a computer game.

- ☑ Programs often have two names, the name on the box, such as WordPerfect, and the abbreviated name you type as a command, such as WP. To run a software program, you type in the program's command name at the DOS prompt and press ENTER.

- ☑ Before you can run a software program, the program must reside on your computer's disk. When you purchase software, the software normally comes on a floppy disk, which you install onto your computer's hard disk. The documentation that accompanied the software will provide you with step-by-step installation instructions.

- ☑ When you run a program, DOS loads the program from disk into your computer's electronic memory. When you end the program, DOS will redisplay its prompt and wait for your next command.

Lesson 4

Learning Basic Troubleshooting Techniques

When you turn on your computer, things don't always go as expected. In this lesson you will learn several steps you can perform to help determine why your system is not starting. By the time you finish this lesson, you will understand how to

- Search for and correct the primary causes that prevent your system from starting
- Learn to understand common DOS error messages

If your computer successfully starts, you might want to continue your reading with Lesson 5. However, the discussion presented in this lesson will cover error messages and problems you will eventually encounter, so you might want to spend a few moments reading this lesson's text.

TROUBLESHOOTING YOUR COMPUTER'S SELF-TEST

You learned in Lesson 2 that each time you turn on your computer's power, your PC runs an internal self-test. During the self-test, your computer examines its electronic components. Should the computer find a component that is not working, the computer might display an error message on your screen, sometimes telling you what to do next, such as press **F1**. Should an error message appear, write down the message on a sheet of paper so you can read it to your retailer later. In some cases, your computer might sound a series of long and short beeps. Count the number of beeps sounded and tell your retailer. Believe it or not, the beeps are meaningful to your retailer's technical support group.

Normally, as soon as you turn on your computer's power, you will hear your computer's fan start to whir. If you do not, check your computer's power cable to ensure that it is securely inserted. Next, double-check the power outlet with a working appliance to ensure that power is available. If the outlet is working, but your computer's power does not come on, your computer will require servicing.

As you have learned, during the power-on self-test, most PCs display the amount of working memory they contain. If your computer does not, your computer may be failing a test that occurs early in the self test. Double-check your monitor to ensure that it is properly connected to the PC, plugged in, and turned on. If your monitor is on and plugged in, notify your retailer that your computer is failing its self-test.

Rescued by DOS

> ### Passing the Power-On Self-Test
>
> If you can hear your computer's fan whirring, and your computer successfully displays the amount of working memory it contains, your computer is passing its internal power-on self-test. If your computer fails to start after passing the self-test, your computer might be experiencing a disk error. Record all messages displayed on your screen and provide them to your computer retailer.

Troubleshooting System Configuration Errors

To help your computer remember certain characteristics such as the current date and time and your disk, monitor, and keyboard type when its power is turned off, the PC uses a small battery called the *CMOS battery*. Periodically, the CMOS battery will die, and your system settings are lost. In such cases, your PC will display an error message during the system startup process. The CMOS battery resides inside your system unit. Should your CMOS battery fail, a local computer store can quickly replace the battery and restore your settings. Likewise, if you know an experienced user, you can purchase a CMOS battery and have the user help you replace the battery. Next, the user can help you reset your system's original settings.

Troubleshooting DOS Startup Errors

You learned in Lesson 2 that, after your computer successfully passes its power-on self-test, the PC will load DOS from disk into memory. If your floppy disk drives do not contain a disk and you have previously started DOS from your hard disk, the startup process will normally be successful. To load DOS into your computer's memory, your computer looks for DOS first on a floppy disk in drive A and then on a disk in drive C. Thus, if your floppy disk drive A contains a disk that doesn't have DOS on it, your computer will very likely display the following message:

```
Non-System disk or disk error
Replace and press any key when ready
```

Should this message appear, check your system to determine if drive A contains a floppy disk. If so, remove the disk and press any key to continue. If the disk in drive A does not contain a floppy, the special files that DOS needs in order to start have been deleted from drive C. Have an experienced DOS user start your system from floppy disk and restore the necessary files.

Finally, should your system display a message stating that it cannot find an operating system, DOS has not yet been installed on your hard disk. If your retailer provided you with DOS disks, follow the documentation included to successfully install DOS onto your hard disk.

4: Learning Basic Troubleshooting Techniques

TROUBLESHOOTING DOS ERROR MESSAGES

As you work with DOS, you will encounter different errors. As a rule, DOS normally displays a message describing the cause of the error. Your trick is to interpret the meaning of the error message so you can correct the situation. For example, you have learned that, to execute a command, you type the command's name at the DOS prompt. To clear your screen display, you would type **CLS** as shown here and press ENTER :

```
C:\> CLS   <ENTER>
```

If you accidentally mistype the command, as CSL, for example, DOS will display an error message, like this:

```
C:\> CSL   <ENTER>
Bad command or file name
```

In this case, the **Bad command or file name** message tells you that DOS could not find a command named CSL. If, as you type in different commands DOS displays this error message, the file containing the command might not reside in your disk's current directory. Lesson 9 discusses directories in detail. To execute your command, you might need to change directories.

In Lesson 6 you will learn to copy, rename, delete, and even display files that reside on your disk. At that time, DOS might display the message **File not found** when you execute a command. Should this message appear, double-check your spelling of the filename. Next, make sure the file resides in the current directory. As you work with the commands presented throughout this book, take time to examine the messages DOS displays. In general, you will encounter a small set of DOS error messages on a regular basis. To help you better understand these messages, the lessons in this book will describe the messages in detail as corresponding topics are discussed.

LEARNING MORE ABOUT DOS COMMANDS

The lessons presented throughout this book introduce many different DOS commands. If, as you execute DOS commands, you run into problems, you can learn more about the command using the HELP command:

```
C:\> HELP   <ENTER>
```

HELP, in turn, will display a menu of the available DOS commands as shown in Figure 4.1.

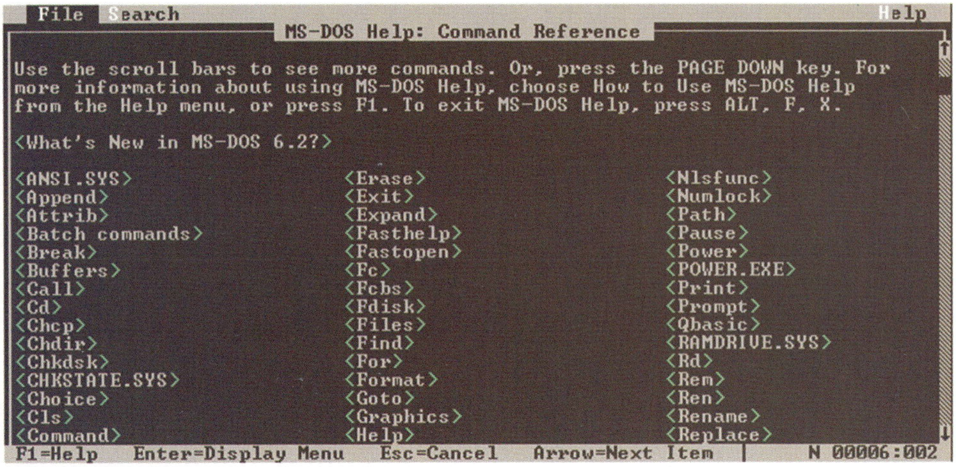

Rescued by DOS

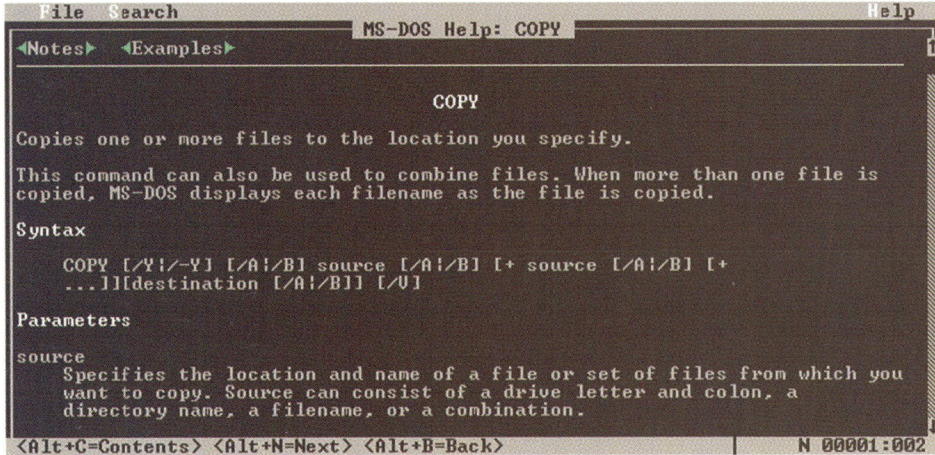

Figure 4.1 The HELP menu of commands.

To get help on a specific command, use your arrow keys to highlight the command name and press Enter. For example, if you highlight the Copy command name and press Enter, HELP will display a summary of the COPY command as shown in Figure 4.2.

Figure 4.2 HELP's summary of the COPY command.

4: Learning Basic Troubleshooting Techniques

HELP divides the information about a command into three parts: syntax, notes, and examples. The syntax discussion shows you the command's format and explains different command line switches. The notes discussion provides you with specifics about the command and when you might want to use different parameters and switches. The example section provides everyday examples of the command's use. To select a specific section, highlight the section name and press Enter:

To return to Help's main menu, press the Alt-C keyboard combination. To display the previous screen of information press Alt-B (for back). Likewise, to display the next screen of infomation, type Alt-N.

As you display information in Help, there may be times when you want to print a copy of the information. To print information about a topic, press Alt-F to select the file menu and choose Print. Lastly, to end your Help session, select the File menu and choose Exit.

WHAT YOU NEED TO KNOW

In Lesson 5 you will learn how to store information in files from one session to another. Before you continue with Lesson 5, make sure that you have learned the following:

- ☑ When your computer first starts, it performs its power-on self-test. If your computer identifies a component that is not working correctly, your computer might display an error message describing the error. Record the message and provide it to your computer retailer.

- ☑ To help your computer remember different system configuration information when the power is turned off, your computer uses a special CMOS battery. Over time, your CMOS battery might fail, and your system configuration will be lost. In such cases, you must purchase and install a new battery and reset your settings. Most new users should have their retailer perform the installation for them.

- ☑ As you work with DOS, you will encounter different error messages. Take time to examine the messages. The DOS manual that accompanied your computer may provide a listing of error messages and the steps you must perform to resolve them. In addition, several of the most common error messages are discussed throughout this book.

Section Two

Understanding and Working with Files

No matter which programs you run, you will eventually need to store information in files from one session to another. The information you store might be a letter you created using your word processor, a spreadsheet, or even the chapter of a book. Just as you use paper files within an office to store information, the computer lets you store electronic files on your disk. The lessons in this section examine files, how you name them, and common operations such as copying, renaming, moving, and even deleting files. Take time to read carefully each lesson presented in this section. As you use your computer, you will eventually need to copy files to floppy disks and locate files on your hard disk. The lessons discuss these operations in detail.

Lesson 5 Getting Started with Files

Lesson 6 Common File Operations

Lesson 7 Working with Groups of Files

Lesson 8 Working with Files on Other Drives

Lesson 5

Working with Files

No matter which programs you run on your computer, you will eventually store information within files on your computer's disk. The information might be a letter or report you created in a word processor, a monthly budget that you calculated in a spreadsheet program, or highest score in a new video game. If you don't store information within a file before turning off your computer, the information will be lost. Files exist to let you save information from one session at the computer to the next. This lesson covers the basics of working with files in DOS. By the time you finish this lesson you will understand how to

- Assign meaningful names to your files
- View the files stored on your disk
- Determine a file's size and the amount of space available on disk

UNDERSTANDING FILENAMES

If you work in an office that uses filing cabinets to store files, you have undoubtedly attached a label to a paper file and place the file into the cabinet. By assigning a unique name to a file, you can quickly locate the file when you need to use it in the future. When you store information on a disk, you place the information within a file. As was the case with the files in the office, you assign unique names to each file you create on your disk. When you work with DOS or any DOS-based program, such as your word processor or even Microsoft Windows, your *filenames* consist of two parts: an up-to-eight-character *basename* and an up-to-three-character *extension*. When you create a filename, you separate a the basename and extension using a period (BASENAME.EXT).

A FILE EXTENSION TELLS YOU THE TYPE OF INFORMATION A FILE CONTAINS

The up-to-three-character extension helps you determine the kind of information your file contains. If the file contains a memo, for example, you might use the MEM extension. Likewise, for a report, you might use RPT. In the case of word processing documents, most users use the DOC extension (an abbreviation for document). Table 5.1 lists several commonly used file extensions and their corresponding file contents.

Extension	File Contents
BAT	DOS batch file
COM	DOS command
DOC	Word processing document

Table 5.1 Common file extensions and their corresponding contents. (continued on next page)

Rescued by DOS

Extension	File Contents
EXE	Executable program file
LTR	A letter
MEM	A memo
RPT	A report
SYS	An operating system file
TXT	An ASCII text file

Table 5.1 Common file extensions and their corresponding contents. (continued from previous page)

THE BASENAME PROVIDES SPECIFICS ABOUT A FILE

The file's up-to-eight-character basename provides the specifics about a file. For example, if you are storing a budget report on disk, you might use the basename BUDGET. By examining the complete filename, BUDGET.RPT, you quickly gain an idea about the file's contents. In a similar way, a file named VACATION.MEM, very likely contains a memo about a company's vacation policy. The file that contained the text for this lesson of this book, for example, used the basename LESSON05. When you choose a filename, it is important that you pick a meaningful name that accurately describe the file's contents. In this way, you can quickly locate the file at a later time. In most cases, you should use all eight basename characters whenever possible to produce the most meaningful name. At first look, the six-character basename in BUDGET.RPT appears meaningful. However, using the last two letters, you could include the year for which the budget was created, such as BUDGET94.RPT. Also, as you create your filenames, try to use a consistent naming structure. For example, assume that you have stored the first five homework assignments from your Spanish class in the following files:

    SPAN_HW1.DOC   SPAN_HW2.DOC   SPAN_HW3.DOC
    SPAN_HW4.DOC   SPAN_HW5.DOC   SPAN_HW6.DOC

If you later change your naming format, such as HW7_SPAN.DOC, you will have difficulty organizing your files.

WHICH CHARACTERS ARE ALLOWED IN FILENAMES?

As you create your filenames, you can use underscore (_) characters to separate parts of a name. You cannot use blanks or spaces within a filename. In addition, you can use all the characters of the alphabet, the numbers 0 through 9, and the following characters:

    ~ ! @ # $ % ^ & ( ) - _ { } '

Using these characters, you can create meaningful the following filenames, as shown here:

    TODO!.LST   SALES$93.RPT   SALE&EXP.DOC

5: Working with Files

> ### UNDERSTANDING DOS FILENAMES
>
> DOS filenames consist of two parts: an up-to-eight-character basename and an up-to-three-character extension. DOS separates the basename and extension with a period, such as BASENAME.EXT. When you assign names to your files, you assign a meaningful basename that accurately describes the file's contents. The up-to-three-character extension describes the file's type. For example, the DOC extension is often used for word processing documents and the RPT extension might be used for reports.

LISTING THE FILES THAT RESIDE ON YOUR DISK

DOS stores the files on your disk in a directory. In the simplest sense, a directory is simply a list of filenames. To view the files that reside in a directory, you use the DIR command. Assuming, for example, that you are using DOS directory that contains your DOS commands, the DIR command would display output similar to the following:

```
C:\DOS> DIR   <ENTER>

 Volume in drive C has no label
 Volume Serial Number is 1B44-6A60
 Directory of C:\DOS

.              <DIR>        05-16-93    4:23a
..             <DIR>        05-16-93    4:23a
DBLSPACE BIN            64,246 09-27-93    6:20a
DBLSPACE EXE           176,424 09-27-93    6:20a
ANSI     SYS            9,065 09-27-93    3:59p
APPEND   EXE           10,774 09-27-93    3:37p
ATTRIB   EXE           11,208 09-27-93    3:38p
CHKDSK   EXE           12,241 09-27-93    3:39p
EDIT     COM              413 03-10-93    6:00a
   :        :             :        :        :
   :        :             :        :        :
TREE     COM            6,945 09-27-93    3:58p
UNDELETE EXE           26,416 08-04-93    9:16a
COMMAND  COM           54,500 09-27-93    6:20a
XCOPY    EXE           16,930 09-27-93    3:59p
      139 file(s)    5,817,429 bytes
                    96,169,984 bytes free
```

Annotations:
- Basename
- Extension
- File size
- File date and time stamp
- Number of files displayed
- Disk space the files consume
- Available disk space

23

Rescued by DOS

Unless told to do otherwise, the DIR command displays filename, file size in bytes, and the date and time each file was created or last changed (the file's date and time stamp). In addition DIR displays a count of the number of files displayed and the amount of disk space the files consume, as well as the amount of available space on the disk. File sizes, disk space consumed, and available disk space are expressed in terms of bytes. In the simplest sense, a byte is a character of information. A file that contains 512 bytes, for example, contains 512 characters of information. Use the following DIR command to display the files in the current directory:

```
C:\> DIR   <ENTER>
```

As you will learn in Lesson 9, your disk normally contains several different directories (file lists). For example, your DOS files reside in the directory name DOS, and your Windows files in a directory named WINDOWS.

To display the files that reside in a specific directory, include the directory name (preceded with a backslash) in the DIR command. For example, issue the following command to display the files that reside in the DOS directory:

```
C:\> DIR  \DOS   <ENTER>
```

As you type the DIR command, make certain that you precede the directory name with a backslash (\), or DOS will look for a file named DOS in the current directory.

> ### DISPLAYING FILES USING DIR
>
> DOS stores the files on your disk in directories. In the simplest sense, a directory is a list of files. To display the files that reside in the current directory, use the DIR command as shown here:
>
> ```
> C:\> DIR   <ENTER>
> ```
>
> The DIR command displays filenames, sizes, and the date and time each file was created or last changed. In addition, DIR displays the number of files in the directory, the amount of disk space that the files contain, and the amount of space available on your disk.

CONTROLLING HOW DIR DISPLAYS THE DIRECTORY LIST

Depending on the number of files in your directory, the file list might scroll past you faster than you can read it. If you include the /P switch in the DIR command, DIR will suspend its output with each screenful of filenames, displaying the following message at the end of the file list:

5: Working with Files

```
Press any key to continue . . .
```

The following DIR command, for example, uses the /P switch to display the files in the DOS directory one screen at a time:

```
C:\> DIR  \DOS  /P   <ENTER>
```

Note that the directory name is preceded by a backslash (\), while the /P switch is preceded by a forward slash.

When you are looking for a specific file, there may be times when you want DIR to display only filenames, suppressing the display the file size and date and time stamp. To display only filenames, invoke DIR using the /W switch as shown here:

```
C:\> DIR  \DOS  /W   <ENTER>
```

As you work with DOS, you will use the DIR command a lot! Take time now to experiment with the DIR commands presented in this lesson.

What You Need to Know

In Lesson 6 you will learn how to use the COPY, RENAME, DELETE, and TYPE commands with the files on your disk. Before you continue with Lesson 6, however, make sure you have learned the following:

- ☑ When you store information on your disk, you place the information in files. If you don't store information in files, the information is lost when you turn off your computer.

- ☑ Each file on your disk has a unique name. DOS filenames consist of two parts: an up-to-eight character basename and an up-to-three character extension. The basename should accurately describe the files contents. The up-to-three-character extension specifies the file's general type, such as a memo (MEM), report (RPT), or word processing document (DOC).

- ☑ DOS stores the files on your disks in directories. In the simplest sense, a directory is a list of filenames. The DIR command displays the name, size, and date and time a file was created or last changed for each file on your disk.

- ☑ If DIR's file list scrolls past you faster than you can read it, invoke DIR with the /P switch. DIR in turn, will suspend its output with each screenful of file, waiting for you to press a key before proceeding.

Lesson 6

Fundamental File Operations

When you store information in paper files, there are times when you must make copies of the file's contents, rename a file, and even throw away a file that is no longer needed. As it turns out, many of these operations also apply to the electronic files you store on your disk. This lesson examines the fundamental files operations you will use on a regular basis with DOS. By the time you finish this lesson, you will understand how to

- Copy one file's contents to another file
- Rename a file
- Delete a file that is no longer needed
- Display the contents of an ASCII file on your screen

No matter how you use your computer, you will perform the operations presented in this lesson a regular basis. Make sure you feel comfortable with each command's format before you continue.

COPYING A FILE'S CONTENTS

One of the most common file operations you will perform is copying one file's contents to another using the DOS COPY command. For example, assume that you want to make a copy of the file BUDGET94.RPT, naming the file copy BUDGET94.SAV. To perform the copy operation, you would use the following COPY command:

```
C:\> COPY  BUDGET94.RPT  BUDGET94.SAV  <ENTER>
```

If the COPY command successfully copies the file, COPY will display the following message:

```
1 file(s) copied
```

You can also copy the contents of a file to a different disk or directory and keep the same name. The following COPY command copies BUDGET94.RPT from drive C to the disk in drive A:

```
C:\> COPY  BUDGET94.RPT  A:  <ENTER>
      1 file(s) copied
```

5: Working with Files

> ### COPYING A FILE'S CONTENTS
>
> As you work with files there will be many times when you need to copy a file's contents to another file. To do so, you can issue the COPY command, as shown here:
>
> ```
> C:\> COPY   FILENAME.EXT   NEWCOPY.EXT   <ENTER>
> ```
>
> In this case, the COPY command will copy the contents of the file FILENAME.EXT, creating a new file named NEWCOPY.EXT.

When you use the COPY command to copy a file's contents, you need to be careful that you don't overwrite an existing file. Prior to DOS 6.2, if the filename you specify for the target of a COPY operation is in use for an existing file, DOS will overwrite the existing file's contents. For example, the following command copies the file PAYROLL.DAT to a file named BUDGET94.SAV:

```
C:\> COPY   PAYROLL.DAT   BUDGET94.SAV   <ENTER>
```

If the file BUDGET94.SAV already exists, the COPY command will overwrite the file's contents, and the file's previous contents will be lost. Beginning with DOS 6.2, however, the COPY command will display the following prompt before overwriting an existing file:

```
Overwrite BUDGET94.SAV (Yes/No/All)?
```

If you type **Y**, COPY will overwrite the file's contents. If you type **N**, the copy will not occur.

RENAMING A FILE

As you work with files, there will be times when you will need to rename a file. For example, assume that you want to rename the file RESCUED6.DOC as LESSON06.DOC. To do so, you would issue the following RENAME command:

```
C:\> RENAME   RESCUED6.DOC   LESSON06.DOC   <ENTER>
```

If the RENAME command is successful, DOS will immediately redisplay its prompt, as shown:

```
C:\> RENAME   RESCUED6.DOC   LESSON06.DOC   <ENTER>
C:\>
```

The RENAME command will not overwrite an existing file. If you try to rename a file using the name of an existing file, the operation will fail, as shown here:

27

Rescued by DOS

```
C:\> RENAME  FILENAME.EXT  LESSON06.DOC  <ENTER>
Duplicate file name or file not found
```

Because of RENAME's frequency of use, DOS lets you abbreviate RENAME as simply REN. As such, the following REN command is identical in function to the previous RENAME command:

```
C:\> REN RESCUED6.DOC  LESSON06.DOC  <ENTER>
```

> ### Renaming a File
>
> When you work with files, there will be times when you will need to rename a file. To rename a file, you can use the RENAME command, as shown here:
>
> ```
> C:\> RENAME  OLDNAME.EXT  NEWNAME.EXT  <ENTER>
> ```
>
> Because of its frequency of use, DOS lets you abbreviate the RENAME command as REN.

Deleting a File That Is No Longer Required

Just as there are times when you throw away a paper file that is no longer needed, there will be times when you will delete files from your disk. The following DEL command, for example, deletes a file named LESSON06.OLD:

```
C:\> DEL   LESSON06.OLD  <ENTER>
```

Because DEL removes files from your disk, you need to use the DEL command with care.

> ### Deleting a File from Your Disk
>
> There will be times when you will no longer need one or more files stored on your disk. To remove a file from your disk, you can use the DEL command. For example, the following command deletes a file named OLDINFO.DAT:
>
> ```
> C:\> DEL   OLDINFO.DAT  <ENTER>
> ```
>
> Should you accidentally delete a file you still need, you might be able to recover the file with the UNDELETE command.

6: Fundamental File Operations

DISPLAYING A FILE'S CONTENTS

Depending on the programs you run, you might create files on your disk that contain information in many different formats. For example, when you create a document with a word processor, the file will contain special characters that are meaningful only to the word processor. These special characters might control **boldface** or *italics*. In a similar way, spreadsheet and database programs might store information in their own formats. In later lessons you will create batch files, which contain the names of commands you want DOS to automatically execute. Likewise, in Lesson 29 you will create a file named CONFIG.SYS, which lets you customize how DOS loads itself in memory. These files are called ASCII files because they contain only standard characters, numbers, and punctuation symbols. To create an ASCII file you can use the EDIT command. The following TYPE command displays the contents of a file named CONFIG.SYS:

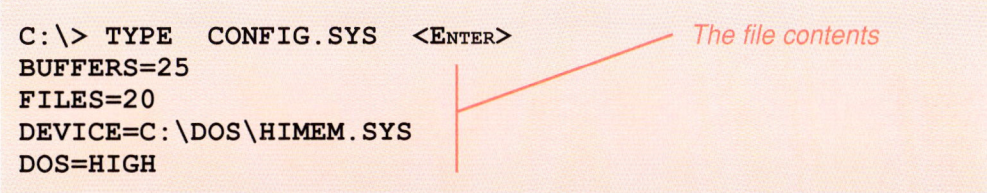

```
C:\> TYPE   CONFIG.SYS   <ENTER>         — The file contents
BUFFERS=25
FILES=20
DEVICE=C:\DOS\HIMEM.SYS
DOS=HIGH
```

> ### DISPLAYING AN ASCII FILE'S CONTENTS
>
> When you work with ASCII files, such as CONFIG.SYS or DOS batch files, you can display the file's contents with the TYPE command:
>
> ```
> C:\> TYPE   FILENAME.EXT   <ENTER>
> ```
>
> TYPE only displays the contents of an ASCII file. If you try to display the contents of a word processing document with TYPE, for example, special characters that have meaning only to the word processor will result in the display of strange characters on your screen display.

WHAT YOU NEED TO KNOW

In Lesson 7 you will learn to use wildcard characters to perform file operations on two or more files. Before you continue with Lesson 7, however, make sure you have learned the following:

- ☑ The DOS COPY command lets you copy one file's contents to another.
- ☑ To rename a file, use the RENAME command. Due to RENAME's frequency of use, DOS lets you abbreviate RENAME as simply REN.
- ☑ The DOS DEL command lets you delete files you no longer need from your disk.
- ☑ An ASCII file contains only letters, numbers, and punctuation symbols. Using the TYPE command, you can display an ASCII file's contents.

Lesson 7

Working with Groups of Files

In Lesson 6 you learn how to copy, move, rename, and delete files that reside on your disk. When you perform file-manipulation operations, there will be many times when you need to perform the same operation on two or more files. For example, you might want to copy all of the files with the RPT extension to a floppy disk, or you might want to delete all the files having the OLD extension. To help you perform file operations on a group of files, DOS provides two wildcard characters that you can place in your file-manipulation commands. These wildcards make it easy for you to issue commands that direct DOS to copy, for example, all files whose extension is DOC. By the time you finish this lesson, you will understand how to

- Use the asterisk (*) wildcard combination to specify several "don't care" character positions
- Use the question mark wildcard to tell DOS you "don't care" about specific character positions

UNDERSTANDING DOS WILDCARDS

When you perform a file operation on a group of files, the format of your commands does not change. In other words, a COPY command still specifies a source file and a target file. What changes in your commands is that you use either the asterisk or question mark *wildcard character* within your source or target filenames. The wildcards tell DOS that you want DOS to perform the operation on all files that match your wildcard specification. For example, assume that you want to list all the files in your current directory that have the RPT extension using the DIR command. Because you don't care about the filenames, you can use the asterisk wildcard, as shown here:

```
C:\> DIR   *.RPT   <ENTER>
```

When you issue this command, DOS will examine all the files in your directory, displaying only the names of those that have the RPT extension. In a similar way, the following DIR command lists the names of all files with the BAT extension:

```
C:\> DIR   *.BAT   <ENTER>
```

When DOS encounters the asterisk wildcard, DOS will ignore the filename character that appears in the same location as the wildcard *and* all the characters that follow. In the case of the previous commands, the wildcard appears in the first character of the filename. As a result, DOS will ignore

7: Working with Groups of Files

the first character of the filename and all the characters that follow, up to the period. In a similar way, the following command directs DIR to display the names of all files that begin with the letter B and that have the RPT extension:

```
C:\> DIR  B*.RPT  <ENTER>
```

In this case, DOS will examine each of the files in your directory displaying only the names of files that begin with the letter B and end with RPT extension. The asterisk wildcard can appear anywhere the file's basename or extension.

> ### UNDERSTANDING THE ASTERISK WILDCARD
>
> To help you perform file operations on a group of two or more files, DOS lets you include wildcard characters in your file commands. The asterisk (*) wildcard directs DOS to ignore specific characters when it matches the filenames to be used in the current command. When DOS encounters the asterisk wildcard, DOS will ignore the character in the filename position that contains the asterisk, as well as the character locations that follow. The following command, for example, uses the asterisk wildcard to direct DOS to display the names of all files with the EXE extension:
>
> ```
> C:\> DIR  *.EXE  <ENTER>
> ```

To direct DOS to ignore one specific character position in your filenames, you can use the question mark (?) wildcard. When DOS encounters the question mark, DOS ignores only the character position that contains the wildcard. For example, assume that your disk contains the following files:

```
C:\> DIR  <ENTER>
 Volume in drive C has no label
 Volume Serial Number is 1B30-A2F8
 Directory of C:\

REPORT88 DOC           183 09-16-88   8:23p
REPORT89 DOC           115 09-22-89   4:01p
REPORT90 DOC        34,694 09-02-90   6:20a
REPORT91 DOC         4,820 07-17-91   5:00a
REPORT92 DOC           183 09-16-92   8:23p
REPORT93 DOC        54,933 09-02-93   6:20a
        6 file(s)       94,928 bytes
                   101,076,992 bytes free
```

Filename characters that differ

Rescued by DOS

As you can see, several of the filenames differ only by two characters. Using the question mark wildcard, you can display a directory listing for your files for 1988 and 1989 like this:

```
C:\> DIR   REPORT8?.DOC    <ENTER>

 Volume in drive C has no label
 Volume Serial Number is 1B30-A2F8
 Directory of C:\

REPORT88 DOC           183 09-16-88    8:23p
REPORT89 DOC           115 09-22-89    4:01p
       2 file(s)            298 bytes
                    101,076,992 bytes free
```

Using the question mark wildcard

Likewise, the following command lets you quickly display your files for the 1990 through 1993:

```
C:\> DIR REPORT9?.DOC   <ENTER>

 Volume in drive C has no label
 Volume Serial Number is 1B30-A2F8
 Directory of C:\

REPORT90 DOC        34,694 09-02-93    6:20a
REPORT91 DOC         4,820 07-17-92    5:00a
REPORT92 DOC           183 09-16-93    8:23p
REPORT93 DOC        54,933 09-02-93    6:20a
       4 file(s)         94,630 bytes
                    101,072,896 bytes free
```

UNDERSTANDING THE QUESTION MARK WILDCARD

DOS wildcards exist to help you perform file operations on a group of two or more files. The question mark wildcard lets you direct DOS to ignore the character that appears in a specific character position when it tries to match files. For example, the following DIR command directs DOS to list all the files with the DOC extension that start with the letters AR and end with the letters DISK:

```
C:\> DIR   AR??DISK.DOC   <ENTER>
```

7: Working with Groups of Files

You can use the DOS wildcards with all file-manipulation commands. For example, the following COPY command would direct DOS to copy all of your REPORT files for 1990 through 1993 to files with the extension SAV:

```
C:\> COPY REPORT9?.DOC  *.SAV  <ENTER>
REPORT90.DOC
REPORT91.DOC
REPORT92.DOC
REPORT93.DOC
        4 file(s) copied
```

In this case, the source file for the copy operation used the question mark wildcard. The asterisk wildcard in the target filename directs DOS to use the same name as the source files. In this case, when DOS copies the file REPORT90.DOC, DOS will create a file named REPORT90.SAV.

WILDCARDS AND THE DEL COMMAND

As you have learned, wildcards let you perform file operations on a group of files. When you use the *.* wildcard combination, DOS will apply the operation to every file in your directory. To prevent you from accidentally deleting all the files in your directory, the DEL (delete) command will display the warning prompt when you use *.*:

```
All files in directory will be deleted!
Are you sure (Y/N)?
```

If you type **Y**, DEL will delete all the files. If you instead type **N**, the files will not be deleted. DEL only displays this prompt when you use the *.* wildcard combination.

WHAT YOU NEED TO KNOW

In Lesson 8 you will learn to copy, move, and delete files using disks other than your current drive. Before you continue with Lesson 8, make sure that you have learned the following:

- ☑ DOS wildcards let you perform file operations on two or more files. The wildcards let you specify "don't care" character positions DOS can ignore as it tries to match filenames for use in the command.

- ☑ The asterisk wildcard directs DOS to ignore the character position containing the wildcard, as well as those that follow. The question mark wildcard directs DOS to ignore a specific character position.

- ☑ You can use the wildcards in most file-manipulation commands.

33

Lesson 8

Working with Files on Other Drives

Computers normally use two types of disk drives, a hard drive, which can store very large amounts of information and smaller floppy drives whose floppy disks you can insert and remove as you require. Floppy drives are commonly used to move files from one computer to another. For example, assume you have just completed a section of your company's annual report. By copying your file to a floppy disk, you can give the section to another user who can add it to the report. This lesson examines file operations that use disks other than the current drive. By the time you finish this lesson you will understand how to

- Identify your computer's disk drives
- Change from one drive to another
- Use drive letters within DOS commands

IDENTIFYING YOUR COMPUTER'S DISK DRIVES

Your computer normally uses one hard drive and one or more floppy drives. The hard drive is contained within your computer's system unit. You cannot actually see the drive itself. Floppy disk drives, on the other hand, are easily accessible. Each disk drive in your computer has a unique, single-letter name. Normally, your floppy disk is named drive A. If your computer has two floppy drives, the upper or leftmost drive (depending on the disk's positioning) is drive A, and the second floppy drive is drive B. Your hard disk is normally drive C. Figure 8.1 illustrates the common location of your computer's disk drives.

USING THE DISK DRIVE NAME

Each of the DOS file-manipulation commands presented in this section, such as DIR, COPY, and DEL let you specify a disk drive letter. When you use a disk drive letter within a command, you place a colon after the letter. For example, use **A:** to refer to drive A, **B:** to refer to drive B, and so on. For example, the following DIR command displays the names of files that reside on drive A:

```
C:\> DIR  A:   <ENTER>
```

To display the files that reside on drive B, use the characters **B:** in the command, as shown here:

```
C:\> DIR  B:   <ENTER>
```

8: Working with Files on Other Drives

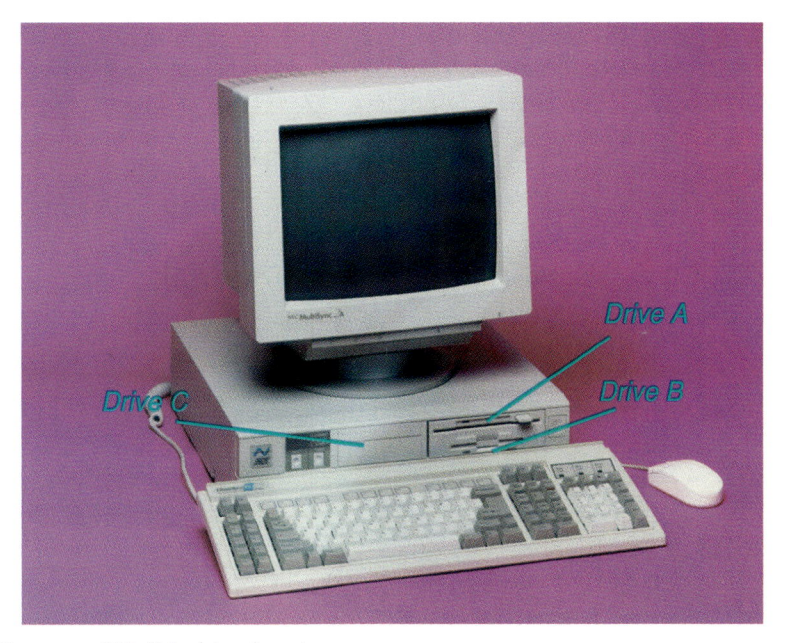

Figure 8.1 Common PC disk drive locations.

USING A DRIVE NAME

The DOS file-manipulation commands let you include a drive letter. When you use a drive letter within a command, you append a colon to the disk drive letter. For example, the characters **A:** refer to drive A. Likewise, **B:** refers to drive B. The following command, for example, lists the files contained on drive A:

```
C:\> DIR  A:   <ENTER>
```

CHANGING FROM ONE DISK DRIVE TO ANOTHER

When you start your computer, DOS will normally select drive C as the current drive. The *current drive* is so named because, unless you specify otherwise, it is the drive DOS uses for all commands. As you work with your computer, there will be times when you need to change from one disk drive to another. For example, if you want to work with the files on the floppy disk contained in drive A, you can select drive A as the current drive. Later, when you are ready to perform your normal operations, you can select drive C as the current drive.

Rescued by DOS

To select a drive as the current drive, simply type the drive letter (and colon) at the DOS prompt and press ENTER. For example, the following command will select drive A as the current drive:

```
C:\> A:   <ENTER>
```
Desired drive and colon

When you press ENTER, DOS will change drives, displaying the new drive letter in the system prompt, as shown here:

```
C:\> A:   <ENTER>
A:\>
```
Displaying the new current drive letter

If you were now to issue the DIR command, DOS would display the names of files residing on the current drive (drive A). To resume your work on drive C later, you can select the drive as shown here:

```
A:\> C:   <ENTER>
C:\>
```

CHANGING THE CURRENT DRIVE

As you work with your computer, you must select one drive as the current drive. Unless you tell DOS otherwise, all the commands you issue affect only the current drive. To change the current drive, type in the drive letter followed by a colon and press ENTER. For example, to select drive A as the current drive, you would type **A:** and press ENTER:

```
C:\> A:   <ENTER>
```

UNDERSTANDING ABORT, RETRY, FAIL?

As you begin to work with floppy disks, there may be times when you reference a disk drive that does not contain a floppy, or the floppy as not yet been formatted for use by DOS. In such cases, DOS will display a message describing an error followed by the **Abort, Retry, Fail?** prompt. For example, the following DIR attempts to display the contents of the disk in drive A when drive A does not contain a disk:

```
C:\> DIR A:   <ENTER>
Not ready reading drive A
Abort, Retry, Fail?
```

8: Working with Files on Other Drives

DOS displays the **Abort, Retry, Fail?** prompt when it needs you to specify how DOS should handle the current error. To respond to the prompt, you must type **A** (for abort), **R** (for retry), or **F** (for fail). If you select the Abort option, DOS will end the command causing the error. In the case of the previous example, DOS will end the DIR command. If you know and can correct the cause of the error, you can choose the Retry option to direct DOS to repeat the operation that caused the error. For example, if drive A does not contain a floppy, you can place a disk in the drive and then choose Retry. The Fail option is the least commonly used option. If, for example, you experience a disk error and you are trying to copy the files that are not yet damaged, you might select the Fail option each time DOS encounters an error so that you can try reading the next file. As a rule, most users simply abort a command when this prompt occurs and then correct the cause, later reissuing the command.

Using a Disk Drive Letter with a Filename

In Lesson 6 you learned how to use the COPY, DEL, REN, and MOVE commands. As it turns out, DOS lets you precede filenames with a disk drive letter. For example, assume that you want to copy the file named BUDGET.RPT from the current drive to drive A. To do so, you simply precede the target filename with the drive letter and colon, as shown here:

```
C:\> COPY   BUDGET.RPT   A:BUDGET.RPT   <Enter>
```

If you don't precede a filename with a disk drive letter, DOS assumes the file resides on the current drive. In this example, DOS will copy the file BUDGET.RPT from the current drive to drive A. In a similar way, assume that you want to delete the file BUDGET.OLD from the floppy disk in drive B. To do so, simply precede the filename with drive letter and colon, as shown here:

```
C:\> DEL   B:BUDGET.OLD   <Enter>
```

Finally, this command moves the file MYREPORT.DOC from the current drive to drive A:

```
C:\> MOVE   MYREPORT.DOC   A:MYREPORT.DOC   <Enter>
```

Common Scenarios

As you create document files using your spreadsheet or word processor, there will be many times when you will need to copy the file to a floppy disk so it can be used by another user. Assuming that your document is in the file REPORT.DOC, you can copy it to the floppy disk in drive A using the following command:

```
C:\> COPY   REPORT.DOC   A:REPORT.DOC   <Enter>
```

Rescued by DOS

Likewise, assume the user makes changes to your document and places the updated document on floppy disk using the filename UPDATE.DOC. If you place the disk in drive A, you can copy the file to your hard disk (you can see by the prompt that C is the current drive) using the following command:

```
C:\> COPY    A:UPDATE.DOC   UPDATE.DOC   <ENTER>
```

> **PRECEDING A FILENAME WITH A DRIVE LETTER**
>
> As you work with files, there may be times when you need to move or copy files from one disk drive to another, or you may need to delete a file that resides on a different disk. To perform such operations, you simply precede the file's name with the desired disk drive. For example, the following command copies the file COMPANY.DOC from drive A to the current drive:
>
> ```
> C:\> COPY    A:COMPANY.DOC   COMPANY.DOC   <ENTER>
> ```

What You Need to Know

In Lesson 9 you will learn how to organize the files on your disk by creating directories. Before you continue with Lesson 9, make sure that you have learned the following:

- ☑ Most PCs use a hard disk and one or more floppy disks. You cannot view the hard disk—it is contained within your system unit. Each PC disk drive is identified by a drive letter. Your first floppy disk drive is drive A. If you have a second floppy, it is drive B. Your hard disk is normally drive C.

- ☑ When you refer to a disk drive within a DOS command, you specify the drive letter followed by a colon. For example, A: refers to drive A. Likewise, B: refers to drive B.

- ☑ As you work, you must select one disk as the current drive. Unless you tell DOS to otherwise, the commands you issue only affect the current drive. To change the current drive, type in the desired drive letter (and a colon) at the DOS prompt and press ENTER.

- ☑ Each of the DOS file-manipulation commands lets you precede filenames with a drive letter, such as A:FILENAME.EXT. By preceding a filename with a drive letter, you can copy or move files between disks or even delete a file that resides on a different drive.

Section Three

UNDERSTANDING DIRECTORIES

Files let you store information from one user session to another. Over time, the number of files that reside on your disk can become very large. As a result, locating a specific file on your disk can become very difficult and time consuming. To help you organize your files, DOS lets you create directories. The best way to visualize a directory is as a drawer within a filing cabinet. By placing related files into a directory, you improve your organization. No matter which programs you run on your PC, you need to understand directories. Take time to understand carefully the lessons presented in this section—they are critical to your success with DOS.

Lesson 9 Organizing Your Files Using Directories

Lesson 10 Creating and Traversing Directories

Lesson 11 Working with Files and Directories

Lesson 12 Common Directory-Manipulation Commands

Lesson 13 Defining a Command Path

Rescued by DOS

Lesson 9

Organizating Your Files Using Directories

As you have learned, files let you store information from one session to another. No matter which programs you use, there will be times when you need to store information within files. To help you organize the files on your disk, DOS lets you create directories. In the simplest sense, a directory is similar to a drawer within a filing cabinet. Using directories you can organize related files. For example, if you need to store files for the office, school, and your own records, you could create three directories named OFFICE, SCHOOL, and RECORDS. In Lesson 10 you will learn how to create, select, and later remove directories from your disk. This lesson simply covers the basics of directories. By the time you finish this lesson you will understand how to

- Determine which directories you need and how to use them
- Further organize your disk using subdirectories
- Understand the use of the current directory
- View the files that reside in a specific directory

DIRECTORIES ORGANIZE YOUR FILES

Every disk starts with one directory called the *root directory.* The root directory is so named, because like a tree, the directories you create to store your files will later grow from the root. Conceptually, you can view the root directory as an empty filing cabinet. DOS uses the backslash character (\), with no names after it, to represent the root directory. As you create files, you could, conceptually, place all of your files into root. Unfortunately, your root directory would soon become cluttered, and finding files would become difficult. In addition, DOS places a limit on the number of files the root directory can store. As a result, you can't get around using directories. Normally, the large programs you install on your disk create their own directories. Thus, your disk may contain directories similar to those shown in Figure 9.1.

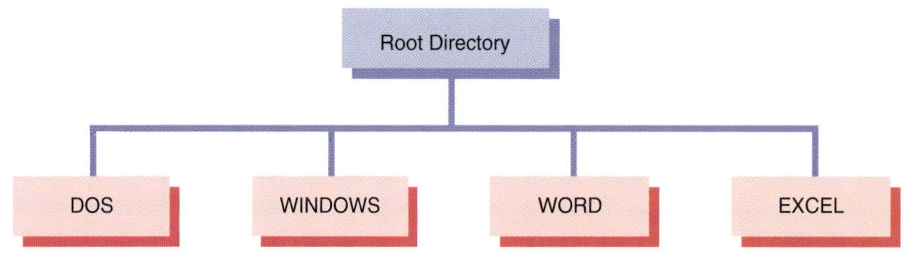

Figure 9.1 Common directories on your disk.

9: Organizing Your Files Using Directories

If you need to store files for your office, school, and personal records, you might add the directories shown in Figure 9.2.

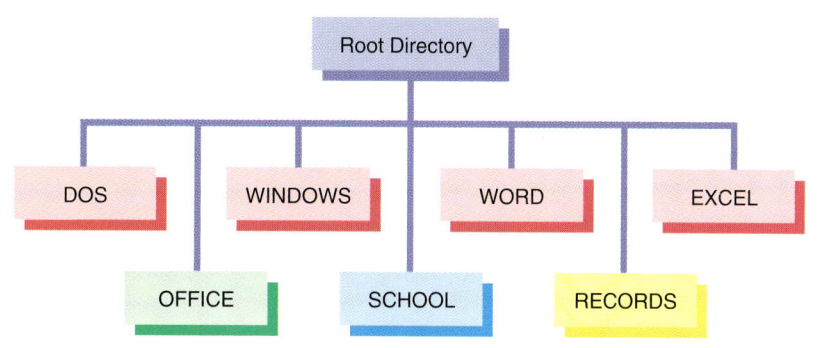

Figure 9.2 Adding the directories OFFICE, SCHOOL, and RECORDS.

The directories OFFICE, SCHOOL, and RECORDS provide you with a first level of organization. You will very likely want to organize your directories further. In the case of your OFFICE files, you might organize files by creating the directories LETTERS, MEMOS, FAXES, and REPORTS. Likewise, you might organize your SCHOOL directory by subject as shown here:

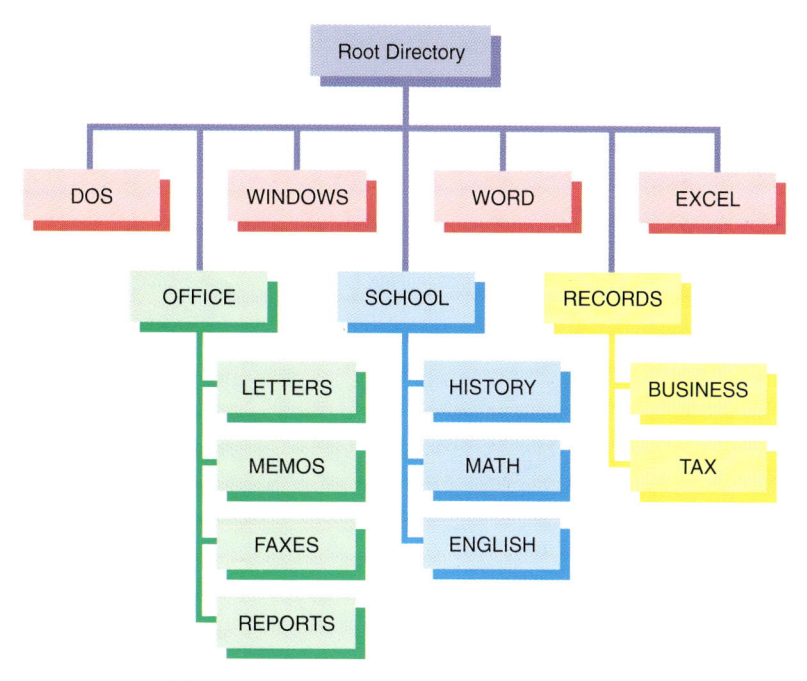

Figure 9.3 Organizing files with additional directories.

41

Rescued by DOS

If you use a word processing program such as WordPerfect or a spreadsheet such as Excel, you should use directories to organize the different type of documents that you create.

Understanding the Current Directory

When you work with paper files in a filing cabinet, you normally open one drawer of the filing cabinet at any given time. In a similar way, when you work with directories on your disk, each disk drive has a *current directory*. For example, your current directory on drive C might be the DOS directory, while the current directory on drive A might be the root directory. The current directory is the directory that, unless told to do otherwise, DOS will search for specified files or within which DOS will place the files you create. As you work within DOS, you can select different directories as the current directory. For example, before you start your word processing program, you might select the directory that contains your WordPerfect files.

Normally, your DOS prompt will display the name of the current drive and directory. For example, the following prompt tells you that the root is the current directory:

```
C:\>          Current directory is the root (\)
```

Likewise, the following prompt tells you the DOS directory is the current directory:

```
C:\DOS>       Current directory is DOS
```

In Lesson 10 you will learn to use the CHDIR command to select a different directory as the current directory. You will learn in Lesson 10 that, as you change from one directory to another, DOS will change the DOS prompt to include the current directory name.

Understanding and Determining the Current Directory

The current directory is conceptually similar to an open drawer in a filing cabinet. DOS keeps track of the current directory for each disk drive in your computer, just as you might have an open drawer in two or more filing cabinets. Unless you tell DOS otherwise, DOS looks for and stores files within the current directory. Normally, the DOS prompt will contain the current directory name. For example, the following prompt tells you that the current directory is WINDOWS.

```
C:\WINDOWS>
```

9: Organizing Your Files Using Directories

Understanding Directory Pathnames

As is the case with filenames, DOS restricts the number of characters in a directory name to eight. Thus, you might need to think of meaningful abbreviations when you create your directories. In most cases, you should find that eight characters is enough to create meaningful directory names.

When you open or save files and the file does not reside in the current directory, you can tell DOS where to place the file on your disk by specifying a complete directory *pathname*. The pathname includes the drive and directory names, as well as the filename. The easiest way to specify a directory name is to start at the root directory (\) and then to specify the directory name and the filename. For example, assume you want to store the file HOMEWORK.DAT in the directory SCHOOL. To specify the complete pathname, start at the root (\), add the name SCHOOL (\SCHOOL), and then append the filename onto it, such as \SCHOOL\HOMEWORK.DAT.

As you can see, you separate directory names using the backslash character. If you wanted to place the file in the subdirectory SPANISH that resides in your SCHOOL directory, you could use the directory name \SCHOOL\SPANISH\HOMEWORK.DAT. As you can see, the name starts at the root, works its way through the SCHOOL and SPANISH directories, followed the filename. As you first work with files and directories, you will probably find it easier to select the desired directory from within the directory list before saving or opening a file.

Displaying the Files a Directory Contains

In Lesson 5 you learned how to display the files on your disk using the DIR command. As it turns out, DIR actually displays the files that reside in a specific directory. If you examine the first few lines of a directory listing, you can determine for which directory the files are being displayed:

```
Volume in drive C has no label
Volume Serial Number is 1B30-A2F8
Directory of C:\
```
────────── *Root directory listing*

```
Volume in drive C has no label
Volume Serial Number is 1B30-A2F8
Directory of C:\DOS
```
────────── *DOS directory listing*

To display the files for a specific directory, you simply include the pathname to the directory within the DIR command. For example, the following command directs DIR to display the files that reside in the DOS directory:

```
C:\> DIR   \DOS   <ENTER>
```

43

Likewise, the next command displays the files that reside in the WINDOWS directory:

```
C:\> DIR  \WINDOWS  <ENTER>
```

If the files scroll past you too quickly, you can include the /P switch to direct DIR to pause with each screenful of files:

```
C:\> DIR  \DOS  /P  <ENTER>
```

Note that a backslash (\) precedes the directory name, while a forward (/) slash the precedes the P in the switch. Finally, because the following command does not specify a directory name, DIR displays the names of files that reside in the current directory (in this case, the root of drive C):

```
C:\> DIR  <ENTER>
```

WHAT YOU NEED TO KNOW

In Lesson 10 you will learn how to use the DOS MKDIR, CHDIR, and RMDIR commands to create, select, and later remove directories on your disk. Before you continue with Lesson 10, make sure that you have learned the following:

- ☑ Directories help you organize the files that reside on your disk. Conceptually, a directory is similar to the drawer of a filing cabinet.

- ☑ When you use a filing cabinet, it is common to further divide the drawers of the cabinet to organize files. In a similar way, you can create subdirectories within the directories that reside on your disk.

- ☑ Regardless of the programs you use, you should use directories to improve your file organization.

- ☑ Each disk in your computer has a current directory, which is similar to an open drawer in the filing cabinet. Unless you tell DOS to do otherwise, DOS always opens and stores files in the current directory.

- ☑ To work with files that reside in a directory other than the current directory, you can specify a complete pathname to the directory. Pathnames start at the root directory (\) and then traverse from one level in the directory tree to the next.

- ☑ To display the names of files that reside in a specific directory, you must simply include the name of the directory within DIR command. If you don't specify a directory name, DIR will display the names of files that reside in the current directory.

Lesson 10

Creating and Traversing Directories

As you learned in Lesson 9, directories exist to help you organize the files that reside on your disk. To help you create, select, and later remove a directory, DOS provides the MKDIR, CHDIR, and RMDIR commands. This lesson examines each of these directory-manipulation commands in detail. By the time you finish this lesson you understand how to

- Create your own directories using MKDIR
- Select the current directory using CHDIR
- Remove a directory when it is no longer needed using RMDIR
- Use relative directory names
- Determine the directories on your disk

No matter how you use your computer, you cannot avoid using directories. Make sure that you understand fully each of the commands presented in this lesson.

CREATING A DIRECTORY WITH MKDIR

When you install new software on your disk, such as a word processor or spreadsheet, the program you run to perform the installation will normally create one or more directories to hold the program's files. As you use the program to create your own files, you can create your own directories to organize your files. The DOS MKDIR command lets you create a directory. As you have learned, most DOS commands are abbreviations. MKDIR is an abbreviation for make directory. Assume, for example, that your directory contains the directories listed in Figure 10.1.

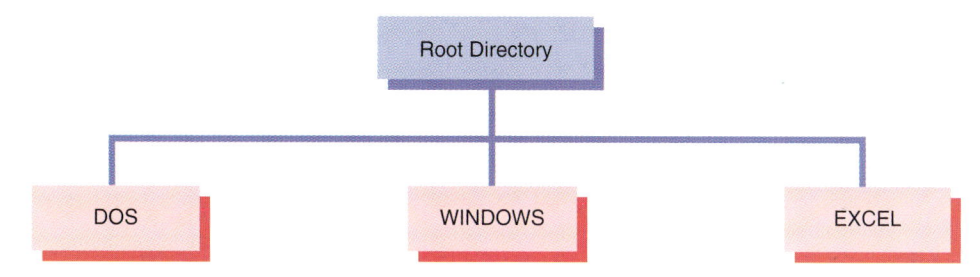

Figure 10.1 A sample directory tree.

Next, assume that you want to create a directory named WORK, into which you will store the files you bring home from the office. To create the directory, invoke the MKDIR command with the directory name you want to create, as shown here:

```
C:\> MKDIR   \WORK   <ENTER>
```

When you execute the command, the previous directory tree will include the WORK directory, as shown in Figure 10.2.

```
                    Root Directory
         ┌──────────┬──────────┬──────────┐
        DOS      WINDOWS      EXCEL      WORK
```

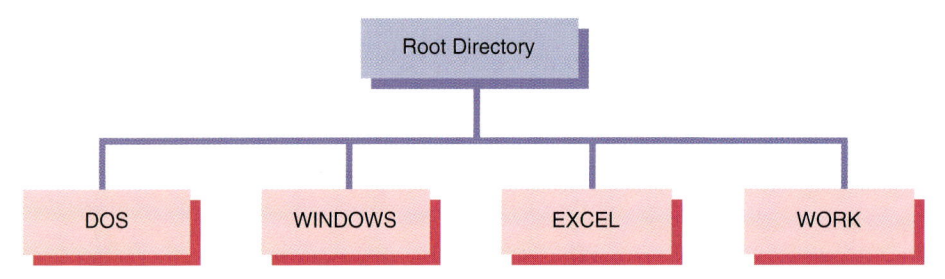

Figure 10.2 Adding the WORK directory to the directory tree.

Next, assume that you want to organize the files in your WORK directory further by those related to expenses and those related to sales. Using the MKDIR command you can create the two subdirectories, as shown here:

```
C:\> MKDIR   \WORK\EXPENSES   <ENTER>
C:\> MKDIR   \WORK\SALES      <ENTER>
```

In this case, the directory tree will add the subdirectories as shown in Figure 10.3. To create the lower-level directories, you simply specify a complete pathname. In the case of the pathname \WORK\EXPENSES, DOS will begin at the root directory (\), locate the directory WORK, and then create the directory EXPENSES.

As you work with DOS, you will use the MKDIR command on a regular basis. Since this command is so common, DOS lets you abbreviate the MKDIR command as simply MD. The following command, for example, creates a directory named SCHOOL, adding it to the directory tree:

```
C:\> MD   \SCHOOL   <ENTER>
```

10: Creating and Traversing Directories

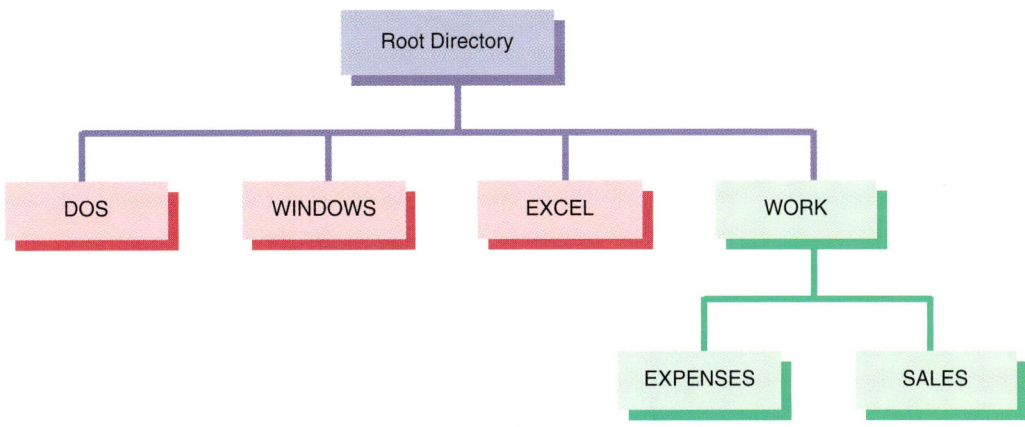

Figure 10.3 Adding the EXPENSES and SALES directories to the directory tree.

CREATING DIRECTORIES WITH MKDIR

As you have learned, directories exist to help you organize files on your disk. Using the MKDIR command, you can create your own directories. For example, the following command creates a directory named MEMOS within your disk's root directory:

```
C:\> MKDIR   \MEMOS    <ENTER>
```

Because of it is so frequently used, DOS lets you abbreviate the MKDIR command as simply MD. Thus, the following MD command is identical to the MKDIR command just shown:

```
C:\> MD    \MEMOS    <ENTER>
```

SELECTING THE CURRENT DIRECTORY WITH CHDIR

When you store files within a filing cabinet, you open a specific drawer into which you place a file. Depending on your file organization, you may further divide files within the drawer. If you need to use other unrelated files, you might need to close the current drawer so you can open a second. In a similar way, when you work with directories on your disk, DOS lets you select the current directory. The *current directory* is so named because unless you tell DOS otherwise, commands such as COPY or DEL only affect the files that reside in the current directory. To select a new current directory you use the CHDIR command. CHDIR is an abbreviation for change directory. Assume, for example, you are using the directory tree previously shown in Figure 10.3. To select the DOS directory as the current directory, you would issue the following CHDIR command:

Rescued by DOS

```
C:\> CHDIR  \DOS   <ENTER>
```

If you use DIR to perform a directory listing, DIR will display your DOS files. Likewise, to select the WINDOWS directory as the current directory, you would use CHDIR as shown here:

```
C:\> CHDIR  \WINDOWS   <ENTER>
```

When you use CHDIR to change the current directory, DOS will normally change the appearance of your DOS prompt, as shown here:

```
C:\> CHDIR  \WINDOWS   <ENTER>     ← The old current directory (the root)
C:\WINDOWS>                         ← The new current directory
```

You have learned that, when you issue the DIR command, DIR displays the files that reside on your disk. A more accurate description of DIR is that it displays the current directory contents or the contents of the directory specified in the DIR command line. If you examine the first few lines of DIR's output, you can determine the directory for which the listing is being displayed, as shown:

```
Volume in drive C has no label
Volume Serial Number is 1B30-A2F8
Directory of C:\WINDOWS          ← Current directory name
```

Because of it is so frequently used, DOS lets you abbreviate the CHDIR command as simply CD. Using CD, the following command selects the directory \WORK\SALES as the current directory:

```
C:\> CD \WORK\SALES   <ENTER>
```

In this case, DOS will begin at the root directory (\), locate the WORK directory, and then select the directory SALES. The best way to visualize this process is to open the drawer of your filing cabinet that is labeled WORK and then to select the file labeled SALES.

Each Disk Has a Current Directory

To simplify your directory operations, DOS keeps track of a current directory for *each* of your disk drives. Most PCs have a hard disk (drive C) and one floppy (drive A). DOS lets you select a directory on each disk as that disk's current directory. For example, the current directory on drive C may be WINDOWS, while the current directory on drive A may be the root. The best way to visualize the current directories for multiple drives is to think of each drive as a unique filing cabinet. Selecting a directory on each drive is similar to opening a drawer in each cabinet.

10: Creating and Traversing Directories

SELECTING A DIRECTORY WITH CHDIR

DOS lets you select one directory as the current directory. The current directory is equivalent to a filing cabinet's open drawer. Unless you tell DOS to use a different directory, the commands you issue only affect files stored in the current directory. The following CHDIR command selects the directory MEMOS as the current directory:

```
C:\> CHDIR   \MEMOS   <ENTER>
```

To simplify the command's use, DOS lets you abbreviate CHDIR as CD. Using CD, the following command is equivalent to the CHDIR command just shown:

```
C:\> CD   \MEMOS   <ENTER>
```

CREATING AND SELECTING A DIRECTORY

To understand the MKDIR and CHDIR commands better, issue the following MKDIR command to create a directory named RESCUED, as shown here:

```
C:\> MKDIR   \RESCUED   <ENTER>
```

Next, use the CHDIR command to select the directory:

```
C:\> CHDIR   \RESCUED   <ENTER>
C:\RESCUED>
```

As you can see, DOS will change the prompt to reflect the selected directory. Next, use the DIR command as shown here to display the directory's files:

```
C:\RESCUED> DIR   <ENTER>

 Volume in drive C has no label
 Volume Serial Number is 1B30-A2F8
 Directory of C:\RESCUED

  .            <DIR>        11-26-93    6:49p
  ..           <DIR>        11-26-93    6:49p
        2 file(s)              0 bytes
                    102,653,952 bytes free
```

49

Rescued by DOS

Because you just created the directory, the directory does not contain any files. As you can see, however, the directory contains the . and .. directory entries. Each time you create a directory, DOS automatically places these entries within the directory. The entries are abbreviations. The single period (.) is an abbreviation for the current directory. The double period (..) is an abbreviation for the directory that resides immediately above the current directory, sometimes called the *parent directory*. In the case of the RESCUED directory, the period corresponds to RESCUED, while the double period corresponds to root (the directory immediately above RESCUED). As you become more familiar with directories, you can use these abbreviations to simplify your commands.

> ### Understanding the . and .. Directory Entries
>
> Each time you create a directory, DOS places two entries within the directory. The first entry, a single period (.) is an abbreviation for the current directory. The second entry, the double period is an abbreviation for the parent directory, which resides immediately above the current directory:
>
> ```
> .          <DIR>        11-26-93     6:49p
> ..         <DIR>        11-26-93     6:49p
> ```

Removing a Directory with RMDIR

Over time, you have directories on your disk that you no longer require. After you delete the files the directory contains, you can use the RMDIR command to remove the directory from your disk. RMDIR is an abbreviation for remove directory. You cannot use RMDIR to remove the current directory or any directory that has files in it. Assuming that you want to remove the directory RESCUED, for example, you must first select a directory other than RESCUED as the current directory. Next, you can use the following RMDIR command to remove the directory:

```
C:\> RMDIR   \RESCUED   <ENTER>
```

You must first delete the files a directory contains (with exception of the . and .. entries) before you can remove directory. If you try to remove a directory that contains one or more files, the command fail, and DOS will display the following error message:

```
C:\> RMDIR   \WINDOWS   <ENTER>
Invalid path, not directory,
or directory not empty
```

10: Creating and Traversing Directories

Because it is frequently used, DOS lets you abbreviate the RMDIR command as RD. For example, the following command uses RD to remove the directory WORK:

```
C:\> RD    \WORK     <ENTER>
```

> ### REMOVING A DIRECTORY WITH RMDIR
>
> Just as there are times when you must remove files from a cabinet when you no longer need them, the same is true for the directories on your disk. When you no longer need a directory, you can use the RMDIR command to remove it. Before you can remove a directory using RMDIR, you must first remove the files the directory contains. In addition, you cannot remove the current directory. Using RMDIR, the following command removes a directory named BUDGET:
>
> ```
> C:\> RMDIR    \BUDGET    <ENTER>
> ```
>
> To simplify the command's use, DOS lets you abbreviate the RMDIR command as RD. Using RD, the following command is equivalent to the RMDIR command just shown:
>
> ```
> C:\> RD    \BUDGET    <ENTER>
> ```

UNDERSTANDING RELATIVE DIRECTORY NAMES

Throughout this lesson you have used complete pathnames to reference each directory you create. For example, you used the following command to select the directory EXPENSES, which resides within the directory WORK:

```
C:\> CHDIR    \WORK\EXPENSES    <ENTER>
```

When you select, make, or remove a directory, you can always specify a complete pathname. However, when the desired directory resides within the current directory you don't need to specify a complete pathname. Instead, you simply specify the directory name. For example, assume that the root directory is the current directory and you want to select the directory WORK. To select the directory, you can simply specify the directory name, as shown here:

```
C:\> CHDIR    WORK    <ENTER>
```

51

Likewise, once you have changed to WORK, if you want to select the directory SALES that resides in WORK, you can simply specify the directory name, as shown here:

```
C:\WORK> CHDIR  SALES  <ENTER>
```

Because the directory SALES resides within the WORK directory, you do not have to specify a complete pathname. When you specify a directory name without a complete pathname, you are specifying a *relative directory name.* In other words, to locate the directory specified the desired directory must be within the current directory.

Assume, for example, that the root directory is the current directory. The following DIR command displays the files contained in the DOS directory:

```
C:\> DIR  DOS  <ENTER>
```

Because the DOS directory resides within the root, you don't have to specify a complete pathname.

Assume, however, that DOS is the current directory and you want to select the directory WORK. Because the work directory does not reside within the DOS directory, you must specify a complete pathname to the directory, as shown here:

```
C:\DOS> CHDIR  \WORK  <ENTER>
```

RECOGNIZING THE DIRECTORIES ON YOUR DISK

When you perform a directory listing, DIR makes it easy for you to identify directories by placing <DIR> after each directory name. For example, select the root as your current directory:

```
C:\DOS> CHDIR  \  <ENTER>
```

Next, issue the DIR command:

```
C:\> DIR  <ENTER>
```

DIR will display the files and directories that reside in the root directory, like this:

10: Creating and Traversing Directories

```
Volume in drive C has no label
 Volume Serial Number is 1B30-A2F8
 Directory of C:\

DOS          <DIR>         05-16-93   4:23a
WINDOWS      <DIR>         05-16-93   4:23a
MOUSE        <DIR>         05-16-93   4:23a
RESBYDOS     <DIR>         09-19-93   3:09p
    :          :               :        :
    :          :               :        :
RESBYWIN     <DIR>         08-31-93   4:30p
COMMAND  COM        54,933 09-02-93   6:20a
CONFIG   SYS           183 09-16-93   8:23p
AUTOEXEC BAT           115 09-22-93   4:01p
RESCUED      <DIR>         09-26-93   6:49p
       21 file(s)        55,231 bytes
                    102,658,048 bytes free
```

<DIR> indicates a directory

As you examine the other directories on your disk, you will encounter entries followed by <DIR>. These entries correspond to directory entries.

WHAT YOU NEED TO KNOW

In Lesson 11 you will learn to perform common file operations with the files that reside in directories. Before you continue with Lesson 11, make sure that you have learned the following:

- ☑ The MKDIR command lets you create a directory on your disk. To simplify the command's use, DOS lets you abbreviate MKDIR as MD.

- ☑ The CHDIR command lets you select a specific directory as the current directory. The current directory is so named because, unless told otherwise, DOS will use it for all file operations. Conceptually, the current directory is similar to the open drawer of a filing cabinet. To simplify the CHDIR command's use, DOS lets you abbreviate the command as CD.

- ☑ When you no longer require a directory, you can use RMDIR to remove it. Before you can remove a directory, you must delete all the files the directory contains. To simplify the command's use, DOS lets you abbreviate the RMDIR command as RD.

- ☑ When you perform file and directory operations, you can always specify complete pathnames. When a directory resides within the current directory, DOS lets you specify a relative directory name, for which DOS searches the current directory for the file or directory specified.

53

Rescued by DOS

Lesson 11

Working with Files and Directories

As you have learned, directories let you organize the files stored on your disk. When you place your files into directories, there will be times when you will need to copy or move a file from one directory to another or you might need to delete one or more files from a directory other than the current directory. In such cases, you must specify complete pathnames to the files. This lesson examines the COPY, MOVE, DEL, and RENAME commands and their use with files that reside in directories. By the time you finish this lesson you will understand how to

- Copy and move files from one directory to another
- Delete files that reside in a different directory
- Rename a file that resides in a different directory

UNDERSTANDING COMPLETE PATHNAMES

As you have learned, a pathname specifies a list of directories DOS must traverse to locate a file or directory. For example, Figure 11.1 illustrates a directory tree.

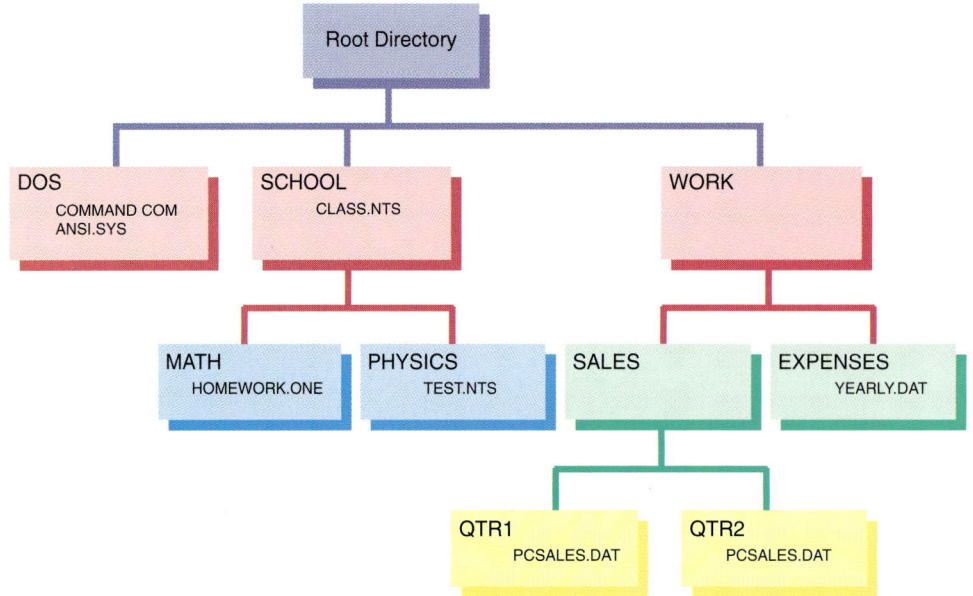

```
                    Root Directory
           ┌────────────┼────────────┐
          DOS         SCHOOL        WORK
      COMMAND.COM   CLASS.NTS    ┌────┴────┐
      ANSI.SYS      ┌────┴────┐ SALES  EXPENSES
                  MATH    PHYSICS         YEARLY.DAT
              HOMEWORK.ONE TEST.NTS
                              ┌────┴────┐
                            QTR1      QTR2
                         PCSALES.DAT  PCSALES.DAT
```

Figure 11.1 Files within a directory tree.

11: Working with Files and Directories

Given the files listed in the directory tree, the following are valid pathnames to files:

\AUTOEXEC.BAT   \DOS\COMMAND.COM
\DOS\ANSI.SYS   \SCHOOL\CLASS.NTS
\SCHOOL\MATH\HOMEWORK.ONE \SCHOOL\PHYSICS\TEST.NTS
\WORK\SALES\QTR1\PCSALES.DAT \WORK\SALES\QTR2\PCSALES.DAT

As you can see, by following the directories listed in a pathname, you can quickly locate a file. When you need to copy or move a file to or from a different directory, you need only specify compete pathnames for source and target files.

COPYING OR MOVING FILES FROM ONE DIRECTORY TO ANOTHER

To copy or move files from one directory to another, you need to specify a complete pathname to the file. For example, assume that your current directory is root and that you need to copy the file CLASS.NTS that resides in the directory SCHOOL to a floppy disk in drive A. To do so, you have two choices. First, you can CHDIR to SCHOOL and then copy the file as shown here:

```
C:\> CHDIR   \SCHOOL    <ENTER>
C:\SCHOOL>  COPY CLASS.NTS    A:CLASS.NTS    <ENTER>
```

Second, you can specify a complete pathname to the file within the COPY command itself:

```
C:\> COPY   \SCHOOL\CLASS.NTS    A:CLASS.NTS    <ENTER>
```

In a similar way, assume that you need to move the file HOMEWORK.ONE from the MATH directory to the PHYSICS directory. To do so, you can specify complete pathnames within the source and target filenames as shown here:

```
C:\> MOVE \SCHOOL\MATH\HOMEWORK.ONE \SCHOOL\PHYSICS\*.* <ENTER>
```

Using the complete pathnames, you can quickly copy or move files from one directory to another.

RENAMING AND DELETING FILES THAT RESIDE IN A DIFFERENT DIRECTORY

Just as there may be times when you need to copy or move files from one directory to another, there may be times when you need to delete one or more files that reside in another directory. To do so, you simply specify a complete pathname to the file or files you want to delete.

For example, given the directory tree previously shown in Figure 11.1, you can delete the file YEARLY.DAT that resides in EXPENSES directory in one of two ways. First, you can select the EXPENSES directory as the current directory, deleting the file as shown here:

```
C:\> CHDIR    \WORK\EXPENSES    <ENTER>
C:\WORK\EXPENSES> DEL    YEARLY.DAT    <ENTER>
```

Second, you can specify a complete pathname to the file, as shown here:

```
C:\> DEL    \WORK\EXPENSES\YEARLY.DAT    <ENTER>
```

Likewise, to delete the file PCSALES.DAT from the QTR2 directory, you would use the following:

```
C:\> DEL    \WORK\SALES\QTR2\PCSALES.DAT    <ENTER>
```

As you have learned, the RENAME command lets you change a file's name. You cannot move a file from one directory to another using RENAME. Thus, you can only specify a pathname in front of the source filename. For example, assume that you want to rename the file TEST.NTS that resides in the PHYSICS directory to LASTEXAM.NTS. To do so, you would issue the following:

```
C:\> RENAME    \SCHOOL\PHYSICS\TEST.NTS    LASTEXAM.NTS    <ENTER>
```

If you precede the target filename with a directory, DOS assumes that you are trying to move the file from one directory to another and the command will fail, as shown here:

```
C:\> RENAME \SCHOOL\PHYSICS\TEST.NTS \SCHOOL\PHYSICS\LASTEXAM.NTS <ENTER>
Invalid filename or file not found
```

What You Need to Know

In Lesson 12 you will examine several common directory-manipulation commands. Before you continue with Lesson 12, make sure that you have learned the following:

- ☑ A complete pathname specifies a list of directories DOS must traverse to locate a specific file. By specifying a complete pathname, you can quickly copy, move, delete, or rename files that reside in another directory.

- ☑ The DOS RENAME command lets you change a file's name. You cannot use RENAME to move a file from one directory to another. To move a file from one directory to another, use the MOVE command.

12: Advanced Directory-Manipulation Commands

Lesson 12

Advanced Directory-Manipulation Commands

As you have learned, directories help you organize the files on your disk. As the number of directories on your disk increases, there may be times when remembering each directory becomes more difficult. In this lesson you will learn how to use the DIR command to display the files in a directory, as well as files in subdirectories that reside within the directory. In addition, you will learn how to display a visual representation of your directory tree using the TREE command. You will also learn how to delete a subdirectory from your disk quickly, deleting all the files the directory contains. By the time you finish this lesson you will understand how to

- Use the /S switch with DIR to display files in subdirectories that reside beneath the current directory
- Display your directory tree using the TREE command
- Delete a directory and the files it contains using the DELTREE command

DISPLAYING SUBDIRECTORY FILES WITH DIR

As you have learned, the DIR command lets you display the names of files that reside in the current directory or in the directory specified. As you organize your files in different levels, there may be times when you not only want to list the files in a directory, but also the files that reside in subdirectories. To display files that reside in subdirectories, include the /S switch in your DIR command. For example, the following command displays all the files in the DOS directory, as well those in any subdirectories the DOS directory contains:

```
C:\> DIR \DOS /S <ENTER>
```

In a similar way, the following DIR command, issued from the root directory, uses the /S switch to display all the files the disk contains:

```
C:\> DIR /S <ENTER>
```

In most cases, the list of files will scroll past you on the screen faster than you can read them. To suspend the DIR's output with each screenful of files, use the /P switch as shown here:

```
C:\> DIR /S /P <ENTER>
```

57

Rescued by DOS

VIEWING A GRAPHIC DIRECTORY TREE

As the number of directories you create on your disk increases, there may be times when your directory tree becomes difficult to remember. To help you visualize the directories your disk contains, you can issue the DOS TREE command. Assuming that your disk contains the directory structure previously shown in Figure 12.1, the TREE command will display the following output:

```
C:\> TREE    <ENTER>
```

When you use the TREE command, you need to keep track of the current directory before you execute the command. By default, the TREE command begins its directory tree display within the current directory. In the case of the previous command, the current directory was the root, so TREE displayed the names of all the directories on the disk. However, had the current directory been DOS or WINDOWS, the output of the TREE command would display on those subdirectories that reside beneath the current directory. By default, the TREE command only displays the names of directories. If you include the /F switch, you can direct TREE to display the name of the files each directory contains, as shown here:

```
C:\> TREE    /F    <ENTER>
```

DELETING A DIRECTORY

In Lesson 10 you learned that the DOS RMDIR command lets you remove a directory from your disk. To use RMDIR, however, the directory must be empty. In other words, you must first delete the files the directory contains before you can remove the directory. If the directory contains subdirectories, you must also remove those directories as well, again removing the files and subdirectories each contains. Assume, for example, your disk contains the directory structure shown in Figure 12.1.

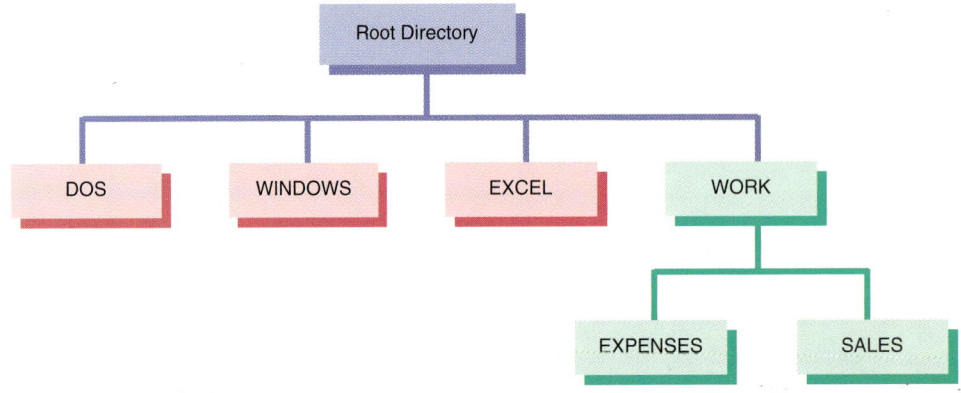

Figure 12.1 A sample directory tree.

12: Advanced Directory-Manipulation Commands

Next, assume that you want to remove the WORK directory. To do so, you must remove the subdirectories SALES and EXPENSES. As you can see, before you can remove those directories, you must first delete other subdirectories. As a result, removing the WORK directory can become complex and time consuming. To simplify such operations, DOS provides the DELTREE command, which lets you delete a directory and all the files and subdirectories the directory contains in one step. For example, to delete the WORK directory, you would invoke DELTREE as follows:

```
C:\> DELTREE   \WORK   <ENTER>
```

The DELTREE command will display the following prompt, asking you to verify that you really want to delete the directory:

```
Delete directory "\work" and its subdirectories? [yn]
```

To delete the directory and *all* the files and directories it contains, type **Y** and press ENTER. DELTREE will display a message telling you that it has deleted the directory and its files:

```
Deleting \work...
```

Note: Take tremendous care when you use the DELTREE command. An errant command can quickly and inadvertently delete files or directories you require. Should you accidentally delete the wrong directory, turn to Lesson 50, which discusses the UNDELETE command, before you do anything else.

WHAT YOU NEED TO KNOW

In Lesson 13 you will learn how to simplify running programs by defining a command path. Before you continue with Lesson 13, make sure that you have learned the following:

- ☑ To display a directory listing of files in a specific directory, as well as files that reside within subdirectories of the desired directory, invoke DIR with the /S switch.

- ☑ As the number of directories on your disk increases, there may be times when you want to display a graphical representation of your directory tree. To do so, use the TREE command.

- ☑ The DOS RMDIR command lets you remove an empty directory from your disk. To remove a directory that contains files or subdirectories, you can use the DELTREE command.

- ☑ Because an errant DELTREE command can quickly erase all the information on your disk, you should execute DELTREE with great care.

Lesson 13

Defining a Command Path

When you install new software on your disk, the installation program normally creates a directory for the software. After the software is installed, you can normally execute the program by simply typing the command's name at the DOS prompt, regardless your current directory. To simplify the steps you must perform to run your commonly used programs, DOS lets you create a *command path*, which defines a list of directories DOS automatically searches for a program file's executable file. In this lesson you will learn how to view and change the command path. By the time you finish this lesson you will understand how to

- Determine which files on your disk contain executable programs
- Execute a program that resides in a different directory
- View the current command path
- Change the command path to include a specific directory

UNDERSTANDING EXECUTABLE FILES

As you have learned, software is a file that contains instructions the computer performs to accomplish a specific task. Files that contains executable programs are sometimes called executable files. DOS uses the EXE (abbreviation for executable) and COM (abbreviation for command) extensions for executable files. The difference, briefly, is that COM files are smaller. If you examine the files in your DOS directory, for example, you will find that many contain the EXE and COM extensions. To list the executable filenames, invoke DIR as shown here:

```
C:\> DIR  \DOS  <ENTER>
```

When you type in the name of executable program at the DOS prompt and press ENTER, DOS will load the program file from disk into memory, allowing your computer to execute the program's instructions. For example, Figure 13.1 illustrates how DOS loads the file TREE.COM from disk into your computer's memory.

13: Defining a Command Path

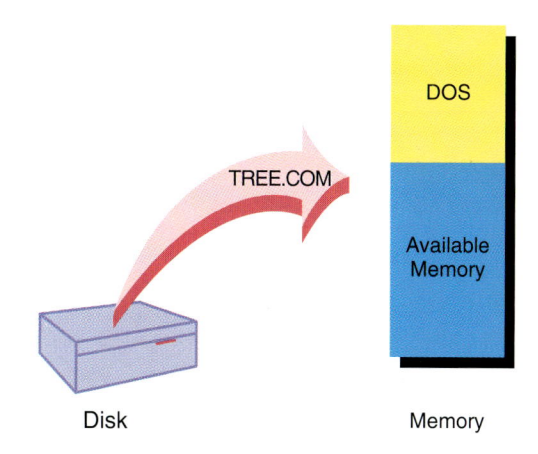

Figure 13.1 DOS loads executable programs from disk into your computer's memory for execution.

When you execute a program, you must tell DOS how to locate the executable file. The easiest way to tell DOS the file's location is to select the directory that contains the program file. For example, to execute the TREE command that resides in the DOS directory, you can use the CHDIR command to first select DOS as the current directory:

```
C:\> CHDIR   \DOS   <ENTER>
```

Next, you can simply type the command name at the DOS prompt:

```
C:\DOS> TREE   <ENTER>
```

Because the file TREE.COM resides in the current directory, DOS will locate the file and load it into memory. The second way to help DOS locate an executable file is to specify a complete pathname to the file when you type in the command. For example, to execute the TREE command, you can precede the command name with a directory path, as shown here:

```
C:\>  \DOS\TREE   <ENTER>
```
Directory containing the command
Command name

USING A COMMAND PATH

If you are using programs such as a word processor or spreadsheet, you may have found that you can execute the program without selecting the program's directory as the current directory and without specifying a complete pathname to the file. To make your commonly used programs easier to execute, DOS lets you define a command path, which lists the names of directories you want

61

DOS to search automatically for program files each time you type a command at the DOS prompt. The DOS PATH command lets you view or display the command path. To view your current command path, type **PATH** at the DOS prompt and press ENTER:

```
C:\> PATH    <ENTER>
```

The PATH command will display a list of directory names that DOS automatically searches for your program files:

```
C:\> PATH    <ENTER>
PATH=C:\DOS;C\WINDOWS;C:\BATCH
```

In this case, the command path contains three directories (DOS, WINDOWS, and BATCH). As you can see, each directory resides on drive C. When you define a command path, DOS will automatically search the directories specified if it fails to first find the program file in the current directory. For example, assume that you are working in the root directory and you type **WIN** to invoke Windows:

```
C:\> WIN    <ENTER>
```

In this case, DOS will first search the root directory for a file named WIN.EXE or WIN.COM. If DOS fails to find the file, DOS will then search the directory C:\DOS for the file. If DOS successfully locates the file, it will execute the corresponding program. Otherwise, DOS will continue its search of the specified directories. DOS searches the directories in the order they are listed in the command path. If, after searching all the specified directories, DOS has still not located a matching file, DOS will display the **Bad command or file name** error message. By adding the names of directories that contain your commonly used commands to the command path, you make the corresponding programs much easier to run.

DEFINING THE COMMAND PATH

In addition to letting you view the current command path, the PATH command lets you specify the directories you want DOS to search automatically. To change the command path, you simply invoke the PATH command with a list of desired directory names. You should precede each directory name with the letter (and colon) that corresponds to the drive on which directory resides. In addition, you should separate the directory names with semicolons (;) and no spaces. The following PATH command, for example, directs DOS to search the DOS and WINDOWS directories:

13: Defining a Command Path

```
C:\> PATH   C:\DOS;C:\WINDOWS   <ENTER>
```

In Lesson 19 you will learn how to use a special file named AUTOEXEC.BAT to list commands that you want DOS to automatically execute each time your system starts. As you will learn, most users will place a PATH command in their AUTOEXEC.BAT file. In this way, DOS automatically knows which directories to search each time your system starts. When you install a new software program, the installation program will normally edit your AUTOEXEC.BAT file adding the new program's directory to the command path. In this way, you can simply type the program's name from the DOS prompt, regardless of your current directory.

> ### WHICH DIRECTORIES BELONG IN THE COMMAND PATH
>
> As a rule, you should only place the directories that contain your commonly used programs into the command path. If you were to place all your directory names into the command path, DOS would spend a considerable amount of time searching directories that are unlikely to contain commonly used commands. In addition, the maximum number of characters you can place your command path is 121. Most users will place the DOS and WINDOWS directories into their command path, along with their most commonly used application programs.

WHAT YOU NEED TO KNOW

In Lesson 14 you will learn how to group two or more DOS commands into a special batch file, which uses the BAT extension. When you type the batch file's name at the DOS prompt, DOS will execute each of the commands, in order, that the batch file contains. Before you continue with Lesson 14, make sure that you have learned the following:

- ☑ A program is a file that contains a list of instructions the computer performs to accomplish a specific task. DOS programs use the COM (an abbreviation for command) and EXE (an abbreviation for executable) extensions.

- ☑ To execute a program file you have two choices. First, you can use the CHDIR command to select the directory, then typing the command name. Second, you can type in a complete pathname to the program file with the command.

- ☑ Each time you type in a command at the DOS prompt, DOS first searches the current directory for the command. If DOS finds the command, DOS will execute it. Otherwise, DOS will search, in order the directories listed in the command path.

- ☑ The DOS PATH command lets you view and change the command path. Most users place a PATH command in the special AUTOEXEC.BAT file, discussed in Lesson 19.

Section Four

DOS Batch Files

As you have learned, files with the EXE and COM extensions contain executable programs. If you type the name of an EXE or COM file at the DOS prompt and press ENTER, DOS will load the corresponding program into memory. As you work with different programs, you might find that there are many times when your repeatedly execute the same series of commands. For example, when you use your word processor, you might first select the directory that contains your word processing software and then run the word processing program. Likewise, if your computer is connected to a local area network, you might have to log into the network before you can access the files and programs the network disk contains. In cases when you execute two or more related commands, you can simplify your operations by creating a batch file. In general, a batch file is a file that contains a list of commands you want DOS to execute. When you type the batch file's name at the DOS prompt, DOS executes each of the commands the batch file contains. Batch files are so named because they batch (group) together, two or more commands. Batch files have the BAT extension. This section introduces you to DOS batch files. As you will learn, creating your own batch files is almost like creating your own commands.

Lesson 14 Concepts and Naming

Lesson 15 Controlling Batch File Messages

Lesson 16 Common Batch Commands

Lesson 17 Decision Making

Lesson 18 Batch Parameters and FOR

Lesson 19 AUTOEXEC.BAT

Lesson 14

Getting Started with DOS Batch Files

As the number of operations you perform increases, you might find that you always seem to execute the same sequence of commands. For example, if you use a word processor, you might first select the directory that contains your word processing files and then start your word processor. If you want to use your spreadsheet program later, you first select the directory that contains your spreadsheet files before your run the spreadsheet program. When you have situations where you normally issue two or more commands in sequence, you can save time and typing by creating a DOS *batch file*. A batch file is a file that contains the names of one or more commands. If you type the batch file's name at the DOS prompt, DOS will execute, in order, each command the batch file contains. This lesson introduces DOS batch files. By the time you finish this lesson you will understand how to

- Create your own simple batch files
- Determine when you should use a batch file
- Assign meaningful names to your batch files

BATCH FILE BASICS

In the simplest sense, a batch file is a file that contains one or more command names. Batch files are so named because they let you group (batch) together related commands. Batch files use the BAT extension. Assume, for example, that you create the following simple batch file named SHOWDIR.BAT:

```
CLS
DIR /W /P
```

In this case, the batch file contains two commands: CLS and DIR. The CLS command will clear the contents of your screen display. Next, the DIR command will display the names of current directory files, five names across the screen (/W), pausing after each screenful for you to press a key before continuing (/P). To run the batch file, you simply type the batch file's name at the DOS prompt:

```
C:\> SHOWDIR  <ENTER>
```
Type the batch filename at the DOS prompt

When you type the batch filename at the DOS prompt and press ENTER, DOS will first execute the CLS command, clearing the current contents of your screen. Next, DOS will execute the directory listing, displaying the current directory filenames. In this case, by typing in the name of the batch file, you were able to execute two different commands.

In a similar way, the following batch file, STARTWIN.BAT, clears the screen display, uses CHDIR to select the WINDOWS directory, and then runs Windows using the WIN command:

```
CLS
CHDIR   \WINDOWS
WIN
```

As before, you would type the batch file's name at the DOS prompt and press ENTER to execute this batch file:

```
C:\> STARTWIN   <ENTER>
```

When DOS recognizes that your command is a batch file, DOS will execute, in order, each command the file contains.

DOS Batch Files Group Commands

A DOS batch file is a file that contains the names of one or more commands. When you type the batch file name at the DOS prompt and press ENTER, DOS will execute each command in the order the command names appear within the file. DOS batch files use the BAT extension.

Creating a DOS Batch File

DOS batch files are ASCII files, which means they consist of letters, numbers, and standard punctuation. Do not create DOS batch files with your word processor. As you know, word processors let you create reports and other documents, using **bold** or *italic* text and aligned margins. To perform these operations, word processors embed special hidden characters within your files. One such character might turn italics on, while a second character turns italics off. Although these special characters are meaningful to your word processor, they will not be understood by DOS. You should use the DOS EDIT command to create your batch files. Assume, for example, that you want to create the batch file SHOWDIR.BAT which contains the following commands:

```
CLS
DIR /W /P
```

14: Getting Started with DOS Batch Files

To begin, invoke EDIT, specifying the filename in command line, as shown here:

```
C:\> EDIT  SHOWDIR.BAT  <ENTER>
```

EDIT will display a blank editing screen. Type **CLS** command and press ENTER. Next, type **DIR /W /P**. Your screen should now appear similar to that shown in Figure 14.1.

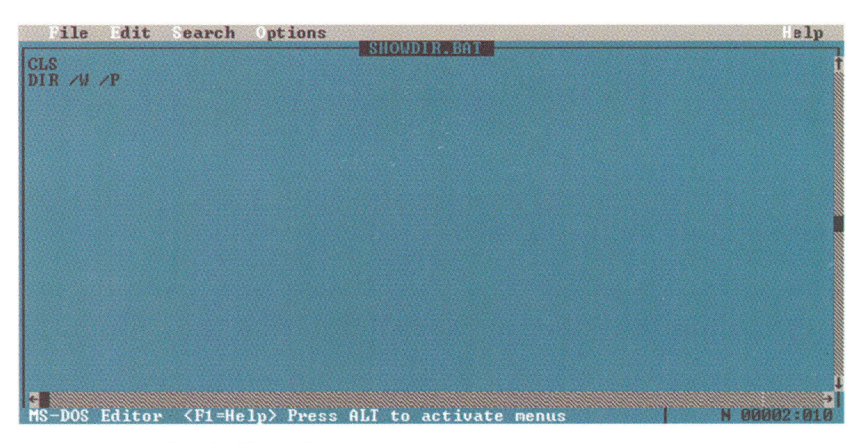

Figure 14.1 Creating a batch file with EDIT.

To save your batch file to disk, hold down the ALT key and press F (or click on the File menu name with your mouse). EDIT will display its File menu. Select the Save option to save your file. Next, select the File menu a second time and select Exit to end your editing session. To execute the batch file, type **SHOWDIR** at the DOS prompt and press ENTER:

```
C:\> SHOWDIR  <ENTER>
```

Using EDIT, you can quickly create batch files. In addition, you can also use EDIT to make changes to a batch file,. For example, assume you want to change the SHOWDIR batch file so it does not use the /W switch with the DIR command:

```
CLS
DIR /P
```

To do so, invoke the EDIT as shown here:

```
C:\> EDIT SHOWDIR.BAT  <ENTER>
```

67

Rescued by DOS

When EDIT displays its editing screen, make your changes to the batch file. Next, select the File menu and choose Save to record your changes to disk. Select the File menu a second time and choose Exit to end your editing session.

Naming Your DOS Batch Files

DOS batch files always use the BAT extension. When you create your batch files, you should choose a name that meaningfully defines the function your batch file performs. For example, if you have created a batch file that runs your company's general ledger accounting programs, you might call your batch file LEDGER.BAT.

Do not use the name of a DOS command for your batch file. Should you create a batch file named CLS.BAT, for example, the batch file would never execute because its name conflicts with the CLS command, which DOS will use instead. To avoid such conflicts, use a name of a file other than an EXE or COM file or a DOS command. If you create a batch file and each time you invoke the batch file a different program runs, your batch filename is conflicting with another command on your disk.

What You Need to Know

In Lesson 15 you will learn how to use the DOS ECHO command to control the display of messages on your screen as your batch files execute. Before you continue with Lesson 15, make sure that you have learned the following:

- ☑ To help you execute two or more related commands in succession with one command, DOS lets you create batch files. In general a batch file is a file that contains the names of one or more commands. When you type in the name of a batch file at the DOS prompt, DOS will execute, in succession, each of the commands the batch file contains.

- ☑ Batch files always use the BAT extension. You should assign meaningful names to your batch files that describe the processing the batch file performs. Do not assign your batch files the same name as a DOS command.

- ☑ Batch files are ASCII files, which contain characters, numbers, and standard punctuation. Do not a use a word processor to create a batch file. Instead, use the DOS EDIT command to create the file. Should you need to later change the batch file, use EDIT to make your changes and then save the changes the disk.

Lesson 15

Controlling Batch File Messages

As you have learned, a batch file is a file that contains the names of one or more DOS commands. When you type the name of a batch file at the DOS prompt, DOS executes each of the commands the batch file contains. Executing commands from within a batch file is really no different than typing the command's name at the DOS prompt. As DOS reads and executes the batch file commands, DOS will display the batch file names on your screen. As your batch files become advanced, you might not want DOS to display each batch file's name on the screen. In this lesson you will learn how to use the ECHO OFF command to direct DOS not to display command names as the batch file executes. In addition, you will learn how to use ECHO to display messages to the user as the batch file executes. By the time you finish this lesson you will understand how to

- Disable the display of command names when a batch file executes
- Display messages to the user during the batch file's execution

Most batch files make extensive use of the ECHO command. Take time to create and use each of the batch files presented in this lesson.

CONTROLLING THE DISPLAY OF BATCH FILE COMMAND NAMES

As you know, a batch file is nothing more than a list of command names. When you type the batch file's name at the DOS prompt, DOS executes each of the commands listed, just as if you typed the commands one at a time at the DOS prompt. To better understand this process, create the batch TODAYIS.BAT, which contains the following commands:

```
CLS
TIME
DATE
```

Execute this batch file at the DOS prompt from the DOS prompt by typing the batch filename and pressing ENTER, as shown here:

```
C:\> TODAYIS   <ENTER>
```

As the batch file executes, the CLS command will clear the contents of your screen, moving the cursor to the upper-left corner of your screen (the home position). Next, DOS will execute the TIME command, as shown here:

69

```
C:\> TIME
Current time is   9:45:55.93p
Enter new time:
```

When you type in a new time or press ENTER, the batch file will continue, and DOS will execute the DATE command, as shown here:

```
C:\> DATE
Current date is Fri 11-19-1993
Enter new date (mm-dd-yy):
```

When you type in a new date or press ENTER to leave the current date unchanged, the batch file will end. As you can see, as the batch file executes, DOS displays the name of each command, as well as the DOS prompt. As your batch files become more complex, you might want to disable the display of command names during the batch file's execution. To do so, include the line @ECHO OFF at the start of your batch files, as shown here:

```
@ECHO OFF
CLS
TIME
DATE
```

The @ECHO OFF command directs DOS not to display command names as the batch file executes. To understand better how the command works, insert the command at the start of the batch file TODAYIS.BAT. Next, invoke the batch file from the DOS prompt. As before, the CLS command will clear the screen contents. Next, the batch file will execute the TIME command, but without displaying the command name. As a result, your screen will display the following:

```
Current time is   9:45:55.93p
Enter new time:
```

When you press ENTER to leave the current time unchanged, the batch file will invoke the DATE command, again without displaying the command name:

```
Current date is Fri 11-19-1993
Enter new date (mm-dd-yy):
```

As you can see, the batch file executes the commands without displaying the corresponding command names.

15: Controlling Batch File Messages

Suppressing Batch File Command Names with @ECHO OFF

By default, when your batch files execute, DOS displays each command's name. As your batch files become more complex, there may be times when the command name display becomes distracting. To turn off the display of command names within your batch files, place the command @ECHO OFF at the start of your batch file, as shown here:

```
@ECHO OFF
CLS
CHDIR \WP60
WP
```

When DOS encounters the @ECHO OFF command, it will continue executing the batch file's commands without displaying the command names.

Displaying User Messages from Within Your Batch Files

As your batch files become more complex, there may be times when you will want the batch file to display messages to the user. To display messages from within your batch files, you can use the DOS ECHO command. For example, assume that you have a batch file named WORDPROC.BAT, which selects the directory that contains your word processor and then invokes your word processor:

```
@ECHO OFF
CLS
CHDIR WP60
WP
```

Next, assume that each time you invoke the WORDPROC.BAT batch file, you want the batch file to remind you to turn on your printer. Using the ECHO command as shown next, your batch file can display the message on to the screen:

```
ECHO Remember to turn on your printer
```

When the batch file encounters the ECHO command, DOS will display the message specified. For example, the following batch file, MESSAGE.BAT, uses the ECHO message to display different messages:

```
@ECHO OFF
CLS

ECHO About to display the system date
```

71

Rescued by DOS

```
DATE
ECHO About to display the system time
TIME
```

When you invoke this batch file, your screen will display the following output:

```
About to display the system date
Current date is Fri 11-19-1993
Enter new date (mm-dd-yy):    <ENTER>
About to display the system time
Current time is  9:45:55.93p
Enter new time:    <ENTER>
```

As you encounter different batch files, you will find many that use the ECHO command to display messages to the user in this way. In addition, many advanced DOS books present ways you can use the ECHO command to select different screen colors using the ECHO command within your batch file. As you will find, batch files make extensive use of the ECHO command.

When you display messages using ECHO, there may be times when you want to display a blank line. In such caeses, simply place a period immediately next to the ECHO command as shown here:

```
ECHO.
```

What You Need to Know

In Lesson 16 you will examine many common batch file commands. Before you continue with Lesson 16, make sure that you have learned the following:

- ☑ A batch file contains a list of command names that DOS executes when you type the batch filename at the DOS prompt and press ENTER. By default, as DOS executes the commands, it will display each command's name.

- ☑ To prevent the command names from distracting the user or cluttering the screen, many batch files place the @ECHO OFF command as the batch file's first command. When DOS encounters the @ECHO OFF command, DOS will not display the names of the commands as the batch file executes them.

- ☑ The @ character has special meaning within your batch files. When DOS encounters the @ character within your batch files, it will not display the name of the command that follows.

Lesson 16

Common Batch Commands

As you have learned, a batch file is simply a list of command names. When you type the batch file's name at the DOS prompt and press ENTER, DOS executes, in order, each command specified. This lesson presents three commands commonly used in most batch files: PAUSE, REM, and @ECHO ON. By the time you finish this lesson, you will know how to

- Display a message to the user, temporarily suspending the batch file's output
- Use ECHO ON along with ECHO OFF to control message display
- Include remarks within your batch file that explain the batch file's purpose and each of the commands the batch file contains

DISPLAYING BATCH FILE MESSAGES WITH PAUSE

Depending on your batch file's purpose, there may be times when you need the batch file to pause for a moment until the user performs a specific task, such as placing a specific paper type in the printer, inserting a disk in drive A, or some other operation that batch file cannot perform itself. In such cases, your batch files can use the PAUSE command.

Using the PAUSE command is very similar to displaying messages to the user with ECHO. You simply place the desired message after PAUSE in the command line. For example, the following batch file, RPT_TO_A.BAT, copies all the current directory files with RPT to the disk in drive A. Before the batch file performs the COPY operation, it uses the PAUSE command to tell the user to insert a floppy disk in drive A:

```
PAUSE Place a floppy disk in drive A
COPY *.RPT   A:
```

When you execute this batch file later, your screen will display the following output:

```
C:\> RPT_TO_A  <ENTER>

C:\> PAUSE Place a floppy disk in drive A
Press any key to continue . . .
```

Rescued by DOS

As you can see, the PAUSE command displays your message and then suspends the batch file, displaying the message **Press any key to continue**. When the user presses a key, the batch file resumes its execution, performing the COPY command. In a similar way, the following batch file, PAYROLL.BAT, uses the PAUSE command to direct the user to insert checks into the printer:

```
PAUSE Make sure the printer contains checks
PAY_EMP
```

When you run this batch file, your screen displays the following output:

```
C:\> PAYROLL   <ENTER>

C:\> PAUSE Make sure the printer contains checks
Press any key to continue . . .
```

Suspending a Batch File with Pause

Before a batch file executes a specific command, there may be times when the batch file needs the user to first perform a manual operation. Using the PAUSE command, the batch file can display a message to the user, suspending the batch file until the user presses any key to continue. For example, the following PAUSE command directs the user to insert the disk containing employee information into drive A:

```
PAUSE Insert the Employee Info disk into drive A
```

When DOS encounters that PAUSE command within your batch file, your screen will display the following output:

```
C:\> PAUSE Insert the Employee Info disk into drive A
Press any key to continue . . .
```

When the user presses any key, the batch file will resume its operation with the next command.

Using @ECHO OFF Causes Problems for PAUSE

In Lesson 15 you learned to place the @ECHO OFF command at the start of your batch files to direct DOS not to display command names as the batch file executes:

```
@ECHO OFF
CLS
TIME
DATE
```

74

16: Common Batch Commands

Unfortunately, if your batch file uses @ECHO OFF and the PAUSE command, DOS *will not* display the message you include the PAUSE command line. For example, the following batch file, changes RPT_TO_A.BAT, to use the @ECHO OFF command:

```
@ECHO OFF
PAUSE Place a floppy disk in drive A
COPY *.RPT   A:
```

Watch what happens to the PAUSE command's output when you execute this batch file:

```
C:\> RPT_TO_A   <ENTER>              ── PAUSE command output
Press any key to continue . . .
```

As you can see, the message **Place a floppy disk in drive A** does not appear on your screen. The reason the message does not appear is that the @ECHO OFF command has suppressed the display of the command name (and in this case the message).

In this case, one solution to this problem is to place the @ character in front of the COPY command instead of using @ECHO OFF at the beginning of the file, as shown here:

```
PAUSE Place a floppy disk in drive A
@COPY *.RPT   A:
```

If your batch file contains many commands with a PAUSE command in the middle, you can place the PAUSE command between ECHO ON and ECHO OFF commands, as shown here:

```
@ECHO OFF
CLS                              ── Turns on command name display
DATE

ECHO ON
PAUSE Place a floppy disk in drive A

@ECHO OFF ─────────────────────── Turns off command name display
COPY *.RPT   A:
TIME
```

In this case, the ECHO ON command enables the display of command names, and the PAUSE command's message will appear on your screen. After the PAUSE command completes, the @ECHO OFF command turns command name display off.

Using Remarks to Explain Your Batch Files

You can use batch files to group two or more related commands or to abbreviate a long command. As the number of commands your batch file increases, you should leave remarks within your batch file that explain the batch file's purpose. In this way, should you or another user view the batch file commands, they can quickly determine the operation the batch file performs. To add remarks to your batch file, you can use the DOS REM command. REM is an abbreviation for remark. When DOS encounters a REM command in your batch file, DOS simply ignores the command. The following batch file illustrates the use of REM to explain the batch file's purpose:

```
@ECHO OFF
REM RPT_TO_A.BAT
REM Copy files with RPT extension to a disk in drive A
REM Written by Kris Jamsa 11/21/93

REM Turn the command name display on and off for PAUSE
ECHO ON
PAUSE Place a floppy disk in drive A
@ECHO OFF

REM Perform the file copy operation
COPY *.RPT   A:
```

By reading the remarks within the batch file, you can determine why the batch file was created, by who and when. In addition, you can understand better why the batch file uses specific commands. Note the batch file's use of blank lines to improve its readability. When DOS encounters a blank line within your batch file, it simply ignores the blank line, continuing with the command that follows. As you create batch files, include remarks that explain the batch file's processing.

What You Need to Know

In Lesson 17 you will learn how to use the DOS IF command to help your batch files make their own decisions. Before you continue with Lesson 17, make sure that you understand the following:

- ☑ The PAUSE command lets your batch files display a message and then wait until the user presses any key to continue.

- ☑ When your batch files use @ECHO OFF and PAUSE, you might need to enable command name display using ECHO ON immediately before the PAUSE command and an @ECHO OFF command after. In this way, the PAUSE command message will not be suppressed.

- ☑ As your batch files increase in complexity, you should include remarks within your batch files that explain the processing they perform. The DOS REM command lets you include such remarks. When DOS encounters a REM command within your batch file, DOS ignores the command.

17: Using Batch Parameters

Lesson 17

Using Batch Parameters

When you execute a DOS command, you can often include additional information, such as a filename, in your command line. As it turns out, DOS also lets you pass information to your batch files within the command line. In this way, you can increase the power of your batch files by letting the same batch file be used with several different files. When you pass information to a batch file, the data you pass to the batch file are called *batch parameters*. By the time you finish this lesson you will understand how to

- Access batch parameters within your batch file
- Use batch parameters to increase the power of your batch files

UNDERSTANDING BATCH PARAMETERS

To better understand how batch parameters work, consider the following batch file, ONEPAGE.BAT, which clears your screen display and then uses the DOS MORE command to display the contents of your AUTOEXEC.BAT file one screenful at a time. If your AUTOEXEC.BAT file is very long, the batch file will stop after displaying each screen, displaying the following message:

```
— More —
```

When you press ENTER, the batch file will display the next screenful of output. The following commands are included in ONEPAGE.BAT:

```
@ECHO OFF
CLS
MORE < C:\AUTOEXEC.BAT
```

To execute this batch file, you type the batch name at the DOS prompt as shown here:

```
C:\> ONEPAGE    <ENTER>
```

In this case, the batch file ONEPAGE.BAT makes it very easy for you to display the contents of your AUTOEXEC.BAT file. A more useful batch file, however, would let you display the contents of any text file. For example, assume that you want to display the contents of your CONFIG.SYS file one screenful at a time. To do so, you could invoke the batch file with the desired filename, as shown here:

77

Rescued by DOS

```
C:\> ONEPAGE CONFIG.SYS  <ENTER>
```
— Batch file name
— Batch parameter

For your batch to support batch parameters, you need to place special symbols in your batch file that represent the parameters. In the case of the batch file ONEPAGE.BAT, you would change the batch file as shown here:

```
@ECHO OFF
CLS
MORE < %1
```
— Batch parameter symbol

In this case, the symbol **%1** represents the first batch parameter. If you invoke this batch file with the filename CONFIG.SYS, DOS will replace the symbol %1 with the filename, as shown here:

```
C:\> ONEPAGE  CONFIG.SYS  <ENTER>

    @ECHO OFF
    CLS
    MORE < %1

        @ECHO OFF
        CLS
        MORE < CONFIG.SYS
```

Likewise, if your invoke the batch file with the filename C:\AUTOEXEC.BAT, the batch file will display the contents of the file AUTOEXEC.BAT one screen at a time.

USING A BATCH PARAMETER

A batch parameter is a value you pass to the batch file when you type the batch filename at the DOS prompt. To support parameters, you must place special symbols within your batch file. The symbol %1, for example, corresponds to your first batch parameter. When you invoke the batch file, DOS will automatically replace each occurrence of the symbol with its corresponding parameter value. For example, the following batch file, CD_LOOK.BAT, selects the directory specified in the command and then uses the DIR command to display the files the directory contains:

```
@ECHO OFF
CD  %1
DIR /P
```

(continued on next page)

17: Using Batch Parameters

> (continued from previous page)
>
> If you invoke the batch file with the directory name DOS, for example, the batch file will select the DOS directory and then list the files the directory contains:
>
> ```
> C:\> CD_LOOK    C:\DOS   <ENTER>
> ```

DOS Supports Parameters %1 Through %9

As you have just learned, to support batch parameters, you need to include special symbols within your batch files. In the case of the batch file ONEPAGE.BAT, you used the symbol %1 to correspond to the first batch parameter. If your batch file requires more than one parameter, you will need to include additional symbols such as %2, %3, and so on through %9.

To better understand how these symbols work, create the following batch file, VIEWPARS.BAT, which displays the value of each batch parameter:

```
@ECHO OFF
CLS
ECHO Parameter one is %1
ECHO Parameter two is %2
ECHO Parameter three is %3
ECHO Parameter four is %4
ECHO Parameter five is %5
ECHO Parameter six is %6
ECHO Parameter seven is %7
ECHO Parameter eight is %8
ECHO Parameter nine is %9
```

As you can see, the batch file uses ECHO to display message to the screen. The symbols %1 through %9 correspond to the batch parameters. When you include parameters within the batch command line, DOS will automatically substitute the symbols with the corresponding parameters.

To understand this process better, invoke the batch file as shown here:

> ```
> C:\> VIEWPARS  Rescued  by  DOS  Jamsa  Press  <ENTER>
> ```

In this case, the batch file will display the following output:

Rescued by DOS

```
C:\> VIEWPARS  Rescued  by  DOS  Jamsa  Press  <ENTER>
Parameter one is Rescued
Parameter two is by
Parameter three is DOS
Parameter four is Jamsa
Parameter five is Press
Parameter six is
Parameter seven is
Parameter eight is
Parameter nine is
```

If you do not specify a value for a specific batch parameter, DOS will replace the parameter with a nonexistent value. In the case of the previous batch command, DOS will assign the nonexistent value to the parameters %6 through %9.

Experiment with the batch file VIEWPARS.BAT, passing to it different parameters and a different number of parameters. For example, you might want to invoke the batch file using the following command lines:

```
C:\> VIEWPARS   <ENTER>
```

```
C:\> VIEWPARS AA BB CC DD EE FF GG HH II JJ KK LL <ENTER>
```

You might notice, in the case of the second command line, that DOS ignores any batch parameters after the ninth one.

WHAT YOU NEED TO KNOW

In Lesson 18 you will learn how to use the DOS IF command to let your batch files make their own decisions. Using the IF command, your batch files can determine whether a specific file exists, whether a command successfully executed, or even whether a batch parameter contains a specific value. Before you continue with Lesson 18, make sure you have learned the following:

- ☑ A batch parameter is information you pass to a batch file, such as a filename.

- ☑ To use batch parameters, your batch file must use the symbols %1 through %9. When you invoke the batch file, DOS will automatically assign the first parameter to %1, the second to %2, and so on.

- ☑ If you do not specify a value for a specific batch parameter, DOS will assign a null or nonexistent value. If you specify more than nine parameters values, DOS will ignore the extras.

Lesson 18

Decision-Making Batch Files

All of the batch files you have created throughout this book have executed their commands in order, from top to bottom. As your batch files become more complex, the batch files themselves can begin to make decisions. For example, if a specific file exists, the batch file might perform one command, and second command if the file does not exist. Likewise, if the previous command ended with an error, you might want the batch file to end immediately, instead of executing the remainder of the batch file commands. This lesson examines the DOS IF command, which lets your batch files make decisions. By the time you finish this lesson, you will understand how to

- Execute a batch command only if a specific file exists
- Execute a batch command depending on the previous command's success
- Execute a batch command if a batch parameter contains a specific value
- Execute a batch command when one of the previous conditions fail
- Skip commands in a batch file using the GOTO command

UNDERSTANDING THE IF COMMAND

The DOS IF command lets your batch files test a condition. If the condition is true, the batch file will execute a specified command. The IF command lets your batch files test three different types of conditions. In general, the IF command consists of two parts: the tested condition and the command the batch file executes if the condition is true:

```
IF   condition   SomeCommand
```

TESTING WHETHER A SPECIFIC FILE EXISTS

Many batch files rely on the existence of a specific file. For example, a batch file that executes payroll commands may test if the file PAYROLL.DAT exists. The following batch file, TESTFILE.BAT, illustrates the use of the IF command to test for the existence of several different files. If the file exists, the IF command displays a message so stating. In this case, the batch file tests for the files CONFIG.SYS and AUTOEXEC.BAT:

```
@ECHO OFF
IF EXIST CONFIG.SYS ECHO The file CONFIG.SYS exists
IF EXIST AUTOEXEC.BAT ECHO The file AUTOEXEC.BAT exists
```

If you invoke this batch file from the root directory (which contains the two files), the batch file will display the following output:

```
C:\> TESTFILE  <ENTER>
The file CONFIG.SYS exists
The file AUTOEXEC.BAT exists
```

If you run the batch file from a different directory, within which the files do not exist, the messages are not displayed.

Testing for a Specific File

To test for the existence of a specific file in your batch files, use the IF EXIST command. If the file specified exists, the batch file will execute the specified command. If the file does not exist, the batch file will not execute the command. The following IF EXIST command, for example, tests for a file named PAYROLL.DAT. If the file exists, the batch file will execute the PAYROLL program:

```
IF EXIST PAYROLL.DAT PAYROLL
```

Testing the Previous Program's Success

As you have learned, the commands you execute do not always succeed. When you issue commands from the DOS prompt, you can determine that the command has failed by reading the error messages displayed. When you execute commands from within a batch file, however, there may be times when the batch file should determine a command's success before executing the remaining commands. To help your batch files perform such operations, many commands provide DOS with an *exit status value* when they end. Depending on the program's success, the exit status value returned to DOS can differ. For example, assume the program PAYROLL.EXE returns the exit status value 0 if an error occurred (such as a file was not found) and 1 if the program is successful. Using the IF ERRORLEVEL command, the following batch file runs the PRINTCHK program only if the PAYROLL program was successful:

```
@ECHO OFF
PAYROLL
IF ERRORLEVEL 1 PRINTCHK
```

When DOS encounters an IF ERRORLEVEL command within a batch file, DOS examines the previous program's exit status value. If the exit value is greater than or equal to the value specified, DOS executes the specified command. In the case of the previous batch file, DOS will only execute the PRINTCHK program if the exit status value of the PAYROLL program is greater than or equal

18: Decision-Making Batch Files

to 1. As you examine different batch files, you might encounter IF ERRORLEVEL commands. To understand the command's purpose, examine the number that follows the word *ERRORLEVEL*. If the preceding program exits with a value greater than or equal to the number, the batch file will execute the specified command. If the exit status value is less than the number, the command will not execute.

> ### TESTING A COMMAND'S SUCCESS
>
> Many batch files only want to execute a specific command when the preceding command was successful. To perform such processing, your batch files can use the IF ERRORLEVEL command. When DOS encounters an IF ERRORLEVEL command, DOS will examine the previous command's exit status value. If the previous command exited with a value greater than or equal to the number specified, the batch file will execute the specified command. However, if the previous programs exits with a status value that is less than the number specified, the command does not execute.
>
> Not all commands provide exit status values to DOS when they end. To determine if a specific command provides an exit status value, use the Help command, discussed in Lesson 4.

TESTING A BATCH PARAMETER'S VALUE

In Lesson 17 you learned how to use parameters within your batch files using the symbols %1 through %9. When you pass parameters to a batch file, there will be times when the batch file will need to know the parameter's value.

For example, assume that you have a batch file named ACCOUNT.BAT, that lets you run your company's payroll, ledger, and cash flow programs. To run the payroll program, for example, you invoke the ACCOUNT with the parameter value PAYROLL, as shown here:

```
C:\> ACCOUNT  PAYROLL  <Enter>
```

Likewise to run the general ledger software you would invoke the batch file with LEDGER:

```
C:\> ACCOUNT  LEDGER  <Enter>
```

Finally, to run the cash flow analysis program, you would invoke the batch file with the parameter CASHFLOW:

```
C:\> ACCOUNT  CASHFLOW  <Enter>
```

Rescued by DOS

Within your batch file, you must test the value of the parameter %1 to determine which program to run. To perform the test, you can use the IF command to compare the parameter's value to a specific string of characters. For example, to test if %1 contains PAYROLL, you can use the IF command as follows:

```
IF  "%1"=="PAYROLL"   PAYROLL
```

In this case, if %1 contains PAYROLL, the IF command will run the PAYROLL program. If %1 contains a different value, the PAYROLL program will not run. The following batch commands test for all three parameter values:

```
@ECHO OFF
IF "%1"=="PAYROLL"  PAYROLL
IF "%1"=="LEDGER"   LEDGER
IF "%1"=="CASHFLOW"  CASHFLOW
```

When you use the IF command to test a parameter's value in this way, the letters tested must match exactly. In other words, DOS will not consider the strings "Payroll" and "PAYROLL" as the same.

You should get into the habit of placing the strings you want to compare within double quotes as previously shown. If you don't include the double quotes and the user invokes the batch file without specifying a value for %1, an error will occur. To understand comparing strings with the IF command better, create the following batch file, STR_TEST.BAT:

```
@ECHO OFF
IF "%1"=="RESCUED"  ECHO Rescued, I've been rescued!
IF "%1"=="By"   ECHO By Whom? By DOS!
IF "%1"=="DOS" ECHO I love DOS!
```

Experiment with this batch file, invoking it with the parameters RESCUED, BY, and DOS, as shown here:

```
C:\> STR_TEST  RESCUED  <ENTER>
Rescued, I've been rescued!

C:\> STR_TEST  BY  <ENTER>
By Whom? By DOS!

C:\> STR_TEST DOS  <ENTER>
I love DOS!
```

Next, invoke the batch file with a different parameter, such as Rescued. Because the DOS will not find an exact match, the batch file will not display any output.

18: Decision-Making Batch Files

There may be times when you need to ensure that the user invokes the batch files with a parameter value. As you read in Lesson 17, if the user does not specify a parameter value, DOS assigns the null value. The following IF command shows you how to test for the null or nonexistent value:

```
IF "%1"=="" ECHO No parameter value specified
```

> ### Testing for Equal Strings
>
> Many batch files need to test the value of different batch parameters. To do so, the batch files can use the IF command to compare a parameter's value to a specific string. When DOS compares strings using IF, the letters within the two strings must match exactly (even in upper and lower cases). If the strings are the same, DOS will execute the command that follows.

Testing for a Failed Condition

Each of the batch files previously shown have used the IF command to execute a command when a given condition was true. There may be times, however, when you will want your batch file to execute a command when a condition is not true. For example, if the file PAYROLL.DAT does not exist, you may want the batch file to display a message notifying the user. To test for conditions that are not true, you simply need to place NOT immediately after the IF, as shown here:

```
IF NOT EXIST PAYROLL.DAT ECHO PAYROLL.DAT was not found
```

You can use the NOT operator with all three IF command types. For example, the following command would display a message if the parameter %1 does not contain PAYROLL:

```
IF NOT "%1"=="PAYROLL" ECHO Parameter is not PAYROLL
```

The following batch file, SHOWAUTO.BAT, uses the TYPE command to display the contents of the file AUTOEXEC.BAT. If you invoke the batch file from the root directory (which contains the file AUTOEXEC.BAT), the batch file will display the file's contents. If you invoke the batch file from a different directory, however, the batch file will display a message telling you AUTOEXEC.BAT was not found:

```
@ECHO OFF
IF EXIST AUTOEXEC.BAT TYPE AUTOEXEC.BAT
IF NOT EXIST AUTOEXEC.BAT ECHO AUTOEXEC.BAT not found
```

As you have learned, IF ERRORLEVEL responds to error levels greater than the IF statement, as well as equal to it. If you want to test for a specific error level, no higher/no lower, such as 1, you must exclude the higher ones specifically with an IF NOT ERRORLEVEL statement, such as this:

85

```
@ECHO OFF
PAYROLL
IF ERRORLEVEL 1 IF NOT ERRORLEVEL 2 PRINTCHK
```

Branching from One Batch File Location to Another

When your batch files make decisions with IF, there are many times when the batch file will need to execute a group of commands when a specific condition is true. In such cases, your batch files can use the GOTO command to jump to a specific location within the batch file that is designated by a label. For example, assume that when the user invokes the batch file ACCOUNT.BAT with the PAYROLL parameter, the batch file executes the commands PAYROLL and PRINTCHK. Likewise, when the user invokes the batch file with LEDGER, the batch file invokes the ACCT_REC, ACCT_PAY, and BALSHEET commands. Finally, should the user invoke the batch file with CASHFLOW, the batch file executes the CASHFLOW and PRINTFLO commands. In this case, you can divide your batch file into three parts, assigning each part a unique label, such as :PAYROLL, :LEDGER, and :CASHFLOW. Note the use of the colon at the start of each label name. Next, the batch file's IF commands will use GOTO to jump to the correct the commands, as shown here:

```
IF "%1"=="PAYROLL" GOTO PAYROLL
IF "%1"=="LEDGER" GOTO LEDGER
IF "%1"=="CASHFLOW" GOTO CASHFLOW
GOTO DONE
```

The last GOTO statement directs the batch file to branch to the label named DONE if none of the other IF commands are true (have found a match). Your entire batch file becomes the following:

```
@ECHO OFF
IF "%1"=="PAYROLL" GOTO PAYROLL
IF "%1"=="LEDGER" GOTO LEDGER
IF "%1"=="CASHFLOW" GOTO CASHFLOW
GOTO DONE

:PAYROLL
PAYROLL
PRINTCHK
GOTO DONE

:LEDGER
ACCT_REC
ACCT_PAY
BALSHEET
GOTO DONE
```

18: Decision-Making Batch Files

```
:CASHFLOW
CASHFLOW
PRINTFLO
GOTO DONE

:DONE
```

Note that after each group of commands completes, they use the GOTO DONE command to jump to the :DONE label. In this way, the batch file immediately ends without executing other commands. As you examine batch files, you will encounter the use of the GOTO command on a regular basis. As you do, simply search the batch file into you find the corresponding label. In this way, you will begin to read larger batch files like a road map, going from one label to another.

> **BRANCHING FROM ONE LOCATION TO ANOTHER**
>
> Many batch files need to execute a group of related commands when a specific condition is true. In such cases, you can divide your batch file into command groups, assigning each group a unique label name. Batch file label names must begin with a colon (:). Using the DOS GOTO command, your batch file can jump to specific locations. When you specify a label name within the GOTO command, you leave off the colon.

WHAT YOU NEED TO KNOW

In Lesson 19 you will learn how to use a special batch file named AUTOEXEC.BAT to execute specific commands automatically each time your system starts. Before you continue with Lesson 19, however, make sure that you have learned the following:

- ☑ Using the DOS IF command, your batch files can make their own decisions. The IF command supports three different condition types. If a condition evaluates as true, DOS executes the specified command.

- ☑ The IF EXIST command lets your batch files determine if a specific file exists.

- ☑ The IF ERRORLEVEL command lets your batch files determine the success of the previous program.

- ☑ The IF *String*==*String* command lets your batch files compare one string's letters to another.

- ☑ When your batch files need to test for a failed condition, you can place the NOT operator immediately after the word IF.

- ☑ Using the GOTO command, you can jump from one location in your batch file to another.

87

Rescued by DOS

Lesson 19

Automatically Executing Commands in AUTOEXEC.BAT

As you have learned, DOS batch files provide a convenient way for you to execute two or more related commands. As it turns out, DOS provides a special batch file named AUTOEXEC.BAT that you can use to specify one or more commands you want DOS to automatically (AUTO) execute (EXEC) each time your system starts. This lesson examines AUTOEXEC.BAT and several commands users commonly place within it. By the time you finish this lesson you will understand how to

- Examine your current AUTOEXEC.BAT file
- Make changes to your AUTOEXEC.BAT file
- Include common commands within AUTOEXEC.BAT
- Protect yourself from inadvertent changes to AUTOEXEC.BAT

LOCATING AND VIEWING AUTOEXEC.BAT

Each time your system starts, DOS examines your disk's root directory for a special file named AUTOEXEC.BAT. If DOS locates the file, DOS automatically executes the commands the file contains. To view the contents of your AUTOEXEC.BAT file, select the root as the current directory:

```
C:\DOS> CHDIR \    <ENTER>
```

Next, use the DOS TYPE command to view the file's contents:

```
C:\> TYPE  AUTOEXEC.BAT  <ENTER>
```

The TYPE command will display the file's contents on your screen, similar to the following:

```
C:\> TYPE  AUTOEXEC.BAT  <ENTER>
PATH C:\DOS;C:\WINDOWS;C:\BATCH
PROMPT $P$G
SET TEMP=C:\TEMP
SMARTDRV
```

19: Automatically Executing Commands in AUTOEXEC.BAT

As you can see, AUTOEXEC.BAT, like all DOS batch files, contains a list of commands DOS will execute in succession. If, for some reason, your disk's root directory does not contain an AUTOEXEC.BAT file, DOS will instead, automatically execute the DATE and TIME commands, briefly discussed in Lesson 3, each time your system starts. If your disk does not have an AUTOEXEC.BAT file, you will need to create one.

> ## Understanding AUTOEXEC.BAT
>
> Each time your system starts, DOS automatically searches your disk's root directory for the file AUTOEXEC.BAT. If DOS locates the batch file, DOS executes the commands it contains. Most users use AUTOEXEC.BAT to execute commands that set up their system in some way, such as defining the command path using the PATH command, or by defining the DOS prompt.

Editing AUTOEXEC.BAT

Like all batch files, AUTOEXEC.BAT is an ASCII file. ASCII files are files that contain only letters, numbers, and standard punctuation symbols. ASCII files do not contain the hidden characters often used by word processors to control text alignment and document formatting. Thus, you should not use a word processor to edit AUTOEXEC.BAT. Instead, use the DOS EDIT command. To begin, invoke EDIT with the filename AUTOEXEC.BAT, as shown here:

```
C:\> EDIT AUTOEXEC.BAT <ENTER>
```

EDIT will display the file within an editing screen, as shown in Figure 19.1.

Figure 19.1 Using EDIT to create or edit AUTOEXEC.BAT.

89

After you have made your desired changes to the file, hold down the ALT key and press **F** to select EDIT's File menu or use your mouse to click on it. Next, use your keyboard arrow keys to highlight the Save option and press ENTER. Select the File menu a second time and choose Exit.

As a rule, you should always make a copy of the current contents of your AUTOEXEC.BAT file before you make any changes to the file. To do so, use the COPY command, as shown here:

```
C:\> COPY   AUTOEXEC.BAT    AUTOEXEC.OLD   <ENTER>
```

Should you later find that your change to the file does not work, you can always restore the file's previous contents.

WHICH COMMANDS BELONG IN *AUTOEXEC.BAT*

AUTOEXEC.BAT lets you specify the commands you want DOS to execute each time your system starts. As a general rule, most AUTOEXEC.BAT files contain a PATH command (discussed in Lesson 13), which defines your command path, and a PROMPT command, which directs DOS to display the current drive and directory name within the prompt. In the case of the AUTOEXEC.BAT file just shown, the following PATH command defined the command path:

```
PATH C:\DOS;C:\WINDOWS;C:\BATCH
```

In this case, DOS will automatically search the directories DOS, WINDOWS, and BATCH for your program files. Likewise, the following PROMPT command directs DOS to display the current drive and directory name within the command prompt:

```
PROMPT $P$G
```

The PROMPT command uses special characters, called *metacharacters*, such as $P and $G, which direct DOS to display different items within the prompt. In this case, the $P metacharacter directs DOS to display the current drive and directory. Likewise, the $G character directs DOS to display the greater-than character (>). For a detailed listing of the PROMPT metacharacters, use the HELP command, discussed in Lesson 4.

The batch file previously shown also included the following commands:

```
SET TEMP=C:\TEMP
SMARTDRV
```

Some programs (such as Windows) create temporary files as they execute. Before the programs create the files, they search a special storage location DOS sets aside in memory called the *environment* for an entry named TEMP that specifies a directory within which they should create

19: Automatically Executing Commands in AUTOEXEC.BAT

the files. In this case, the programs would create their temporary files in a directory named TEMP, which resides on drive C. The DOS SMARTDRV command installs special software that improves your system performance by reducing the number of slow disk read and write operations your computer must perform. Lesson 54 discusses SMARTDRV in detail. Finally, many users like to start Microsoft Windows automatically each time they turn on their system. To do so, they simply place the WIN command at the end of their AUTOEXEC.BAT file.

If your AUTOEXEC.BAT contains commands other than those presented here, do not remove the commands until you fully understand each command's use.

PROTECTING YOUR AUTOEXEC.BAT FILE

You should always make a copy of your AUTOEXEC.BAT file before you change the file in any way. In addition, you should make a copy of the file before you install new software. Many software installation programs make changes to your AUTOEXEC.BAT file. Should the program's change to AUTOEXEC.BAT create an error, you still have your original copy.

Note: *Should a change you make to your AUTOEXEC.BAT file prevent your system from starting, turn your computer's power off and on. As DOS begins to start, press the* **F8** *function key. DOS will let you type Y or N to control the processing of each entry in your CONFIG.SYS and then will let you type Y or N to control whether or not it executes each command in your AUTOEXEC.BAT file. For more information on CONFIG.SYS, turn to Lesson 29.*

WHAT YOU NEED TO KNOW

In Lesson 20 you will examine your computer's common hardware components. Before you continue with Lesson 20, however, make sure that you have learned the following:

- ☑ Each time your system starts, DOS searches your disk's root directory for a special batch file named AUTOEXEC.BAT. If the batch file exists, DOS executes each command it contains, in order. If, the file does not exist, DOS executes, instead, the DATE and TIME commands.

- ☑ Before you make any changes to your AUTOEXEC.BAT file, make sure you first create a backup copy of the file's contents. Should your change to the file create an error, you can restore the original file's contents.

- ☑ Most AUTOEXEC.BAT files contain a PATH command, which defines the command path, and a PROMPT command, which controls the appearance of the DOS prompt.

Section Five

GETTING TO KNOW YOUR HARDWARE

Your computer uses hardware such as your keyboard, screen, and printer, and software such as DOS, Windows, a word processor, and spreadsheet. Although the sizes and shapes of PCs and notebook computers might differ, most use similar pieces of hardware. In this section you will learn how to use such common hardware as your keyboard, monitor, mouse, printer, and disks.

Lesson 20 Common PC Hardware

Lesson 21 Using Your Keyboard

Lesson 22 Using Your Monitor

Lesson 23 Working with a Mouse

Lesson 24 Using Your Printer

Lesson 25 Understanding Computer Ports

Lesson 26 Storing Information on Disk

Lesson 27 Working with Floppy Disks

Lesson 28 Working with Hard Disks

Lesson 20

Common PC Hardware

Hardware is your computer's physical components, such your monitor, keyboard, printer, and even the cables that connect them. This lesson introduces the common hardware found on most PCs. Before you can feel comfortable with your computer, you need to understand the function each piece of hardware provides. By the time you finish this lesson you will understand how to

- Identify your computer's primary components and their functions
- Note the similarities between a desktop and notebook or laptop computer
- Understand the operation of your computer's monitor, mouse, keyboard, and printer
- Recognize your computer's disk drives

As you will find, understanding your computer's hardware is very easy.

COMPARING PC COMPONENTS

Whether you are using a desktop computer or a small notebook computer, your computer uses a system unit, keyboard, monitor, and disk drives. Figure 20.1 illustrates a standard desktop computer computer.

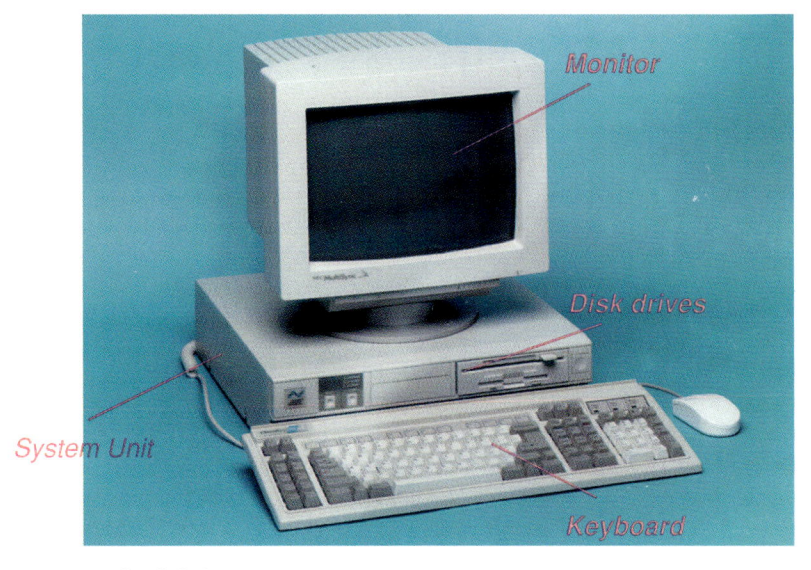

Figure 20.1 A standard desktop computer.

Rescued by DOS

As you can see, the primary difference between the standard desktop and tower-based computer is the chassis that holds the system unit. The *system unit* contains your computer's electronic brain—the central processing unit or *CPU*. In addition, the system unit houses your computer's memory and the chips and electronic boards that let your computer display information to the screen or send information to your printer. If you have limited space on your desk or if you plan to add many different hardware boards to your computer such as scanner, CD-ROM drive, or multimedia sound board, you might find the tower-based system unit more convenient. Other than size and shape, there is no difference between the two system unit chassis. In a similar way, Figure 20.2 illustrates a tower-based PC. As you can see, the components are very similar.

Figure 20.2 A standard desktop and tower-based computer.

Figure 20.3 illustrates a *notebook computer*. Notebook computers are so named because there size and weight allow you to carry the computer with you, much as you would carry a notebook. As you can see, the notebook computer has a keyboard, monitor, and system unit.

20: Common PC Hardware

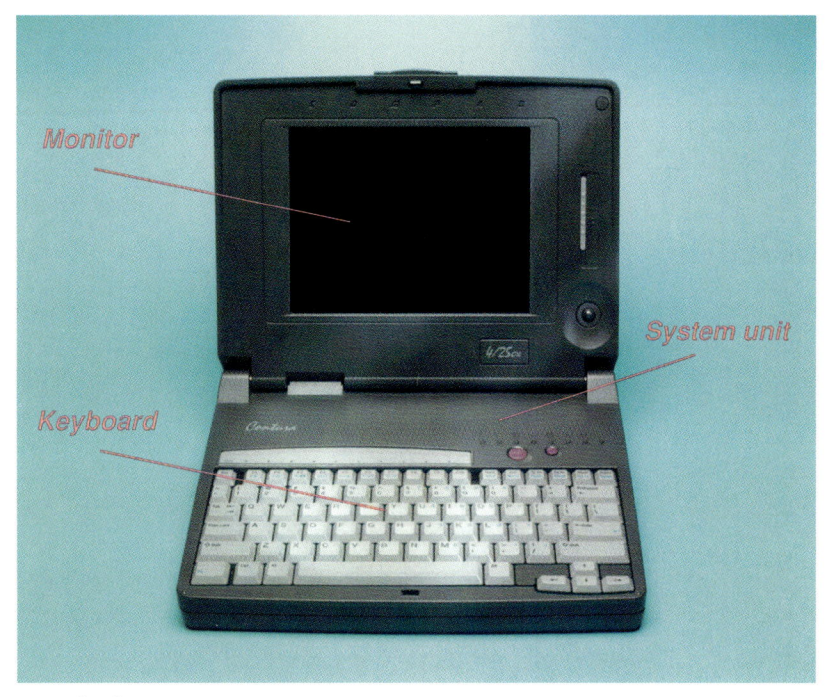

Figure 20.3 *A notebook computer.*

ADDITIONAL HARDWARE DEVICES

As you will learn in Lesson 23, many programs let you use a mouse to select menu entries or quickly perform other operations by aiming a *mouse pointer* at objects that appear on your screen. The mouse pointer normally appears on your screen as a small rectangle or arrow-shaped object. As you move the mouse on your desk, the mouse pointer moves in same direction on your screen. If you are using Microsoft Windows, for example, you are probably very familiar with the mouse. Unfortunately, not all DOS-based programs support a mouse. When a program does not support a mouse, you must use your keyboard to perform all operations.

As you will learn in Lesson 24, your printer lets you create *hard copy*, printouts of your reports, memos, letters, and other documents you create. Normally, you will use the program within which you created the document for printing. A word processing program, for example, places special symbols within your document files that control formatting, italics, paragraph alignment, and so on. These special symbols are meaningful only to your word processor. If you tried to print the word processing document file from within a different program, or even from DOS, your printout would very likely contain many strange characters.

Inside the System Unit

Note: *Working inside the system unit can be dangerous, not only to your computer, but to yourself. If you need to add a new hardware board or additional memory to your computer, make sure that you unplug your system unit before you begin. Next, have an experienced user or your computer retailer assist you.*

Several of the lessons that follow discuss different system unit components, such as disk drives and your computer's electronic memory. The system unit also houses your computer's electronic brain or central processing unit. The CPU is an electronic chip about an inch square that oversees all operations within your computer. The CPU is normally named using a number such as the 386 or 486. The CPU's number helps you determine your computer's speed and capabilities. When the IBM PC was first released in 1981, it used a chip called the 8088. In 1984, IBM upgraded the PC using a faster and more power 80286 or simply 286 for short. Since that time, the 386 was introduced and then replaced by the powerful 486. Recently, Intel released the very fast and powerful Pentium processor. The Pentium processor is many hundred times faster than the original 8088.

What You Need to Know

In Lesson 21 you will learn how to use your computer's keyboard. Before you continue with Lesson 21, make sure that you have learned the following:

- ☑ Hardware is your computer's keyboard, monitor, system unit, and even the cables that connect them and the nuts and bolts that hold them together.

- ☑ Regardless of your computer's type, all PCs use a monitor, keyboard, and system unit.

- ☑ Your computer's system unit houses your computer's electronics, such as the central processing unit and memory.

- ☑ Most new users do not have a reason to open their system unit. Should you ever need to work inside the system unit, unplug the unit and have an experienced user assist you.

Lesson 21

Using Your Keyboard

No matter which programs you run, you're going to have to type. This lesson examines the PC keyboard and its difference between a standard typewriter keyboard. By learning some keyboard secrets, you still may not enjoy typing, but you may find it easier. By the time you finish this lesson you will understand how to

- Locate the standard, numeric, cursor control, and function keys
- Determine when you should use a SHIFT key versus CAPS LOCK
- Understand CTRL and ALT key combinations
- Enable and disable your keyboard's numeric keys
- Quickly repeat your previous DOS command using F1 and F3

TAKING A LOOK AT YOUR KEYBOARD

Figure 21.1 illustrates a standard keyboard. If you look closely at the keyboard, you will find that it contains four different types of keys: standard keys, numeric keys, function keys, and cursor control keys.

Figure 21.1 Key types on a standard keyboard.

Rescued by DOS

In a similar way, Figure 21.2 illustrates a small notebook computer. Although the keys are positioned much closer, you can still quickly identify different key types.

Figure 21.2 Key types on a notebook computer keyboard.

Using the Standard Keyboard Keys

Your keyboard's standard keyboard keys are positioned and behave very much like a typewriter keyboard. If you examine your keys closely, you will find the keys **QWERTY** appear along the top row of letters, just as they would on a typewriter. To type uppercase letters, you simply hold down a right or left SHIFT key as you type. If you need to type several letters in uppercase, your keyboard provides a CAPS LOCK key. The first time you press the CAPS LOCK key directs your PC to type everything in uppercase (to type a lowercase letter you must hold down the SHIFT key). The second time you press the CAPS LOCK restores the keyboard to normal operations.

Correcting errors with a computer is much easier than with a typewriter. Should you mistype a letter, simply press the BACKSPACE key to erase the letter. If you need to erase several letters, press the BACKSPACE key the required number of times. As you type, your computer will advance a small cursor on your screen to help you track your current position. As you will learn next, many programs let you press the keyboard's cursor control keys to position the cursor.

21: Using Your Keyboard

Using the Cursor Control Keys

As you type, your PC displays a small cursor on your screen, which indicates your current position. The next character you type will be displayed at the current cursor position. When you use your PC to create a letter or report, there may be times when you need to move throughout the report either to add or delete text or to correct existing text. To do so, you simply move the cursor to the desired location using the cursor control keys. If you examine your keyboard closely, you will find cursor control keys that contain an up, down, right, or left arrow. Each time you type one of these keys, your PC will move the cursor one character position in the direction of the key's arrow. Unlike the BACKSPACE key, which erases characters, pressing an arrow key places the cursor next to a specific character. Assume for example, that you wanted to add a word to a sentence three lines up. To do so, you would press the UP ARROW key three times and then use the RIGHT ARROW or LEFT ARROW key to position the cursor at the desired location. Depending on your keyboard, your cursor control keys might play a dual role, depending on the state of the NUMLOCK key, discussed next.

Using the Numeric Keypad

To make it easy for you to type numbers quickly, your keyboard contains a set of keys called the *numeric keypad*. The keypad contains keys for the numbers 0 through 9 and keys for addition, subtraction, multiplication and division, similar to those you would find on a ten-key adding machine. On most keyboards, the numeric keys also have arrow keys that you control the cursor. Before you can use the numeric keys to type in numbers, you must first press a special key labeled NUMLOCK. When you press the NUMLOCK key, your PC might illuminate a small light, indicating that the NUMLOCK is active. If you later want to use the keys for cursor positioning, press the NUMLOCK key a second time. The NUMLOCK light will turn off, and the keys will move the cursor.

Using the Keyboard Function Keys

To make common operations easier to perform, many of the software programs you will run make use of your keyboard's function keys, which typically appear near the top of your keyboard. Depending on your keyboard, you may have functions named **F1** through **F10**, or possibly through **F12**. When you use a word processing program to create a letter, for example, you might press the **F5** key to print your letter and the **F6** key to spell-check it. The meaning of the function keys depends on your current program. If you are using DOS the **F1** and **F3** function keys let you quickly repeat the previous command. For example, assume that you used the DIR command to list the files on drive A as shown here:

```
C:\> DIR  A:  <ENTER>
```

Each time you press the **F1** function key, DOS will display one letter of the previous command. For example, if you press **F1** one time, DOS will display the first letter of the last command, which in this case is D:

Rescued by DOS

```
C:\> D
```

If you press **F1** two more times, DOS will display the letters I-R, as shown here:

```
C:\> DIR
```

Press the ENTER key to execute the DIR command. Next, when DOS redisplays its prompt, press the **F3** function key. DOS will immediately recall the entire pressed command. Using **F1** and **F3** within DOS, you can quickly repeat commands. Other programs will use the function keys differently.

USING CTRL AND ALT KEY COMBINATIONS

Just as many programs assign different operations to your keyboard's function keys, many programs will also assign different operations to CTRL and ALT key combinations. The key combinations are so named because you must hold down either the CTRL or ALT key and then press another letter. For example, you can end many DOS commands using the CTRL-C keyboard combination. To press CTRL-C, hold down the CTRL key and press C (either in upper- or lowercase). Likewise, many programs use the ALT-F *key combination* to select a File menu. To press ALT-F, you hold down the ALT key and press F. As you work with more software programs, you will encounter different keyboard combinations. Normally, you simply hold down the specified keys in the order listed.

WHAT YOU NEED TO KNOW

In Lesson 22 you learn how to control your PC's monitor and video display. Before you continue with Lesson 22, make sure that you have learned the following:

- ☑ Most keyboards consist of four parts: standard, numeric, function, and cursor-control keys. Your keyboard's standard keys are very similar to those found on a typewriter keyboard.

- ☑ Numeric keys help you quickly type numbers. The numeric keypad is arranged similarly to that of an adding machine. To use the numeric keys, you may need to first press the NUMLOCK key.

- ☑ Your keyboard contains keys labeled **F1** through **F12**. Depending on the program that is currently running, the operation of these keys performs will differ.

- ☑ A keyboard combination is a collection of keys that you hold down at the same time. Many keyboard combinations include the CTRL or ALT key. To press the CTRL-C keyboard combination, for example, you would first hold down the CTRL key and then press C.

Lesson 22

Using Your Monitor

Your computer's monitor exists to display a program's output and the information you type at the keyboard. To display output on the monitor, your computer's system unit contains a video card from which you attach a cable to the monitor. Depending on your monitor type and the video card type, the number of colors your monitor can display and the sharpness of the images that appear on the screen will differ. This lesson examines the basics behind the PC's video display. By the time you finish this lesson you will understand how to

- Control your monitor's brightness and contrast
- Understand how resolution affects image sharpness
- Understand how video display cards such as EGA, VGA, and SuperVGA differ

UNDERSTANDING RESOLUTION

Your monitor displays images by illuminating small dots. If you have a color monitor, each dot can be assigned a different color. The more dots your screen contains, the sharper the images will appear. Your screen's *resolution* defines the number of dots that can be used to display an image. The higher your screen resolution, the more dots, and hence the sharper the image. Your screen's resolution is measured using X (horizontal) and Y (vertical) values. For example, if your screen has a resolution of 640 × 480, your screen has 640 dots across the x or horizontal axis and 480 vertically.

UNDERSTANDING VIDEO COLORS

If you are using a color monitor and color video card, your programs can display their output in color. It is important to note that, some programs, such as most of the DOS commands, do not use color. However, those programs that support color, normally let you chose the colors with which you want to work. Depending on your video card, the number of different colors your screen can display at one time will range from two (black and white) to as many as 16 million! In most cases, as the number of colors you are displaying increases, your resolution decreases. However, many newer video cards support high resolution and up to sixteen million colors. Figure 22.1, for example, illustrates a high-resolution graphic that contains a multitude of colors.

Figure 22.1 A high-resolution, high-color image.

YOUR VIDEO CARD AND MONITOR ARE A TEAM

Because images appear on the monitor screen, it is easy to think that the monitor controls the image resolution and colors. Actually, however, color and resolution is controlled by a video card contained inside your computer's system unit. Video cards have names, such as EGA, VGA, and SuperVGA, that describe their capabilities. Each year, as technology increases, so too does the number of colors and resolution the video cards can display. When you purchase a video card, you need to ensure that the card supports the resolution and number of colors you desire. Next, you must ensure that your monitor will work with the card and that the monitor's capabilities won't restrict those of the card.

Most newer monitors are *multisynch*, which means you can attach them to any of the video cards listed in Table 22.1 and they will work. However, monitors have two characteristics that affect the quality of your image display. The first is the monitor's *refresh rate*, which controls how many times a second the monitor redraws (refreshes) the image on your screen. For the image refresh to be undetectable to the human eye, you want the image refreshed 60 or more times per second. To achieve this refresh rate at higher resolutions, many monitors use a technique called *interlacing*, for which they only refresh every other line with each pass. For the sharpest image quality, you want noninterlacing. Second, monitors have a *dot pitch* value, which, determines the distance between two successive red, green, or blue dots, as shown in Figure 22.2. The smaller the dot pitch, the sharper your image. Most users will find a dot pitch near 0.25mm to be very good.

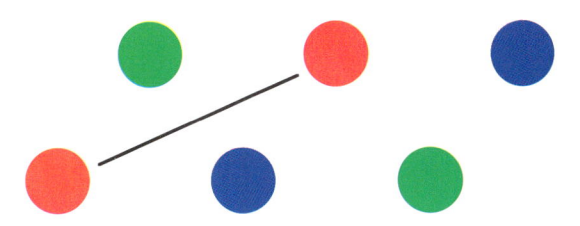

Figure 22.2 The monitor's dot pitch controls image sharpness.

Controlling Your Monitor's Brightness and Contrast

Your computer's monitor is very similar to the your television set, in that it converts incoming signals into images that appear on your screen. In addition, like your television, your monitor should have one or more knobs that let you control the brightness and contrast. If your monitor is near a window and periodically suffers from glare caused by reflecting light, you might want to adjust the brightness or contrast.

What You Need to Know

In Lesson 23 you will learn how to use your mouse within DOS-based programs. Before you continue with Lesson 23, make sure that you have learned the following:

- ☑ Most monitors provide knobs that let you adjust your monitor's brightness and contrast. In addition, many let you adjust the picture height and width, and let you fine-tune colors.

- ☑ The sharpness of images on your screen depends on the resolution of your video card. The higher your video card resolution, the greater the number of dots used to display the image.

- ☑ Depending on your video card, your monitor can display from two to sixteen million colors. As the number of different colors on your screen increases, the monitors resolution normally decreases.

- ☑ Your monitor and video card work as a team to display images. When you shop for a monitor or video card, make sure that your monitor compliments and does not restrict your video card capabilities.

Lesson 23

Working with a Mouse

If you have used Microsoft Windows, you are probably very familiar with how to use a mouse to select menu options, choose files, or to respond to dialog boxes. If you have not used Windows, or if you are having trouble using your mouse within DOS-based programs, this lesson will get you up and running. By the time you finish this lesson, you will understand how to

- Install software that lets your DOS-based programs use your mouse
- Perform common mouse operations

INSTALLING A MOUSE DRIVER

Unless you tell DOS to do otherwise, DOS does not support mouse operations. However, many DOS-based programs such as a word processor, spreadsheet, and even several DOS commands will let you use a mouse. Before you can use the mouse, however, you must run a special software program called a *mouse driver*, which, lets your DOS-based programs use the mouse. Normally, the name of the mouse driver program is MOUSE.EXE. If a mouse came with your computer, your computer retailer or manufacturer should have placed the mouse driver program on to your hard disk. If they did not, they may have provided a floppy disk that contains the program. To determine if the mouse driver is on your disk, select the root directory using CHDIR. Next, issue the following DIR command to search the directories on your disk for the file:

```
C:> DIR   MOUSE.*   /S   <ENTER>
```

If DOS displays the message **File not found**, your disk does not contain the mouse driver program. Contact your manufacturer and request a mouse driver. If the DIR locates the file, note the directory within which the file resides. If your mouse driver is not on your hard disk, but you have a copy of the program on floppy, create a directory named MOUSE on your hard disk and copy the driver file from your floppy disk into the directory. Lesson 19 discussed the special AUTOEXEC.BAT, which lets you run specific programs automatically each time your system starts. Because you may use the mouse on a regular basis, you should consider adding a command within AUTOEXEC.BAT that invokes the driver.

USING THE MOUSE

After you install the mouse driver, nothing will appear differently on your screen until you run a program that supports the mouse. At that time, a small shape such as a rectangle or arrow will appear on your screen:

23: Working with a Mouse

Mouse cursors

The shape is your mouse cursor. As you move your mouse across the your desk, the mouse cursor will move in the same direction across your screen. Figure 23.1 illustrates a mouse. Most mice have two buttons, called select buttons. To use the mouse to select a menu option, for example, you move the mouse across your desktop until the mouse pointer is aimed at the desired option. Then, you normally *click* the left mouse button by pressing and releasing the button. Some mouse operations require a double-click operation. To *double-click* your mouse, press and release the mouse select button twice in quick succession. If you are left handed, many programs let you switch the mouse buttons so you can click on objects by pressing the right mouse button.

Right select button
Left select button

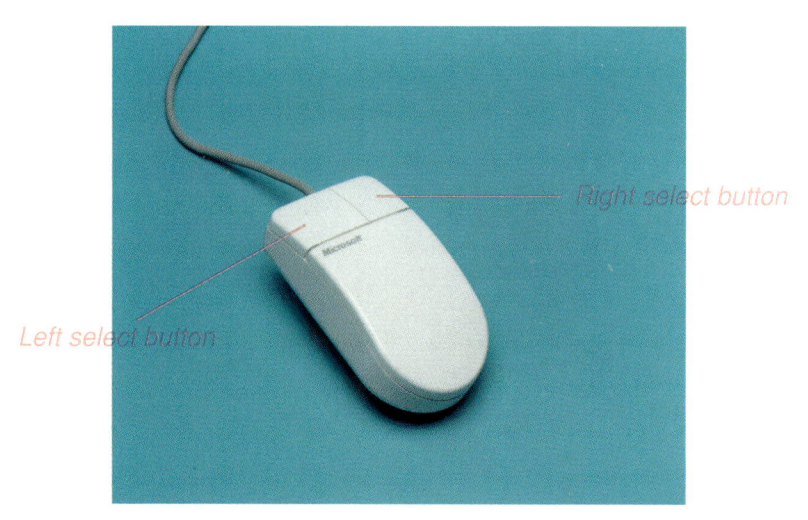

Figure 23.1 A common PC mouse.

MICE AND NOTEBOOK COMPUTERS

If you have notebook computer, your system might contain a small *trackball*, similar to the one shown in Figure 23.2. A trackball behaves similarly to a mouse in that you move the track ball to position the mouse cursor on your screen. Most notebook computers also have one or two buttons near the track ball that function as the mouse select buttons. To perform mouse click and double-click operations, you simply press and release these buttons.

105

Rescued by DOS

Figure 23.2 A trackball on a notebook computer.

What You Need to Know

In Lesson 24 you will learn how to use your printer within DOS. Before you continue with Lesson 24, make sure that you have learned the following:

- To use a mouse within your DOS-based programs, you must first install a mouse driver program. Normally, the name of the mouse driver program is MOUSE.EXE.

- Most users invoke the mouse driver program from within their AUTOEXEC.BAT file.

- When you use a program that supports a mouse, a small shape, called the mouse cursor will appear on your screen. As you mouse the mouse across your desk, the cursor will move across your screen in the same direction.

- To select a menu option or other object using your mouse, aim the mouse cursor at the object and then click your mouse's left select button.

- Some operations require a mouse double-click. To perform a double-click operation, press and release the mouse select button twice in quick succession.

Lesson 24

Working with a Printer

When you create documents with a word processor or spreadsheet, you will normally want to print hard copies of the documents on paper. Normally, you will use the program within which you created the document to print it. However, as you will learn, DOS does provide a PRINT command, with which you can print ASCII files such as the batch files discussed in Section 4 or the CONFIG.SYS file discussed in Section 6. By the time you finish this lesson you will understand how to

- Determine if your printer is connected to a parallel or serial port
- Use the PRINT command to print files
- Print your current screen contents

UNDERSTANDING YOUR PRINTER TYPE

Figure 24.1 illustrates a commonly used laser printer. Likewise, Figure 24.2 illustrates a dot matrix printer. In general, the two printers work in the same way, letting your print your documents from DOS or from within your software programs. The primary differences between a laser and dot matrix printer are price, quality, noise, and the ability to print graphics. Table 24.1 summarizes the differences between the laser and dot matrix printer.

Figure 24.1 A laser printer.

Rescued by DOS

Figure 24.1 A dot-matrix printer.

Feature	Status
Cost	Laser printer is the most expensive.
Noise	Laser printer is much quieter.
Quality	Laser printer has higher quality.
Graphics	Some dot-matrix printers cannot print graphics.
Multipart Forms	Require a dot matrix printer.

Table 24.1 General differences between a laser printer and a dot matrix printer.

Regardless of your printer type, the steps you must perform to use the printer within DOS or your application programs are the same. To begin, you need to know to which port your printer is connected.

DETERMINING YOUR PRINTER PORT

If you examine the back of your computer, you will find several ports to which you can connect devices to your computer. Lesson 25 examines your computer ports in detail. For now, however, you are concerned only with the port to which your printer is connected. If you examine the cable that connects your printer to your computer, you should find that the cable plugs into a 25-pin female parallel port connector.

24: Working with a Printer

If your printer is attached to a similar port, you can assume that your printer is connected to a parallel port named LPT1. Parallel ports are commonly used to connect line printers to your computer. Thus, the designation LPT (an abbreviation for line printer) is used within the parallel port names. The number 1 indicates that LPT1 is the first parallel port on your system. Your PC can contain up to three parallel ports. If your printer is connected to LPT1, you can use the name LPT1 or PRN (which assumes that your printer is a parallel printer) to refer to the printer. If your printer does not attach to a parallel port but, instead, connects to a 25- or 9-pin male connector, your printer is connected to serial port. Your PC can contain up to four serial ports. If your printer is connected to a serial port, you can assume it is connected to a port named COM1. In the past, serial ports were commonly used for data communications between computers over modems. Thus, the letters COM (an abbreviation for communications) are used within the serial port names.

Note: *Lesson 25 discusses the difference between parallel and serial ports. As you will learn, using a parallel port for printer operations will improve your performance, letting your output print much faster.*

PRINTING ASCII FILES

When you create a document with a word processor, the word processor embeds special hidden characters within the document file that control paragraph alignment, spacing, font selection, and so on. Unfortunately, these hidden characters are known only to your word processor. Thus, if you create a document with a word processor, you will need to print the document from within the word processor. If you tried to print the word processing document using the DOS PRINT command, the hidden special characters would not be understood, and your printout would appear garbled.

An *ASCII file* is a file that contains only letters, numbers, and standard punctuation symbols. Your batch files are good examples of ASCII files. Using the DOS TYPE command, you can display an ASCII file's contents on your screen. Likewise, using the DOS PRINT command, you can print an ASCII file. To print an ASCII file using PRINT, type **PRINT**, followed by the filename. For example, the following command directs PRINT to print a copy of the file AUTOEXEC.BAT:

```
C:\> PRINT   AUTOEXEC.BAT    <ENTER>
```

The PRINT command will display the following prompt, asking you to which port your printer is connected:

```
Name of list device [PRN]:
```

If your printer is connected to LPT1, you can press simply press ENTER to start printing the file. If your printer is connected to a different port, such as COM1, type in the port name and press ENTER. The file should begin printing. The PRINT command will only display this prompt one time. After you specify the port name, PRINT will use that port until you turn off your computer.

Rescued by DOS

UNDERSTANDING YOUR PRINTER'S ON LINE BUTTON

When your printer is connected to your computer and ready to print, your printer will normally illuminate a small ON LINE light. However, when your printer runs out of paper, it will normally go off line, turning off the light. After you add paper to the printer, you may need to press the on-line button before the printer will print. Should you try to print a document from DOS or from within a software program and nothing happens, make sure your printer is plugged in. Next, make sure the ON LINE light is lit.

PRINTING FROM WITHIN YOUR APPLICATIONS

If you create a document from within an application program such as a word processor, you should print the file using the application. If your printer is connected to LPT1, you can normally print from within the application without performing any other operations. If your printer is connected to a different port, you will need to tell your printer which port to use. In such cases, refer to the documentation that accompanied your software to determine the steps you must perform to specify the correct printer port. Most application programs provide a File menu from which you can save and open files. In addition, the File menu normally contains a Print option, which lets you print your files. Using the Print option you can quickly print your documents.

WHAT YOU NEED TO KNOW

In Lesson 25 you will learn to identify each of the ports that appear on the back of your computer. Before you continue with Lesson 25, make sure that you have learned the following:

- ☑ Whether you are using laser printer or dot matrix printer, the steps you must perform to print using DOS or from within your application programs are the same.

- ☑ You can attach your printer to a parallel or serial port, depending on the type of printer. Using a parallel port will improve the speed at which your printouts print.

- ☑ Most printers are connected to the parallel port LPT1 or the serial port COM1.

- ☑ An ASCII file is a file that contains only letters, numbers, and common punctuation symbols. DOS batch files are a good example of an ASCII file. Using the DOS PRINT command you can print ASCII files.

- ☑ If you create a document within an application program such as a word processor, you should use the application to print the file. Most applications provide a File menu Print option, which lets you print your documents.

Lesson 25

Understanding Computer Ports

As you know, your computer's monitor, keyboard, printer, and mouse are connected to the back of your computer by cables. The locations to which the cables connect are called *ports*. This lesson identifies common PC ports. By the time you finish this lesson you will understand how to

- Recognize the different PC port types
- Recognize male and female connectors
- Determine printer and monitor types by examining only the connectors

EXAMINING YOUR PC PORTS

If you examine the back of your computer, you will find many different connector types similar to those shown in Figure 25.1. The connectors are called *ports* because they allow you to connect devices to your computer. By spending a few moments becoming familiar with and by labeling your ports, you can make it very easy to connect hardware devices in the future.

Figure 25.1 Common PC ports.

Rescued by DOS

As you examine the ports and cables, you will find male and female connectors similar to those shown in Figure 25.2. When you connect a device to a port, you need to ensure that you connect a male cable to a female connector or a female cable to a male connector.

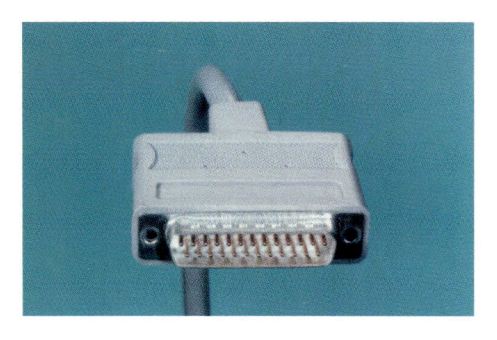

Male connector

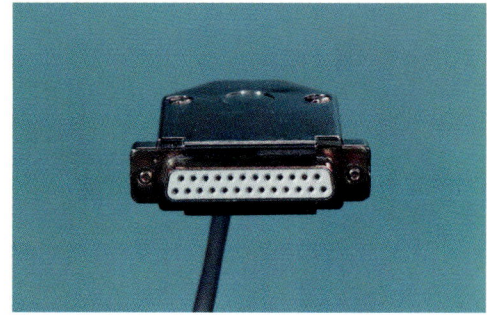

Female connector

Figure 25.2 Female and male port connectors.

UNDERSTANDING SERIAL COMMUNICATION PORTS

Many hardware devices such as a mouse, modem, or even some printers connect to a serial port which can be 9 or 25-pin connectors. Serial port connectors are *always* male connectors. In older PCs, serial ports were often used for data communications using modems. As such, many users refer to serial ports as "com ports." The PC can support up to four serial ports. Serial ports are named COM1, COM2, COM3, and COM4.

Most PCs, however, use only two (COM1 and COM2). Unfortunately, you may have to experiment a little to determine which serial port is which. There is no standard that manufacturers have to follow when they position the ports. Hopefully, the documentation that accompanied your computer will specify the port locations. If, however, you attach a mouse to COM1, for example, and your mouse driver software fails to locate a mouse, try moving the mouse to the other serial port. *Serial ports* are so named because they send and receive information down the wire one bit (a zero or one value) at a time, in series. As such, they are slower than parallel ports, discussed next, which can send up to eight bits (along eight wires) at one time.

25: Understanding Computer Ports

Note: *If your computer uses a 9- or 25-pin serial port and the cable to which you need to attach to the port uses just the opposite, you can purchase a new cable or you can buy a small adapter that changes a 9-pin cable to 25 pin or vice versa.*

> ### Serial Port Names
>
> If you have connected a mouse, modem, printer, or other device to a serial port, you will need to tell your software the name of the port to which the device is connected. Serial ports are named COM1, COM2, COM3, and COM4. Most PCs, however, only have two serial ports, COM1 and COM2. Serial ports can be 9 or 25-pin connectors. They are always male connectors.

Understanding Parallel Ports

Although you can connect most printers to a serial port (just discussed), you will improve the speed at which your documents print by connecting your printer to a parallel port. Parallel ports are 25-pin female connectors. *Parallel ports* are so named because they simultaneously send information over eight wires, in parallel. As such, parallel ports are much faster than serial ports. Parallel ports typically connect line printers to your computer. As such, their names contain the letters LPT (an abbreviation for line printer), such as LPT1, LPT2, and LPT3. Most PCs may only have one parallel port (LPT1). When you connect a printer to this port, you might need to inform your software later of the port's use. Most word processors, and even DOS itself, send printer output to LPT1 by default. The parallel port connector on the back of your PC will always be a 25-pin female connector. When you purchase a parallel cable, however, you need to know what type of connector is present on your printer. As shown in Figure 25.2, your printer may use a standard 25-pin connector, or it may use a Centronics connector.

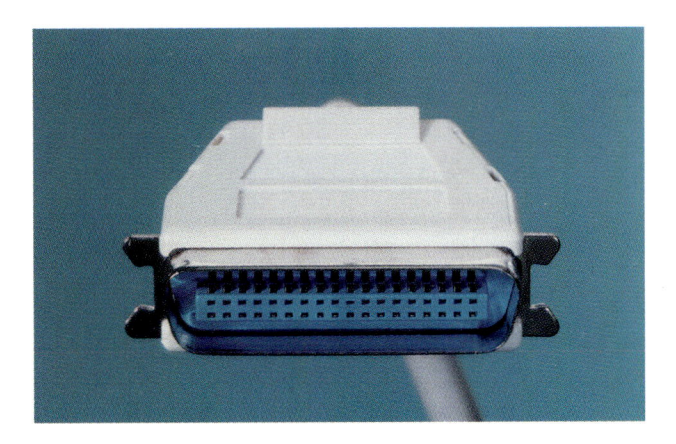

Figure 25.2 *Centronix printer connector types.*

Rescued by DOS

> ### Parallel Port Names
>
> Parallel ports let you connect a printer to your computer. DOS supports up to three parallel ports named LPT1, LPT2, and LPT3. Most computers, however, only have one parallel port. Parallel port connectors are 25-pin female connectors. When you purchase a parallel cable, make sure that the cable you select contains the proper connectors for your printer.

What You Need to Know

In Lesson 26 you will learn how your computer stores information on disk and how to recognize your computer's different disk drives. Before you continue with Lesson 26, make sure that you have learned the following:

- ☑ To attach devices such as a mouse, printer, or modem to your computer, you connect a cable between the device and the computer to ports that appear on the back of the computer.

- ☑ Port connectors and cables are classified as male and female depending on the appearance of their receptacles. Before you purchase a cable, make sure you know whether you need a male or female cable.

- ☑ The most common PC ports are serial and parallel ports. Serial ports are male and can use 9 or 25 pins. Parallel ports on the other hand are female and use only 25-pin connectors.

- ☑ Serial ports are commonly used for data communications and use names such as COM1, COM2, COM3, and COM4. Parallel ports are normally used to connect printers and use the names LPT1, LPT2, and LPT3.

- ☑ When you attach a device to specific parallel or serial port, you may need to inform your software of the port name.

Lesson 26

Storing Information on Disks

When you use your computer for word processing, to create and save spreadsheets, or to create store other types of information, you will store the information on your computer's disk. Computers use two types of disks: *floppy disks* and *hard disks*. The hard disk is contained within your computer's system unit and can store tremendous amounts of information. Floppy disks, on the other hand, store less information but can be easily moved from one computer to another, so you can share files. This lesson examines storing information on disk. By the time you finish this lesson you will understand how to

- Identify your computer's floppy and hard disks
- Determine how much information a disk can store
- Take care of your disks

IDENTIFYING YOUR COMPUTER'S DISK DRIVES

Most computers use hard and floppy disk drives. The hard drive resides inside your system unit. You cannot see the hard drive's disk itself. If you were to open your system unit, you would find a sealed drive unit that contains the platters on which information is recorded. Floppy disks, on the other hand, can be inserted and removed from your computer's disk drive. Lesson 27 examines floppy disks in detail. Depending on your computer, you may have a 3 1/2-inch drive, a 5 1/4-inch drive, or both. Each disk drive on your computer is identified by a unique letter. Your first floppy drive is named drive A. If you have two floppy drives, they will be named drives A and B. Drive A is normally the top or leftmost floppy. Your hard disk is normally drive C.

HOW DISKS STORE INFORMATION

When you run a program, DOS loads the program into your computer's electronic memory. When you later end the program and turn off your computer, the information stored in memory is lost. This is because the electronic memory requires constant power to store information. Likewise, each time you run a program, the new program is loaded into memory, overwriting the memory's previous contents. If you want to store information from one session to another, you must store the information in a file on disk. Disks store information by recording the information on to a magnetic surface, much like a tape recorder or VCR records information on tape. After the information is recorded on disk, you can end the program, turn off your computer's power, or even move the disk from one computer to another.

Rescued by DOS

Because the information is magnetized on to the disk's surface, the disk does not require constant power. Because your files store different types of information, such as letters, memos, reports, numbers, programs, and even art images, the size of your files is expressed in *bytes*. In general, a byte corresponds to a character of information. The word *byte*, for example, would require four characters or four bytes of storage. A single-spaced typed page, for example, would require about 4,000 bytes. Hard disks can store hundreds of millions of bytes. The letters Mb (an abbreviation for *megabyte*) specify how many million (actually 1,048,576) bytes the disk can store. For example, a 100Mb hard disk can store approximately 100 million bytes.

When you use the DIR command to examine the files stored on a disk, the last line of DIR's output will tell you the amount of disk space currently available for use:

```
101,453,824 bytes free
```

If you want to determine how much information your disk can store, as well as the amount currently in use, you can issue the CHKDSK command, as shown here:

```
C:\> CHKDSK   <ENTER>

Volume MS-DOS       created 06-05-1993 9:58p
Volume Serial Number is 1B30-A2F8          ── Total disk capacity

   208,916,480 bytes total disk space      ── Disk space in use
    20,344,832 bytes in 9 hidden files
       229,376 bytes in 45 directories
    86,908,928 bytes in 2738 user files
   101,433,344 bytes available on disk
                                           ── Available disk space

         4,096 bytes in each allocation unit
        51,005 total allocation units on disk
        24,764 available allocation units on disk

       655,360 total bytes memory
       548,560 bytes free
```

TAKING CARE OF YOUR DISKS

The information you store on your computer's disk will remain safe in tact for a very long time if you treat your disks with care. Even so, you should regularly make backup copies of your files, as discussed in Section 9. Because your disks are magnetic, you need to keep your disks away from magnets and other large electronic devices such as a copy machine (or even a telephone or stereo

26: Storing Information on Disks

speakers) that are capable of generating a magnetic flux. In addition, you keep your disks out of direct sunlight and from experiencing severe temperature changes. Finally, smoke is common cause of disk failure because the smoke particles can scratch the disk's surface. If you smoke, do so away from your computer.

Many users ask about airport x-ray machines and their disks. As a rule, an x-ray cannot damage the information stored on your disk. However, the motor that drives the conveyer belt that brings items beneath the x-ray can generate a magnetic flux that can damage your disk. If you were to run the computer through the x-ray machine 100 times, you might be successful each time. However, the one failure may cause you to lose all the information your disk contains. As a rule, I always request a "hand check" of my computer at the airport, bypassing the x-ray machine.

WHAT YOU NEED TO KNOW

Lesson 27 examines floppy disks in detail. Before you continue with Lesson 27, make sure that you have learned the following:

- ☑ To store information from one computer session to another, you must record the information on your disk.

- ☑ Each disk drive on your computer has a unique drive letter. Your first floppy disk is named drive A. Your hard disk is normally named drive C. If you have two floppy drives, they will be named drives A and B.

- ☑ Disks store information by recording the information on to a magnetic surface. As such, you need to keep your disks away from magnets or other sources of magnetic flux.

- ☑ Your disk's storage capacity is expressed in terms of bytes. Most floppy disks can store around one million bytes. Hard disks on the other hand, can store hundreds of millions of bytes. The letters Mb are used to abbreviate megabyte (approximately one million bytes).

- ☑ To determine your disk's storage capacity, use the DOS CHKDSK command.

Rescued by DOS

Lesson 27

Working with a Floppy Disk

As you work with your computer, there will be times when you need to store information on a floppy disk so you can provide the information to another user. To help you better understand floppy disks, this lesson takes a close look at 3 1/2-inch and 5 1/4-inch floppies. By the time you finish this lesson you will understand how to

- Determine and understand your disk's storage capabilities
- Determine the difference between different floppy disk types
- Label your floppy disk so you can quickly determine the disk's contents
- Write-protect a floppy disk to prevent it from being changed
- Store your floppy disks properly to protect them

WORKING WITH FLOPPY DISKS

Floppy disks come in two sizes: 3 1/2 inches and 5 1/4 inches. Floppies store their information using a specially coated magnetic plastic disk. Because the plastic disk is thin and flexible, the disks are named floppy disks. Depending on your PC type, your computer may have a 3 1/2-inch, a 5 1/4-inch floppy drive, or possibly both. Figure 27.1 shows a computer with both floppy drive sizes.

Figure 27.1 A computer with 3 1/2 and 5 1/4 inch floppy disk drives.

27: Working with a Floppy Disk

If your computer contains two floppy disk drives, either the 5 1/4- or 3 1/2-inch drive can be drive A or drive B. Normally, the uppermost or leftmost drive is drive A. When you insert a floppy disk into the drive, you do so with the disk label facing up and end of the disk containing the label inserted last. If you are using an unlabeled 3 1/2-inch disk, insert the disk with the metal end first and the all-plastic side (without the little metal circle in the middle) of the disk facing up. Likewise, if you are using an unlabeled 5 1/4-inch disk, insert the disk so that side of the disk with the small notch is on the left and inserted last.

UNDERSTANDING FLOPPY DISK STORAGE CAPACITY

As discussed in Lesson 26, disk storage capacities are expressed in terms of bytes. In the simplest sense, a byte is a single character of data. Most newer floppy disks can store over one million bytes of information, a *megabyte*. When users discuss floppy disk sizes, they often use the term *density*. A disk's density specifies how close together the disk can store information. The higher the disk's density, the more information the disk can store. The two most common disk densities are double density and quad density. To help you better understand how a disk's density corresponds to the disk's storage capacity, examine the entries in Table 27.1. As you can see, depending on the disk's density, a 3 1/2- inch disk can store 720Kb (737,280 bytes) or 1.44Mb (1,457,664 bytes). Likewise, a 5 1/4-inch disk can store 360Kb (368,640 bytes) or 1.2Mb (1,213,952 bytes).

Disk Size	Density	Storage Capacity
3 1/2	Double	720Kb
3 1/2	High	1.44Mb
5 1/4	Double	360Kb
5 1/4	Quad	1.2Mb

Table 27.1 Floppy disk densities and storage capacities.

If you are using 5 1/4-inch disks, the only way you can determine the disk's storage capacity is to examine the disk's contents or to possibly read an attached label that specifies the size. If you are using 3 1/2-inch disks, however, you can quickly determine if the disk is a 720Kb or 1.44Mb disk through the presence or absence of the high-density (1.44Mb) notch, shown in Figure 27.2.

USING THE DISK ACTIVATION LIGHT

If you examine your floppy disk drives closely, you should find a small light on the front of the drive. Each time your computer reads information from or writes information to the disk in the drive, the computer will illuminate this *disk activation light*. When the disk is done with the read or write operation, the disk will turn off the activation light. Never remove a floppy disk while the disk activation light is illuminated. Doing so can damage your disk and the files it contains.

Rescued by DOS

Figure 27.2 The high-density notch indicates a 1.44Mb floppy disk.

How a Floppy Disk Stores Information

To store information, a floppy disk drive records data on to a specially coated plastic disk, much like the tape in an audio or video cassette. When you work with a floppy disk, never touch the plastic disk. Touching the disk may scratch its surface, damaging the disk and losing the information the disk contains.

Labeling Your Floppy Disk

When you store information on floppy disks, you will insert specific disks into the drive as you require them. To determine the information the disk contains, you need to attach a label to the disk that describes the files on the disk. As Figure 27.3 shows, you should never write on a label that is attached to a disk. Instead, first write your label and then place the label on the disk. If you write on labels attached to a disk, you might damage the disk and the files the disk contains. Should you ever need to change a disk's label, simply create a new label, placing it over the existing label.

Write-Protecting Your Disk

Depending on the information you store on your floppy disks, there may be times when you want to *write-protect* a disk to prevent the disk's contents from being overwritten or changed. If you are using a 5 1/4-inch floppy disk, you can place a small write-protect tab over the disk's write protect notch. If you are using a 3 1/2-inch floppy disk, you can write-protect the disk by sliding the small write-protect tab that appears on the right side of the disk. If the write-protect tab is open, allowing you to look through a hole in the disk, the disk is write- protected.

27: Working with a Floppy Disk

Figure 27.3 Never write on a label that is attached to a disk.

If you cannot see through the disk, the disk *is not* write-protected, and its contents can be changed. By write-protecting a floppy disk you prevent the disk's contents from being changed. If you try to copy a file to a write-protected disk, DOS will display an error message, as shown:

```
C:\> COPY   FILENAME.EXT   A:   <ENTER>
Write protect error writing drive A
Abort, Retry, Fail?
```

If you try to save file to a write-protected disk from within a program such as your word processor, the program will display an error message, and the file save operation will fail.

WRITE-PROTECTING YOUR DISK

When you work with floppy disks, there may be times when you want to prevent the disk's contents from being changed. To do so, you can write-protect the floppy disk. If you are using a 5 1/4-inch disk, you can write-protect the disk by placing a small tab over the disk's write-protect notch. If you are using a 3 1/2-inch disk, you can write-protect the disk by sliding up the disk's small write-protect tab to expose a hole through the disk. Should you later want to change the disk's contents, you can remove the small tab that covers the 5 1/4-inch disk's write-protect notch. Likewise, if you are using a 3 1/2-inch disk, simply slide the write-protect tab down covering the small write-protect hole.

Rescued by DOS

Formatting a Floppy Disk for Use

If, when you try to perform a directory listing of a floppy or copy files to or from a floppy, DOS displays the following message, the disk has not yet been formatted for use by DOS:

```
General failure reading drive A
Abort, Retry, Fail?
```

Type **A** to abort the current command. Next, you must format the floppy for use by DOS. To format the floppy, issue the FORMAT command, as shown here:

```
C:\> FORMAT   A:    <ENTER>
```

FORMAT will ask you place the disk you want to format in drive A, as shown here:

```
Insert new diskette for drive A:
and press ENTER when ready...
```

Place the floppy disk in drive if you have not already done so. When you press ENTER, FORMAT will begin preparing the disk. When the format operation completes, FORMAT will ask you to type in a disk volume label:

```
Volume label (11 characters, ENTER for none)?
```

Press ENTER, bypassing the volume label. FORMAT will display information about the disk's storage capacity, as shown in this example, where drive A holds a 3 1/2-inch floppy:

```
    1,457,664 bytes total disk space
    1,457,664 bytes available on disk

          512 bytes in each allocation unit.
        2,847 allocation units available on disk.

Volume Serial Number is 3234-19DA
```

Next, FORMAT will ask you if you want to format another disk:

```
Format another (Y/N)?
```

27: Working with a Floppy Disk

If you want to format an additional disk type **Y**. FORMAT will prompt you to insert a new floppy disk in drive A. If you don't want to format a disk, type **N**. Your disk is now ready for use by DOS.

PREPARING A DISK FOR USE BY DOS

Before DOS can store information on a disk, the disk must be formatted for use. To format a floppy disk in drive A, issue the following FORMAT command:

`C:\> FORMAT   A:   <ENTER>`

Should you accidentally format a disk that contains information you require, you may be able to recover the disk's contents with the UNFORMAT command, discussed in Lesson 51.

HAT YOU NEED TO KNOW

In Lesson 28 you examine hard disks in detail. Before you continue with Lesson 27, make sure that you have learned the following:

- ☑ Floppy disks let you quickly move files from one computer to another. Floppy disks come in two sizes: 5 1/4-inch and 3 1/2-disks.

- ☑ Floppy disks store information by magnetizing the information on to a specially coated plastic disk. Never touch the disk's surface.

- ☑ A floppy disk's density describes how closely the disk can store information. The higher the density, the more information the disk can store. A high-density 3 1/2-inch disk can store 1.44Mb. Likewise, a high-density 5 1/4-inch disk can store 1.2Mb.

- ☑ When your computer reads or writes information using a floppy disk, the disk drive illuminates a small light called the disk activation light. Never remove a floppy disk from the drive while the disk activation light is in use.

- ☑ To prevent the contents of a floppy disk from being change or overwritten, you can write-protect your disk. If you are using a 5 1/4-inch disk, you can write-protect the disk by placing a small tab over the disk's write-protect notch. If you are using a 3 1/2-inch disk, you can write-protect the disk by sliding the disk's write- protect tab up to expose a small hole through the disk.

Lesson 28

Working with a Hard Disk

As you know, your programs and the files you create normally reside on your computer's hard disk. As was the case with floppy disks, the hard disk stores information by magnetizing it on to the disk's surface. Unlike the floppy disk, your hard disk is much faster and can store many times as much information. This lesson takes a close look at hard disk capabilities. By the time you finish this lesson your will understand how to

- Determine your hard disk's storage capacity
- Know how hard disks differ from floppies
- Understand why some users with hard disks have more than drive C
- Reduce your possibility of a disk crash

DETERMINING YOUR HARD DISK'S STORAGE CAPACITY

In Lesson 27 you learned that floppy disks record their information on a flexible (floppy) plastic storage media. Hard disks, on the other hand, are so named because they store information on hard specially coated, rigid aluminum platters, which can spin much faster than floppy disks. Unlike the flexible floppy disks, hard disk mechanisms are much more precise.

As a result, hard disks are capable of storing information much closer together than a floppy can, which helps the hard disk store much more information. Unlike floppy disks that you can insert and remove from your floppy disk drive, hard disks are enclosed within your system unit. You cannot see the hard disk unit itself. Instead, the most you will see a small disk activation light that tells you when the disk is in use.

As you learned in Lesson 27, floppy disks typically store about 1,000,000 bytes of information, a *megabyte*. Hard disks, on the other hand, can store hundreds of megabytes. In fact, your can now purchase (for more than a thousand dollars) PC hard disks that store over one billion bytes, a *gigabyte*. The easiest way to determine your hard disk's storage capacity is to invoke the CHKDSK command, as shown here:

28: Working with a Hard Disk

```
C:\> CHKDSK  <ENTER>
Volume Serial Number is 1B30-A2F8

  208,916,480 bytes total disk space
   20,344,832 bytes in 9 hidden files
      233,472 bytes in 46 directories
   87,384,064 bytes in 2,781 user files
  100,937,728 bytes available on disk

        4,096 bytes in each allocation unit
       51,005 total allocation units on disk
       24,643 available allocation units on disk

      655,360 total bytes memory
      593,616 bytes free
```

Total disk space
Space available for use

The first and most obvious difference between floppy and hard disks is storage capacity. A typically floppy disk can store about 250 pages of single spaced typed text. A 100Mb hard disk, on the other hand can store about 25,000 pages! The second difference between a hard disk and a floppy is speed. When you insert a floppy disk into a drive, the floppy begins spinning within the drive at 300 revolutions per minute. A hard disk, on the other hand, spins at a rate of up to 5,400 revolutions per minute. Your computer can access the information the hard disk contains much faster than it can information on a floppy.

WHY SOME USERS HAVE DRIVES C, D, AND EVEN E

Most PCs have only one hard disk. However, periodically, you will encounter systems that provide a drive D, E, and possibly even others. These systems appear to have multiple hard disks. In most cases, however, the user has simply partitioned their one hard disk into multiple drive letters. To store information, your disk, as shown in Figure 28.1 is first divided into hundreds of *cylinders*. Depending on your disk size, the number of cylinders your disk contains will differ.

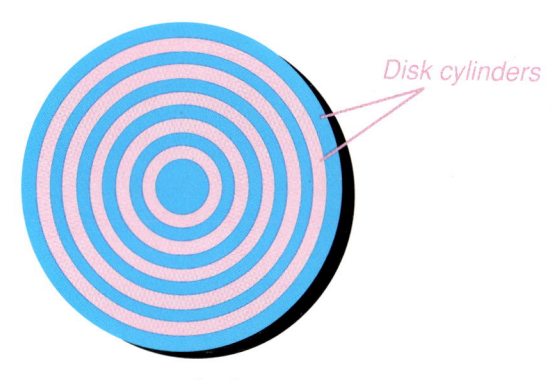

Figure 28.1 Your disk contains many concentric cylinders.

125

Rescued by DOS

Depending on their needs and disk size, many users use a special DOS program to divide their disk's cylinders to regions called *partitions*. Each partition is later assigned a disk drive letter. For example, Figure 28.2 illustrates three partitions in a 200Mb hard disk. Two of the partitions are 50Mb each and one contains 100Mb. To the user, the single hard disk now appears as drives C, D, and E.

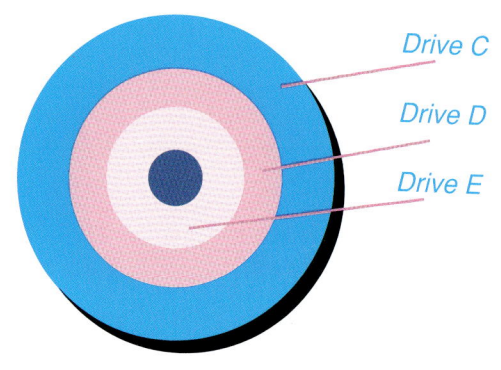

Figure 28.2 Dividing a disk into partitions.

The advantage of dividing your disk into multiple partitions is that a command you issue on one disk will not affect files stored on another. In this way, an errant command can erase or damage fewer files. Using disk partitions in this way, DOS lets you create *logical disk drives* with the letters C through Z. The drives are called logical drives because they don't really exist physically. In the case of the disk shown in Figure 28.3, the user can use the logical drives C, D, and E, but the user really only has one physical hard disk.

The process of partitioning your disk is beyond the scope of this book. This lesson presented disk partitions to help you understand how a computer with only one hard disk appears to have several different drives. The easiest way to determine if a computer has logical drives such as drive D and E is to simply attempt a directory listing using DIR:

```
C:\> DIR  D:   <ENTER>
```

In this case, if the computer has a logical drive D, DIR will display the files that reside in the disk's current directory. If drive D is not present, DOS will display an **Invalid drive specification** error message, as shown here:

```
C:\> DIR  D:   <ENTER>
Invalid drive specification
```

28: Working with a Hard Disk

Understand a Disk Crash

To store and retrieve information stored on the disk's magnetic surface, the disk drive uses a small read/write head. As the disk spins rapidly beneath the read/write head, the disk drive moves the head in and out over the surface the disk. The read/write head floats on a cushion of air just above the surface of the disk. The head does not touch the disk media itself. If the head were to come in contract with the disk's surface, a disk crash would occur and, the specially coated disk surface would be scraped off the disk by the read/write head, causing the information stored on the disk to be lost.

To reduce the possibility of a disk crash, you must keep your PC in a clean environment. Should dust or smoke particles get inside your drive, you greatly increase the chance of disk crash. Also, never move your PC while it is turned on. When you turn off the PC's power, your hard disk will stop spinning, and the read/write head will eventually touch down gently onto the disk's surface. Because the disk is not spinning, the surface is not harmed. When you later turn on your PC's power, the head is again lifted off the surface as the disks start to spin. If you move your PC with the power on, you are almost asking for a disk crash.

Should a disk crash occur, you will normally lose all the information your disk contains. To minimize the amount of data lost, you need to perform regular disk backup operations, as discussed in Lesson 44.

What You Need to Know

In Lesson 29 you will learn how to customize your system using a special root directory file named CONFIG.SYS. Before you continue with Lesson 29, make sure that you have learned the following:

- ☑ Hard disks are so named because they record information on hard (nonbending), specially coated aluminum disks.
- ☑ Hard disks can store hundreds of times as much information as a floppy disk and can access the information much faster.
- ☑ The easiest way to determine your disk's storage capacity is to use the DOS CHKDSK command.
- ☑ Some advanced users will divide their disks into logical regions called partitions. Each disk partition is assigned its own drive letter. In this way, a computer that contains only one hard disk can appear to have several different drives.
- ☑ Never move your computer with the power on. In so doing, you greatly increase the chance of disk crash, which will destroy your disk and the information the disk contains.

Section Six

Customizing DOS with CONFIG.SYS

Over 120 million PCs currently run DOS. Of those millions of PCs, users have many different requirements. To help meet everyone's needs, DOS lets you customize many of its settings, such as the number of files you can open at the one time, how memory is used, and for what devices DOS loads special software. To let you customize your system settings, DOS lets you create a special file in your disk's root directory named CONFIG.SYS. Each time your system starts, DOS searches the root directory for the CONFIG.SYS file. If DOS finds the file, it processes the entries the file contains. Otherwise, DOS uses its own default settings. The lesson in this section will show you how to use CONFIG.SYS to customize your system settings. Using different CONFIG.SYS settings, you can quickly improve your system performance.

Lesson 29 Understanding CONFIG.SYS

Lesson 30 Common CONFIG.SYS Settings

Lesson 31 Working with Device Drivers

Lesson 32 Advanced Options

Lesson 29

Understanding CONFIG.SYS

To help you customize your system, DOS lets you create a special root directory file named CONFIG.SYS. Each time your system starts, DOS searches the root directory the file. If DOS finds the file, DOS uses the entries the file contains to configure itself in memory. Using CONFIG.SYS, you can specify the number of files DOS lets you open at one time, how DOS uses your computer's memory, and for which devices DOS loads special software into memory. This lesson introduces the CONFIG.SYS file. By the time you finish this lesson, you will understand how to

- Determine if your system has a CONFIG.SYS file and, if so, the entries the file contains
- Recognize different CONFIG.SYS entries
- Edit the CONFIG.SYS file to change or add one or more entries

DETERMINING WHETHER YOUR DISK CONTAINS CONFIG.SYS

To determine if your disk contains a CONFIG.SYS file, first select your disk's root directory as the current directory, as shown here:

```
C:\> CHDIR  \   <ENTER>
```

Next, issue the following DIR command:

```
C:\> DIR  CONFIG.SYS   <ENTER>
```

If your disk contains a CONFIG.SYS file, DIR will display a file listing similar to the following:

```
C:\> DIR  CONFIG.SYS   <ENTER>

 Volume in drive C has no label
 Volume Serial Number is 1B30-A2F8
 Directory of C:\

CONFIG    SYS         183 11-16-93    8:23p
        1 file(s)           183 bytes
                    100,970,496 bytes free
```

If your disk does not contain the CONFIG.SYS file, DOS will display the **File not found** message, and you will need to create one as discussed later in this lesson.

Viewing the Contents of CONFIG.SYS

If your disk contains a CONFIG.SYS file, you can use the following TYPE command to view the file's contents:

```
C:\> TYPE  CONFIG.SYS  <ENTER>
```

Although the contents of your CONFIG.SYS file might differ, the file will contain a series of single-line entries, as shown here:

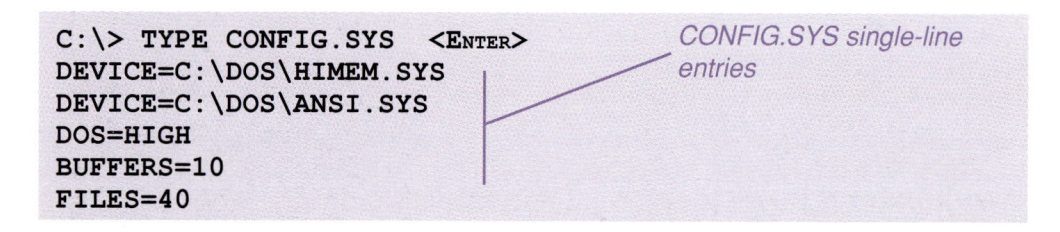

```
C:\> TYPE CONFIG.SYS  <ENTER>
DEVICE=C:\DOS\HIMEM.SYS
DEVICE=C:\DOS\ANSI.SYS
DOS=HIGH
BUFFERS=10
FILES=40
```
CONFIG.SYS single-line entries

As you can see, the CONFIG.SYS file contains a series of single-line entries. In Lesson 30, you will take a closer look at several common entries. For now, simply understand that CONFIG.SYS contains single-line entries that DOS reads each time your system starts. Using the entries, DOS configures itself in memory.

Editing Your CONFIG.SYS File

As you learn more about DOS, you will add and change CONFIG.SYS entries. Before you change the contents of your CONFIG.SYS file, make sure that you make a backup copy of the file's current contents. For example, the following command copies the file's contents to a file named CONFIG.SAV:

```
C:\> COPY  CONFIG.SYS  CONFIG.SAV  <ENTER>
```

Should the changes that you make to CONFIG.SYS cause an error, you can restore the original file's contents.

29: Understanding CONFIG.SYS

CONFIG.SYS is an ASCII file that contains only characters, numbers, and standard punctuation symbols. Do not edit your CONFIG.SYS file with a word processor. As you have read, a word processor can embed hidden characters within your file that DOS does not understand. As a result, when your system starts and DOS tries your read your CONFIG.SYS file, errors will occur. If you need to edit your CONFIG.SYS file, use the EDIT command as shown here:

```
C:\> EDIT  CONFIG.SYS  <ENTER>
```

EDIT will display the file's contents, as shown in Figure 29.1.

Figure 29.1 Editing the contents of CONFIG.SYS.

After you make your changes to CONFIG.SYS, press the ALT-F keyboard combination to select EDIT's File menu. Use the Save option to save your changes. To print a copy of your CONFIG.SYS file, select EDIT's File menu and choose Print. To exit EDIT, select the File menu's Exit option.

CREATING A CONFIG.SYS FILE

If your disk does not contain a CONFIG.SYS file, you can use EDIT to create one. To begin, invoke EDIT as shown here:

```
C:\> EDIT  CONFIG.SYS  <ENTER>
```

Next, type in the following entries:

```
FILES=30
BUFFERS=25
```

For now, the file only contains two entries. As you read the lessons presented in this section and in Section 7, you might find yourself adding entries. Use the File menu's Save option to save your file's contents and the File menu's Exit option to exit EDIT.

Restarting Your System for CONFIG.SYS Changes to Take Affect

The only time DOS uses the contents of your CONFIG.SYS file is when your system starts. Thus, each time you make a change to CONFIG.SYS, you must restart DOS for the change to take effect. To restart DOS without turning your computer's power off and on, you can press the CTRL-ALT-DEL keyboard combination. When you press CTRL-ALT-DEL, your screen will clear, and DOS will restart, just as if you turned your computer off and back on. As DOS restarts, DOS will read and use the changes you have made to CONFIG.SYS.

> ### Restarting DOS Using Ctrl-Alt-Del
>
> When you make changes to your CONFIG.SYS file, you must restart DOS in order for your changes to take effect. To restart DOS without turning off your computer's power, you can press the CTRL-ALT-DEL keyboard combination. The process of restarting your system using CTRL-ALT-DEL is called a warm boot. When you start DOS by turning your computer's power off and on, you perform a cold boot.
>
> Do not press CTRL-ALT-DEL when DOS is running a program. If you do so and the program has open files, the files can be damaged, and the information they contain lost.

What You Need to Know

In Lesson 30 you will examine several common CONFIG.SYS entries. Before you continue with Lesson 30, make sure that you have learned the following:

- ☑ Each time your system starts, DOS searches your disk's root directory for a special file named CONFIG.SYS. If DOS locates the file, it uses the entries the file contains to configure itself in memory. If the file does not exist, DOS uses default settings.

- ☑ CONFIG.SYS is an ASCII file, which means you can display the file's contents using the TYPE command and edit the file using EDIT.

- ☑ Each time you change CONFIG.SYS, you must restart DOS for your changes to take effect. To restart DOS without turning your computer off and on, you can press the CTRL-ALT-DEL keyboard combination.

Lesson 30

Common CONFIG.SYS Settings

As you have learned, the CONFIG.SYS file contains single-line entries that DOS uses to customize your system. Although CONFIG.SYS supports several different entries, most users will use similar entries and will assign similar values. This lesson examines the most commonly used CONFIG.SYS entries. By the time you finish this lesson you will understand how to

- Recognize commonly used CONFIG.SYS entries and their values
- Determine proper settings for common entries
- Identify the purpose of the remaining entries

ASSIGNING VALUES TO COMMON ENTRIES

As you have learned, CONFIG.SYS entries consist of an entry name and value, as shown here:

```
FILES=20
```
─ Entry name
─ Entry value

When you place entries into your CONFIG.SYS file, you will specify a name, followed by an equal sign and a value. If you use the TYPE command to display the contents of your CONFIG.SYS file, you might find entries similar to the following:

```
FILES=20
BUFFERS=30
REM Install support for extended memory
DEVICE=C:\HIMEM.SYS
DOS=HIGH
```

The sections that follow examine these common entries in detail.

SPECIFYING THE NUMBER OF FILES DOS CAN OPEN

No matter how you use your computer, you will eventually store and retrieve information that is stored in a file. The CONFIG.SYS FILES entry specifies the maximum number of files that DOS can open at one time. If you do not place a FILES entry in your CONFIG.SYS file, DOS can only open three files at any given time. Most users will use a value between 20 and 30 for the FILES entry:

```
FILES=30
```

If you use a database program such as Microsoft Access, you might want to increase the number of open files to 50 or more. DOS lets you specify a value up to 255. However, each file you allow DOS to open consumes memory. If you specify a large number of files and the most files you ever open at one time is 20, you will waste memory.

Note: *Many newer programs that require more than 30 files handles automatically update your FILES entry when you install the software.*

SPECIFYING THE NUMBER OF DISK BUFFERS

When your programs work with the information stored in a file, DOS first reads the information from disk into a location in your computer's electronic memory called a *buffer*. The CONFIG.SYS BUFFERS entry lets you specify the number of buffers into which DOS can read and write disk information. If you don't specify a BUFFERS entry in CONFIG.SYS, DOS will select a default value based on the amount of conventional memory in your computer. If your computer has 640Kb, DOS will use 15 buffers as the default value. The number of buffers you should use depends on your system type, the kinds of programs you run, and whether or not you are using the SMARTDRV disk cache, discussed in Lesson 54. If you are not using SMARTDRV, use the values listed in Table 30.1 as your guideline. If you are using SMARTDRV, set the number of buffers to 3, as shown here:

```
BUFFERS=3
```

CPU Type	Number of Buffers
8088	20
80286	25
80386	30
80486	35
Pentium	45

Table 30.1 Values for the CONFIG.SYS BUFFERS entry.

USING REMARKS TO EXPLAIN ENTRY VALUES

In Section 4 you used the DOS REM command to place remarks within your batch files that explained their processing. In a similar way, as you place entries in your CONFIG.SYS file, you can use REM statements to explain your entries and why you chose to assign specific values. In addition, you can place blank lines between entries to make your file easier to read. When DOS encounters a REM statement within your CONFIG.SYS file, it ignores the entry from the word *REM* to the end of the line:

30: Common CONFIG.SYS Settings

```
REM Provide support for 20 open files
FILES=20

REM Not using SMARTDRV so increase the buffer count
BUFFERS=30

REM Install support for extended memory
DEVICE=C:\HIMEM.SYS

REM Load DOS into the high memory area
DOS=HIGH
```

As you work with CONFIG.SYS entries in the future, there may be times when you want to disable an entry. Rather than deleting the entry from your file, you can type **REM** in front of the entry to turn it off, as shown here:

```
REM BUFFERS=30
```

If you later want to enable the entry, you can simply remove the word *REM*.

INSTALLING A DEVICE DRIVER

As you have learned, DOS lets you store information on disk, type at the keyboard, display information on your screen, and even print documents. In other words, DOS provides software that lets you use common devices such as your keyboard, screen, printer, and disks. When you want to use other devices such as mouse or CD-ROM, you must provide software that lets your programs use the device. This additional software is called a *device driver*. Lesson 31 examines device drivers in detail.

For now, think of a device driver as nothing more than a set of instructions (like a program) DOS follows to use a device. To load the device driver instructions into your computer's memory, you must place a DEVICE entry in your CONFIG.SYS file. For example, the following entry directs DOS to load the device driver contained in the file HIMEM.SYS:

```
DEVICE=C:\DOS\HIMEM.SYS
```

When you place a DEVICE entry in CONFIG.SYS, you should specify a complete pathname to the device driver file. (Since DOS reads CONFIG.SYS before it reads AUTOEXEC.BAT, it won't have read your PATH statement by the time it reads the DEVICE declaration.) When you purchase a new hardware device, you might receive a floppy disk that contains the device driver file. Create a directory for the device driver on your hard disk and then copy the file from the floppy into the directory.

OTHER CONFIG.SYS ENTRIES

Several of the lessons that follow look at specific CONFIG.SYS entries in detail. Thus, you may be able to find references to a specific entry within this book's index. In addition, Table 30.2 briefly describes the function of each CONFIG.SYS entry. For more specifics on each entry, refer to the book *DOS the Complete Reference, Fourth Edition*, Osborne/McGraw-Hill, 1993.

Entry	Function
BREAK	Turns extended CTRL-BREAK checking on or off. Most users should omit this entry.
BUFFERS	Specifies the number of available disk buffers.
COUNTRY	Selects a specific international country code for international users.
DEVICE	Installs a device driver.
DEVICEHIGH	Installs a device driver into upper memory, freeing conventional memory.
DOS	Loads DOS into the high memory area and specifies the desired support for the upper memory area. See Lessons 36 and 38.
DRIVPARM	Assigns specific settings to disk drive. Most users will not use this entry.
FCBS	Provides support for file control blocks for older programs. Most users will not use this entry.
FILES	Specifies the number of files DOS can open at one time.
INCLUDE	Directs DOS to use a CONFIG.SYS menu configuration block. Most users will not use this entry.
INSTALL	Loads one of the following memory-resident programs into memory: FASTOPEN, KEYB, SHARE, or NLSFUNC. Most users should use the LOADHIGH command instead (from within their AUTOEXEC.BAT).
LASTDRIVE	Specifies the last logical drive letter DOS can assign to a disk drive.
MENUCOLOR	Specifies the color of the CONFIG.SYS startup menu.
MENUDEFAULT	Specifies the default option in a CONFIG.SYS startup menu.
MENUITEM	Defined an item on the startup menu.
NUMLOCK	Specifies whether the NUM LOCK key is set ON or OFF when your computer starts.

Table 30.2 The function of each CONFIG.SYS entry. (continued on the next page)

30: Common CONFIG.SYS Settings

Entry	Function
REM	Specifies a remark.
SET	Places an entry in the DOS environment.
SHELL	Specifies the location of the DOS command processor (COMMAND.COM).
STACKS	Specifies the amount of memory DOS sets aside to handle hardware interrupts.
SUBMENU	Specifies more menu options within a CONFIG.SYS startup menu.
SWITCHES	Directs DOS to treat an enhanced keyboard as a conventional keyboard to support older programs.

Table 30.2 The function of each CONFIG.SYS entry. (continued from previous page)

What You Need to Know

In Lesson 31 you will learn how to install device driver support in your CONFIG.SYS file. Before you continue with Lesson 31, make sure you have learned the following:

- ☑ CONFIG.SYS entries always use the form *EntryName=EntryValue*. When you change a CONFIG.SYS entry, you must restart your system for the change to take effect.

- ☑ The CONFIG.SYS FILES entry specifies the number of files DOS can have open at one time. Most users will set the FILES entry to 20 or more.

- ☑ The CONFIG.SYS BUFFERS entry specifies the number of disk buffers DOS can use for file read and write operations. If you are using the SMARTDRV disk cache, set the number of buffers to 3.

- ☑ The CONFIG.SYS REM entry lets you place remarks in your CONFIG.SYS file that explain the values you assigned to each entry.

- ☑ To make your CONFIG.SYS file easier to read, you might want to place blank lines between entries.

Lesson 31

Working with Device Drivers

As you have learned, DOS exists to let you run programs, store information on disk, and use devices such as your printer. When you add a new hardware device such as a mouse, scanner, or possibly a CD-ROM, you must provide DOS with additional software that DOS in turn, will use to let your programs access the device. This special software is called a *device driver*. Normally, when you purchase a new hardware device, you will receive a floppy disk that contains the device driver software. Likewise, DOS itself provides several device drivers you can use or choose not to use. In this lesson you will learn how to install device drivers with your CONFIG.SYS file. By the time you finish this lesson you will understand how to

- Determine the device driver files provided by DOS
- Install a device driver using CONFIG.SYS
- Install a memory-resident program as a device driver

Understanding Device Driver Files

As you have learned, a program is nothing more than a file containing a list of instructions the computer performs to accomplish a specific task. In a similar way, a device driver is a file containing instructions the computer must perform to use a specific device. For example, to use a mouse with DOS, you must install a mouse device driver. Device driver files often use the SYS extension. Using the following DIR command, you can list the device driver files provided with DOS:

```
C:\> DIR  \DOS\*.SYS  <ENTER>
```

Depending on your DOS version, DIR will display files similar to those shown here:

```
C:\> DIR  \DOS\*.SYS  <ENTER>

 Volume in drive C has no label
 Volume Serial Number is 1B44-6A60
 Directory of C:\DOS

ANSI        SYS         9,065  09-27-93   3:59p
COUNTRY     SYS        17,646  09-27-93   3:59p
```

31: Working with Device Drivers

```
DBLSPACE SYS      22,496 09-27-93   6:20a
DISPLAY  SYS      15,789 09-27-93   3:59p
EGA      SYS       4,885 03-10-93   6:00a
DRIVER   SYS       5,406 09-27-93   4:00p
RAMDRIVE SYS       5,873 03-10-93   6:00a
HIMEM    SYS      29,040 09-27-93   4:03p
KEYBOARD SYS      34,598 09-27-93   4:04p
         9 file(s)       186,398 bytes
                      94,007,296 bytes free
```

Before DOS can use a device driver file, you must install the driver using the CONFIG.SYS DEVICE entry, discussed next.

> ### UNDERSTANDING DEVICE DRIVER FILES
>
> A device driver is a file that contains the instructions DOS must perform in order to use a specific hardware device. For example, if you are using a mouse, a CD-ROM disk, or even a network, you will need to install a device driver for each. Device driver files normally use the SYS extension. When you purchase a new hardware device, you will normally receive a floppy disk that contains the corresponding device driver file.

INSTALLING A DEVICE DRIVER

Before DOS can use a device, the device driver software must be loaded into your computer's memory. To load a device driver, you place a DEVICE entry in your CONFIG.SYS file. Assume, for example, that you want to install the ANSI.SYS device driver, which resides in your DOS directory. To do so, you would place the following entry in your CONFIG.SYS file:

```
DEVICE=C:\DOS\ANSI.SYS
```

When DOS encounters the DEVICE entry in your CONFIG.SYS file, it uses the pathname that follows to locate the device driver file. In this case, DOS will search the DOS directory for a file named ANSI.SYS. To place the entry in CONFIG.SYS, first select the root directory as the current directory and then edit the CONFIG.SYS file as shown here:

```
C:\> EDIT   CONFIG.SYS   <ENTER>
```

When EDIT displays the file's contents, place the entry near the bottom of the file, as shown here:

```
BUFFERS=30
FILES=40
DEVICE=C:\DOS\ANSI.SYS
```

Next, use the ALT-F keyboard combination to select EDIT's File menu. Choose the Save option to save your changes to CONFIG.SYS. Select the File menu a second time and choose Exit. Press the CTRL-ALT-DEL keyboard combination to restart your computer. When DOS restarts, the device driver will be loaded as required. Several of the lessons presented in Section 7 require you to install different device drivers. Follow the steps just presented to place DEVICE entries for the drivers in your CONFIG.SYS file.

USING THE CONFIG.SYS DEVICE ENTRY

To install a device driver for use by DOS, you must place a DEVICE entry in your CONFIG.SYS file. To specify a device driver using a DEVICE entry, you simply place an entry in CONFIG.SYS that is similar to the following example:

```
DEVICE=C:\DOS\HIMEM.SYS
```

When you place a DEVICE entry in CONFIG.SYS, make sure you specify a complete pathname to the device driver file.

NOT ALL DEVICE DRIVERS REQUIRE CONFIG.SYS

In all the lessons presented in this book, you will install device drivers using the CONFIG.SYS DEVICE entry. In some cases, however, device drivers take the form of computer programs that you execute from the DOS prompt or from within your AUTOEXEC.BAT file. For example, the device driver MOUSE.COM is commonly used to provide DOS with software your programs can use to take advantage of a mouse. Likewise, many networks use similar program-like device drivers. If you need to install a similar device driver, place the corresponding command within your AUTOEXEC.BAT file.

WHAT YOU NEED TO KNOW

In Lesson 32 you will learn advanced techniques you can perform to control how DOS processes your CONFIG.SYS entries. Before you continue with Lesson 32, make sure you have learned the following:

- ☑ A device driver is a file containing the instructions DOS performs to let your software use a device. Device drivers normally use the SYS file extension.

- ☑ To install a device driver, you must place a DEVICE entry in your CONFIG.SYS file. The DEVICE entry specifies the complete pathname DOS must follow to locate a device driver file.

- ☑ Some device drivers come in the form of computer programs that you execute from the DOS. In such cases, place the device driver command in your AUTOEXEC.BAT file.

Lesson 32

Controlling CONFIG.SYS Processing

As you have learned, each time your system starts, DOS searches your disk's root directory for the CONFIG.SYS file. If DOS locates the file, it processes each entry the file contains. If DOS does not find the file, it uses its own default system settings. In the past, when a CONFIG.SYS entry caused an error that prevented the system from starting, users had to locate a bootable floppy disk to start their system. Next, the user had to edit the CONFIG.SYS file, correcting or removing the errant entry and then restarting their system. Beginning with DOS 6, users can direct DOS to bypass the processing of CONFIG.SYS and AUTOEXEC.BAT. By the time you finish this lesson you will understand how to

- Bypass CONFIG.SYS and AUTOEXEC.BAT processing
- Select individually the CONFIG.SYS and AUTOEXEC.BAT entries you want DOS to process

BYPASSING *CONFIG.SYS* AND *AUTOEXEC.BAT*

Each time your system starts, DOS displays the following message on your screen:

```
Starting MS-DOS...
```

If, when this message appears, you press the **F5** function key, DOS will bypass the CONFIG.SYS and AUTOEXEC.BAT processing, displaying instead, the DOS prompt.

When you bypass CONFIG.SYS and AUTOEXEC.BAT processing by pressing **F5**, DOS will start a minimal system. You will not have a command path defined. Likewise, you cannot open more than three files at any given time. Bypassing the system startup in this way provides you with an opportunity to correct errors within CONFIG.SYS or AUTOEXEC.BAT.

Assume, for example, that an entry in your CONFIG.SYS file is causing an error that hangs your system. To correct the error, restart your system. When DOS displays its starting message, press the **F5** function key. DOS will start, displaying its DOS prompt. Next, use the following EDIT command to edit the contents of your CONFIG.SYS file:

```
C> \DOS\EDIT  CONFIG.SYS  <ENTER>
```

Rescued by DOS

Note that the command includes a complete pathname for the DOS EDIT command. When you bypass CONFIG.SYS and AUTOEXEC.BAT processing, you bypass the PATH command (in AUTOEXEC.BAT), which establishes the command path. Likewise, note the prompt only contains the drive letter and a greater-than sign. Like the PATH command, the PROMPT command, which normally appears in the AUTOEXEC.BAT file to customize your DOS prompt, has been bypassed. After you correct the CONFIG.SYS entry, restart your system using the CTRL-ALT-DEL keyboard combination.

> ## Bypassing CONFIG.SYS and AUTOEXEC.BAT
>
> If you find that an entry in your CONFIG.SYS or AUTOEXEC.BAT is causing an error that prevents your system from starting, you can direct DOS to bypass its processing of these files. To bypass CONFIG.SYS and AUTOEXEC.BAT, press the **F5** function key when DOS displays the following message:
>
> ```
> Starting MS-DOS...
> ```
>
> DOS will start a minimal system, from which you can change CONFIG.SYS or AUTOEXEC.BAT as required. After you make your changes, you can restart your system using the CTRL-ALT-DEL keyboard combination.

Processing Specific CONFIG.SYS and AUTOEXEC.BAT Entries

As you just learned, by pressing the **F5** function key when your system starts directs DOS not to process CONFIG.SYS and AUTOEXEC.BAT. In a similar way, by pressing the **F8** function key when your system starts, you can select specific CONFIG.SYS and AUTOEXEC.BAT entries for processing. For example, assume that your CONFIG.SYS file contains the following entries:

```
FILES=20
BUFFERS=30
DEVICE=C:\DOS\HIMEM.SYS
```

If, when your system starts, you press the **F8** function key, DOS will display a prompt for each entry, asking you if you want to process the entry, as shown here:

```
FILES=20 [Y,N]?
```

If you type **Y**, DOS will process the FILES entry. If you instead type **N**, DOS will ignore the entry, as if the entry was not in the file. Next, DOS will display a similar prompt for the BUFFERS entry:

```
BUFFERS=30 [Y,N]?
```

32: Controlling CONFIG.SYS Processing

DOS will perform this processing for each entry in the CONFIG.SYS file. Next, DOS will display the following message asking you if you want to process the AUTOEXEC.BAT entries:

```
Process AUTOEXEC.BAT [Y,N]?
```

If you type **Y**, DOS will display a prompt for each command in the AUTOEXEC.BAT file, letting you select the commands you want to execute. If you instead type **N**, DOS will not process any of the commands in the AUTOEXEC.BAT file.

> ### Controlling CONFIG.SYS and AUTOEXEC.BAT Processing
>
> Depending on your CONFIG.SYS or AUTOEXEC.BAT entries, there may be times when you want DOS not to process one or more entries. To perform such processing, press the **F8** function key when your system starts. DOS in turn, will prompt you for each entry in your CONFIG.SYS and AUTOEXEC.BAT files:
>
> ```
> FILES=20 [Y,N]?
> ```
>
> If you type **Y**, DOS will process the entry or command. If you instead type **N**, DOS will ignore the entry.

What You Need to Know

In Lesson 33 you will examine your computer's electronic memory. Before you continue with Lesson 33, make sure you have learned the following:

- ☑ If you make a change to your CONFIG.SYS or AUTOEXEC.BAT file that causes an error that prevents your system from starting, you can press the **F5** function key when you first start your system to direct DOS to ignore CONFIG.SYS and AUTOEXEC.BAT.

- ☑ If you use the **F5** function key to bypass CONFIG.SYS and AUTOEXEC.BAT, DOS will start a minimal system. From the DOS prompt, use the EDIT command (specify a complete pathname to invoke EDIT) to make your changes to CONFIG.SYS or AUTOEXEC.BAT. When you have finished, press the **Ctrl-Alt-Del** keyboard combination to restart your system.

- ☑ In some cases, you might want DOS to process (or not process) specific CONFIG.SYS and AUTOEXEC.BAT entries. To do so, press the **F8** function key as your system starts. DOS in turn, will display a prompt for each CONFIG.SYS and AUTOEXEC.BAT entry. To process the entry, type **Y**. To bypass the entry, type **N**.

Taking Advantage of the PC's Memory

Section Seven

You have learned that, before a program can run, DOS must load the program into the PC's electronic memory. The lessons in this section examine the PC's memory in detail. You will learn that, depending on your PC type (286, 386, and so on), your PC will support different memory types. By using these different memory types, you give your programs more memory within which they can load their data (the information with which they are working). As a general rule, the more memory you let a program use, the faster the program will run. Memory management is the process of controlling your PC's memory use to maximize your system performance. In this section you will find that once you know a few secrets, memory management is actually very easy.

Lesson 33 Understanding Your Computer's Memory

Lesson 34 Understanding the PC's Different Memory Types

Lesson 35 Using Extended Memory

Lesson 36 Using High Memory

Lesson 37 Using Expanded Memory

Lesson 38 Using Upper Memory

Lesson 39 Running MemMaker

Lesson 33

Understanding PC Memory

As you have learned, before a program can run, the program must reside in your computer's electronic memory. When you type in a command name or execute a command from within a batch file, DOS loads the program from disk into your computer's memory. This lesson introduces the PC's random access memory or RAM and commands you can use to determine your computer's memory use. By the time you finish this lesson you will understand how to

- Recognize memory chips
- Determine how much memory your computer contains
- Display your computer's memory use using MEM

UNDERSTANDING RAM

When computer users talk about PC memory, they often use the term *RAM*. In short, RAM, an abbreviation for random access memory, is your computer's electronic memory. RAM is so named because the computer can access the value stored in any location (randomly access, as opposed to accessing in sequential order, as on a cassette tape) in the same amount of time. As Figure 33.1 shows, your computer's memory (or RAM) is made up of computer chips. The memory chips reside within your system unit.

Figure 33.1 RAM is made up of computer chips.

Rescued by DOS

Because memory chips are electronic, the information the chips hold is lost when you turn off your computer's power. Thus, to store information from one user session to another, you must record the information your computer's magnetic disk.

LOADING A PROGRAM INTO MEMORY

You have learned that, when you run a program, DOS loads a program into your computer's electronic memory. For example, assume you run a word processor named WORDPROC. DOS will load the program from disk into your computer's electronic memory.

As you use the word processor to create a document, the program will hold the document in memory, as shown in Figure 33.2.

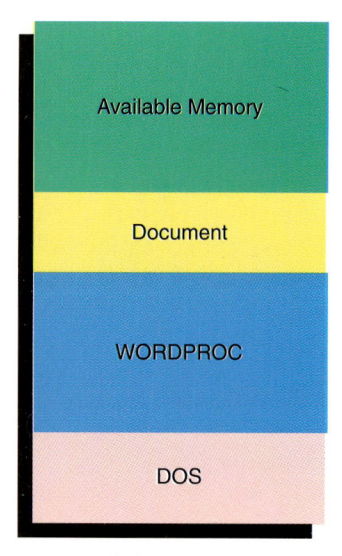

Figure 33.2 A word processing program and document in memory.

When you have finished with your word processing document, you must store the document within a file on disk. If you do not, the document will be lost when you exit the word processor.

Assuming you end the word processor and then run a spreadsheet program, DOS will load your spreadsheet into your computer's memory without regard for the memory's previous contents, as shown in Figure 33.3.

33: Understanding PC Memory

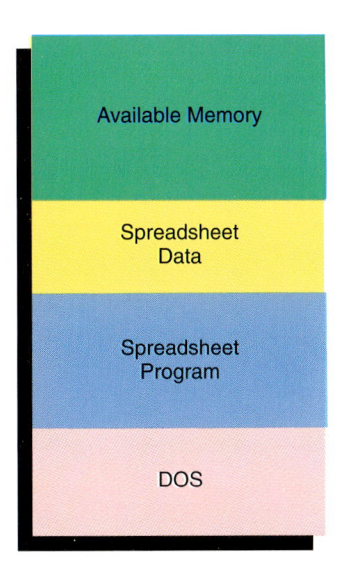

Figure 33.3 Loading a spreadsheet program into your computer's memory.

If, while you are working with the spreadsheet program, your computer loses power or you restart DOS, the information you have not yet saved is lost.

DETERMINING HOW MUCH MEMORY YOUR SYSTEM CONTAINS

Each time you turn on your computer's power, the PC displays a count of the amount of working memory it contains. By noting the value displayed, you can determine how much RAM your computer contains. As you will learn in Lesson 34, the PC uses several different types of memory. The lessons presented in this section help you make the best use of the memory your PC contains.

DISPLAYING YOUR PC'S MEMORY USE

Several of the lessons presented in this section discuss ways to use the PC's memory. To help you determine your PC's memory use, you can use the MEM command, shown here:

```
C:\> MEM    <ENTER>

Memory Type            Total  =   Used   +   Free

Conventional           640K       52K        588K
Upper                    0K        0K          0K
```

147

Rescued by DOS

```
Reserved              128K        128K         0K
Extended (XMS)      7,424K      2,112K     5,312K

Total memory        8,192K      2,292K     5,900K

Total under 1 MB      640K         52K       588K

Largest executable program size    588K  (602,256 bytes)
Largest free upper memory block      0K       (0 bytes)
MS-DOS is resident in the high memory area.
```

In some cases, you will want to know which programs are using your computer's memory and the amount of memory each is consuming. To do so, invoke MEM using the /CLASSIFY switch (which can be abbreviated as /C), as shown here:

```
C:\> MEM   /CLASSIFY   <ENTER>
```

In Lesson 34 you will learn that the PC uses conventional, upper, extended, expanded, and high memory. As you can see, the previous MEM /CLASSIFY command displays how your PC uses these memory areas.

WHAT YOU NEED TO KNOW

In Lesson 34 you will learn about the PC's different memory types. Before you continue with Lesson 34, however, make sure you have learned the following:

- ☑ When you run a program, DOS loads the program from disk into your computer's electronic memory (RAM).

- ☑ If you turn off your computer's power or restart DOS, the information contained in your computer's electronic memory is lost.

- ☑ When you end one program and run another, DOS loads the second program into memory, overwriting the previous memory contents.

- ☑ To determine how much memory your computer contains, note the amount of memory displayed when you turn on your computer's power.

- ☑ If you need to determine how your computer's memory is being used, issue the DOS MEM command. If you include the /CLASSIFY switch, MEM will display each program currently using memory and the amount used. In addition, MEM will display a summary of your PC's different memory types.

34: Understanding the PC's Memory Types

Lesson 34

Understanding the PC's Memory Types

When you run a program, DOS loads the program from disk into your computer's memory. Throughout this book, we have referred to the computer's memory as RAM, memory, or even electronic memory. No matter what we have called the memory, you know that when you turn off your PC's power or restart DOS, the contents of your memory is lost. Likewise, when one program ends and you run a second, DOS overwrites the previous program's memory with the new program. As it turns out, the PC actually uses several different types of memory. This lesson briefly examines each. The lessons that follow look at each memory type in detail and show you how you can use each memory type. By the time you finish this lesson you will understand

- The differences between conventional, extended, expanded, high, and upper memory
- What's so special about the PC's CMOS memory
- How ROM differs from RAM
- How to determine the different memory types your PC contains

UNDERSTANDING CONVENTIONAL MEMORY

When the original IBM PC was first released in 1981, the PC supported 1Mb of memory, called *conventional memory*. As Figure 34.1 shows, part of the conventional memory is available for program use, and part is reserved for use by your video display and other hardware devices.

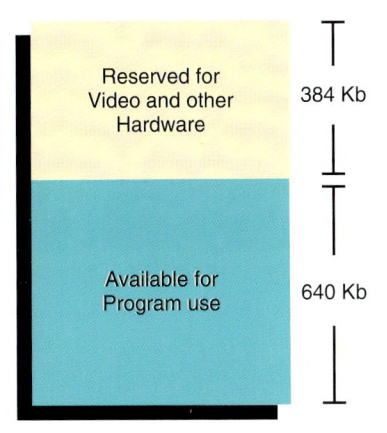

Figure 34.1 Conventional memory is the PC's first megabyte of memory.

149

Rescued by DOS

When you start your computer, the computer loads DOS into the lower portion of conventional memory. When you later run other programs, DOS loads the program from disk into memory, as shown in Figure 34.2.

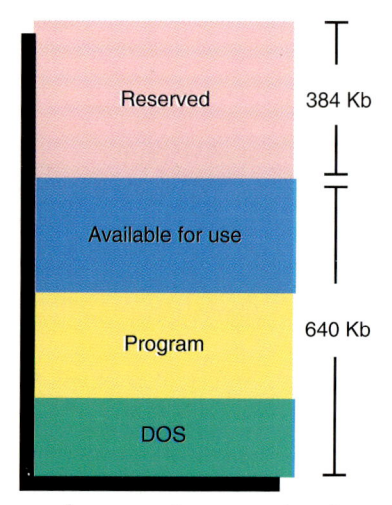

Figure 34.2 DOS-based programs always run in conventional memory.

Every PC, 8088, 80286, 80386, 80486, or even Pentium uses the 1Mb conventional memory. No matter how much memory your computer has, DOS-based programs always run within the 640Kb conventional memory program space. If a program cannot fit within the 640Kb memory region, DOS cannot run the program. As you will learn, however, your programs can store their data in extended and expanded memory, leaving more room in the 640Kb region for program instructions. When users perform memory management within DOS, their goal is to free up as much of the 640Kb region as possible for use by their programs.

Understanding Conventional Memory

Conventional memory is the PC's first megabyte of memory. All PCs have conventional memory. Conventional memory consists of two parts: a 640Kb region used by your programs and a 384Kb region reserved for use by your video display and other hardware devices. When you run programs within DOS, the program's instructions must reside within the 640Kb conventional memory area.

34: Understanding the PC's Memory Types

UNDERSTANDING EXTENDED MEMORY

As programs have become more powerful, they have grown in size. Many programs cannot hold their instructions and data in the 640Kb program area. Beginning with the 286, the PC can use a second memory type called *extended memory*. Depending on the processor type, PCs can hold up to 64Mb of extended memory! Actually 386-based computers (and higher) support up to 4Gb (gigabytes) of memory, however, today's PC's cannot hold this much memory, and you would run out of money trying to buy it!

Your programs can use extended memory to hold their data, such as a spreadsheet or large word processing document, as shown in Figure 34.3.

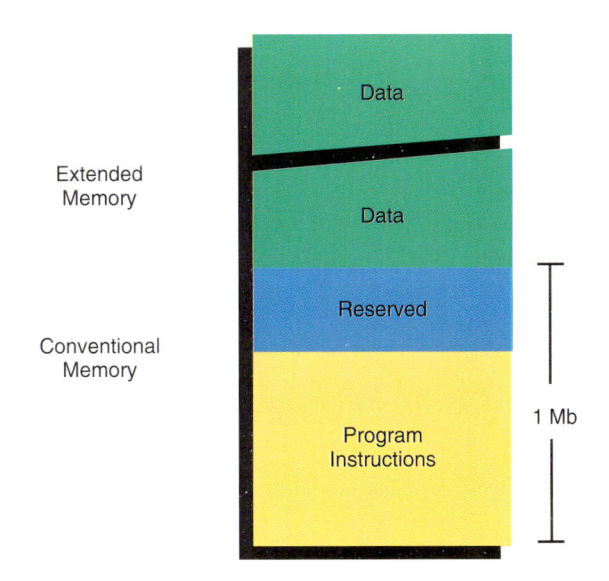

Figure 34.3 *Extended memory is the memory beyond 1Mb and can be used to hold data.*

When you turn on your PC's power, the PC will display a count of your computer's working memory. By examining the value displayed, you can determine how much extended memory your computer holds. For example, assume your computer displays the value 8096 (8Mb). If you subtract the 1Mb of conventional memory, you will find that your computer holds 7Mb of extended memory. Lesson 35 examines extended memory in detail.

Understanding High Memory

If you are using a 386-based computer (or higher) and your computer has extended memory, as just discussed, you can take advantage of the first 64Kb of extended memory, called the *high memory area* to hold DOS. As Figure 34.2 previously showed, DOS is normally loaded into the 640Kb program space in conventional memory. In this way, DOS itself, consumes memory that could be used by your programs. By moving DOS into the high memory area, you free up more of the 640Kb region for your program use. Lesson 36 examines the high memory area in detail.

Understanding Expanded Memory

The original 8088-based IBM PC released in 1981 cannot access memory beyond 1Mb. Thus, the PC cannot use extended memory. To help users run large programs or programs that used large amounts of data (such as a spreadsheet), *expanded memory* was created. Expanded memory is a technique that combines a special hardware board called an expanded memory board with software to trick the PC into accessing memory outside of its 1Mb limit by swapping *pages*, large blocks, of the extra memory, for existing memory when it is called for. The only PC that needs to use expanded memory is the original 8088-based PC. All other PCs should use the much faster extended memory. When the PC used expanded memory, it only did so to store data. As always, program instructions had to reside in the PC's 640Kb conventional memory area. Some PC's contain extended and expanded memory. As a rule, you should only use expanded memory as a last resort. Extended memory is much faster. Most PC's however, only contain conventional and extended memory.

Understanding Upper Memory

You have learned that the PC reserves the top 384Kb of conventional memory for use by the video display and other hardware devices. As it turns out, parts of this 384Kb region, called the *upper memory area*, are not used, so DOS lets you load device drivers and memory-resident programs into these unused areas (called *upper memory blocks*). Normally, DOS loads device drivers and memory-resident programs into the 640Kb program space. By moving these programs to the upper memory area, you free up more of the 640Kb program space for use by your programs. Lesson 38 examines upper memory in detail.

CMOS, A Special Memory

Each of the memory types previously discussed are electronic memory, which means they lose their contents if you turn off the PC's power or restart DOS. In addition to these electronic memories, the PC uses a special battery-powered *CMOS memory*. The CMOS stores information about your PC such as your disk drive types and capacities, your monitor and keyboard types, as well as the current system date and time. Because the CMOS memory is battery powered, the CMOS retains its contents when you turn off the PC's power. Over time, however, the CMOS battery will fail,

34: Understanding the PC's Memory Types

and you will have to replace it. If, when you start your system, your screen displays a message about invalid system settings, your CMOS battery has failed. Have your computer retailer or an experienced user replace the battery and restore your system settings for you.

How ROM Differs from RAM

Your computer's electronic memory is often called RAM, which is short for random access memory. The memory is so named because your computer can access (at random) any memory location in the same amount of time. Your computer's RAM consists of conventional, expanded, extended, upper, and high memory. When you turn off your PC's power, the contents of RAM is lost. In addition to RAM, your computer has memory called *ROM*, which is short for read-only memory. In general, ROM is a computer chip that contains information your PC can read but cannot change (read-only). Your computer's basic input and output system (or *BIOS*), which DOS uses to read characters from keyboard or to write characters to the screen display, is stored in ROM. Because DOS cannot change or move ROM, we normally do not consider ROM when we perform memory-management operations.

What You Need to Know

In Lesson 35 you will learn how to use your computer's extended memory. Before you continue with Lesson 35, however, make sure you have learned the following:

- ☑ Your computer's electronic memory (or RAM) may consist of conventional, extended, expanded, upper, and high memory.

- ☑ All PC's have a 1Mb conventional memory area. Conventional memory consists of two parts: a 640Kb program space that holds DOS and programs you run and 384Kb region that is reserved for your video display and other hardware devices.

- ☑ Extended memory is the memory above 1Mb used to hold program data. In DOS, extended memory cannot hold program instructions.

- ☑ Expanded memory is a technique that combines hardware and software to trick the original 8088-based IBM PC into using memory beyond its 1Mb limit. Expanded memory is much slower than extended memory and should not be used by most PCs.

- ☑ Upper memory is the 384Kb region of reserved conventional memory. If you are using a 386 or higher, DOS lets you load device drivers and memory-resident programs into unused regions of upper memory to free up the 640Kb conventional memory program space for your program use.

- ☑ High memory is the first 64Kb of extended memory. By loading DOS into the high memory area, you free up part of the 640Kb program space for your program use.

Rescued by DOS

Lesson 35

Using Extended Memory

When the IBM PC was first released in 1981, the PC could only use 1Mb of memory. When the IBM PC AT (a 286-based computer) was released in 1984, the PC AT could use up to 16Mb. At that time, developers introduced extended memory, which was memory that began beyond the PC's 1Mb conventional memory. This lesson examines the PC's extended memory and how you can use it within DOS. By the time you finish this lesson, you will understand how to

- Determine how much extended memory your PC contains
- Install the HIMEM.SYS device driver to access extended memory
- Use extended memory for a SMARTDRV disk cache or RAM drive

UNDERSTANDING EXTENDED MEMORY

Extended memory is the memory beyond the PC's 1Mb conventional memory, as shown in Figure 35.1.

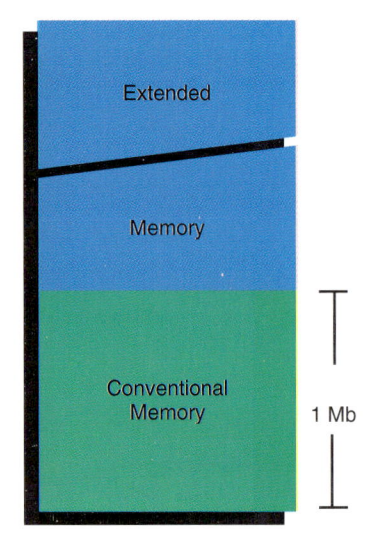

Figure 35.1 Extended memory begins immediately beyond the PC's 1Mb conventional memory.

154

35: Using Extended Memory

If you are using a 286-based machine, your PC can hold up to 16Mb. If you are using a 386-based PC or higher, your system can hold up to 4Gb of extended memory! However, most PCs only provide space for 32 to 64Mb of memory.

When you purchase a PC, the PC will normally come with 4 to 8Mb of memory. The first 1Mb of this memory is your PC's conventional memory area. When you add memory to your computer, you will usually purchase memory chips called SIMMs. The SIMM chips install on your system's motherboard, which resides within your PC's system unit. Although SIMMs are fairly easy to install, the slots into which you install them are very fragile. I strongly recommend that you let your retailer install the SIMM chips for you. In this way, you will reduce your risk of damaging your computer.

Determining How Much Memory Your System Contains

As you know, each time you turn on your PC's power, the PC examines all of its memory, displaying on your screen the amount of memory it encounters. To determine how much memory your system contains, simply watch the last value displayed. Later in this lesson, you will learn how to use the MEM command to display your system's memory use.

How DOS Uses Extended Memory

When you run a DOS-based program, the program's instructions must reside in your computer's conventional memory. Many programs, however, allow their data to reside in extended memory. Figure 35.2 illustrates how DOS uses extended memory.

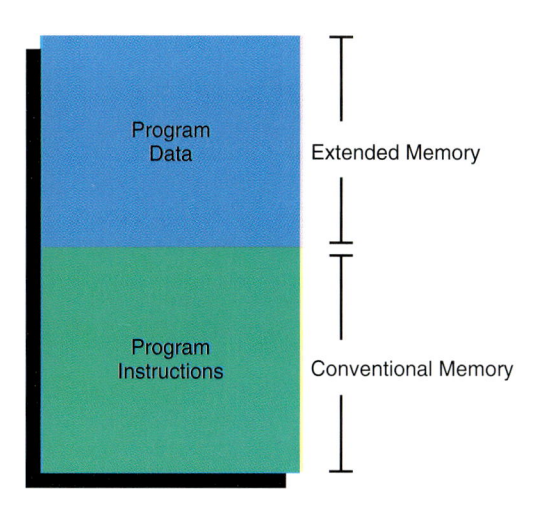

Figure 35.2 DOS programs use extended memory to hold data.

155

Rescued by DOS

INSTALLING AN EXTENDED MEMORY DEVICE DRIVER

Before DOS can use extended memory, you must install the HIMEM.SYS device driver in your CONFIG.SYS file as shown here:

```
DEVICE=C:\DOS\HIMEM.SYS
```

After you place this entry in your CONFIG.SYS file, you must restart your system for the device driver to take effect. To restart your system, use the CTRL-ALT-DEL keyboard combination.

VIEWING YOUR EXTENDED MEMORY USE USING MEM

As you have learned, the MEM command lets you display your system's memory use. For example, the following MEM command displays the amount of extended memory your system contains:

```
C:\> MEM <ENTER>

Memory Type            Total   =   Used   +   Free

Conventional            640K        52K        588K
Upper                     0K         0K          0K
Reserved                128K       128K          0K
Extended (XMS)        7,424K     2,112K      5,312K    Summary of
                                                       extended
Total memory          8,192K     2,292K      5,900K    memory use

Total under 1 MB        640K        52K        588K

Largest executable program size       588K  (602,256 bytes)
Largest free upper memory block         0K       (0 bytes)
MS-DOS is resident in the high memory area.
```

PUTTING EXTENDED MEMORY TO USE

Not all software programs can take advantage of extended memory. Thus, most users will use a portion of their extended memory for a RAM drive and a second portion for a SMARTDRV cache. A *RAM drive* is an electronic drive with its own drive letter with which you can store files. Because the drive is electronic and not mechanical, the drive is very fast. Unfortunately, when you turn off your computer or restart DOS, the information the RAM drive contains is lost. Most users use RAM drives to hold temporary files and then copy the files to their hard disk before they turn off

35: Using Extended Memory

their computer or restart DOS. To create a RAM drive using your computer's extended memory, you must place the RAMDRIVE.SYS device driver in your CONFIG.SYS file. The following entry, for example, directs DOS to create a 1Mb RAM drive in extended memory:

```
DEVICE=C:\DOS\RAMDRIVE.SYS  1024  /E
```

Assume, for example, that your computer has a floppy disk and a hard drive (drives A and C). When you install the RAM drive, DOS will create drive D, an electronic drive. Using the drive letter D, you can copy files to the RAM drive, select the RAM drive as the current drive, or use the RAM drive just as you would use your floppy or hard drive. However, you must remember to save the information to your hard disk before you turn off your computer or restart DOS.

Lesson 54 discusses the SMARTDRV disk caching software in detail. At that time, you will learn that you can improve your system performance by using much of your extended memory as a large disk buffer.

How DOS Uses Extended Memory

DOS-based programs must reside in your computer's conventional memory. However, many programs let their data reside in extended memory. The two most common ways DOS users take advantage of extended memory is to create a RAM drive or to create a large disk buffer using SMARTDRV. If you use Windows, however, Windows program instructions and data can reside in extended memory. As a rule, the more extended memory a system contains, the faster Windows will run.

What You Need to Know

In Lesson 36 you will learn how to free up conventional memory by loading DOS into the high memory area. Before you continue with Lesson 36, make sure you have learned the following:

- ☑ Extended memory is the memory beyond the PC's 1Mb conventional memory.
- ☑ Before DOS can use extended memory, you must place the HIMEM.SYS device driver in your CONFIG.SYS file.
- ☑ DOS-based program instructions must reside in your computer's conventional memory. However, many programs let their data reside in extended memory.
- ☑ The two most common ways users take advantage of extended memory are to create a RAM drive or to create a large disk buffer with SMARTDRV.

Lesson 36

Using the High Memory Area

If you are using a 286 or higher (a 386 or 486)-based PC, DOS lets you take advantage of the first 64Kb of extended memory, called the *high memory area*. You have learned that, in order to run, a program must reside in your computer's first 640Kb of *conventional memory*. A goal of memory management is to leave as much of this 640Kb conventional memory unused as possible for program use. One way users make more conventional memory available for program use is to move DOS itself into the high memory area. In this lesson you will learn how to load DOS into the high memory area. By the time you finish this lesson you will understand how to

- Place entries in CONFIG.SYS that load DOS into the high memory area
- Determine how much memory you save by loading DOS into the high memory area

UNDERSTANDING THE HIGH MEMORY AREA

As you have learned, most PCs contain at least 1Mb of memory. As Figure 36.1 shows, up to 640Kb of this memory is available for your program use and the remaining 384Kb is reserved for hardware use. When your computer loads DOS, part of the 640Kb memory region is used.

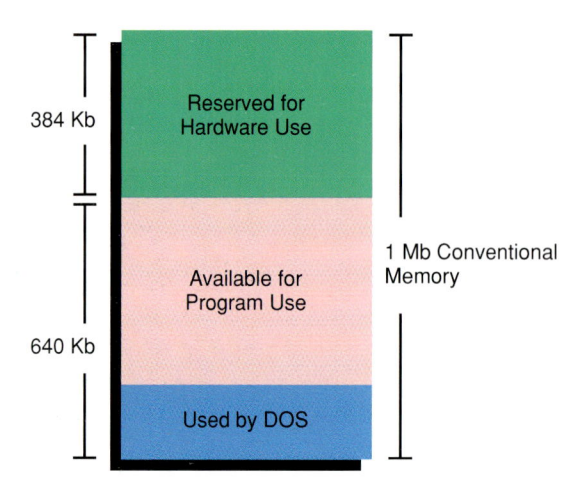

Figure 36.1 A PC's conventional memory use.

36: Using the High Memory Area

If you are using a 286 or higher, you can install extended memory into your computer. When you use DOS, programs can store their data in the extended memory. The program instructions, however, must still reside in the 640Kb conventional memory. As shown in Figure 36.2, the first 64Kb of extended memory is called the *high memory area*.

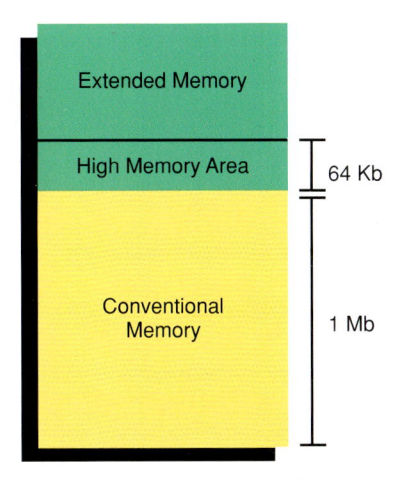

Figure 36.2 *The first 64Kb of extended memory is the high memory area.*

In this lesson, you will learn to move DOS into the high memory area, freeing up conventional memory for your program use, as shown in Figure 36.3.

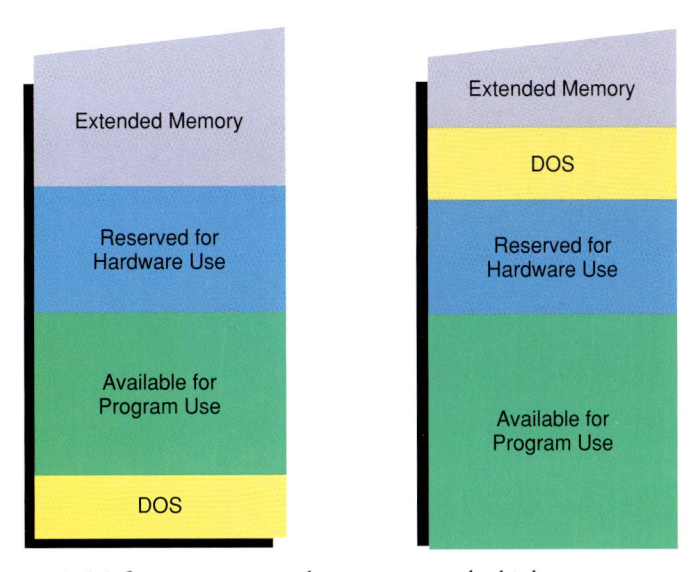

Figure 36.3 *Moving DOS from conventional memory into the high memory area.*

159

Rescued by DOS

Note: *To determine whether your computer has extended memory, watch the amount of memory the computer displays on your screen when you turn on the PC's power. If your computer displays a memory count higher than 1024, your PC contains extended memory, and you can use the steps discussed next to take advantage of the high memory area.*

LOADING DOS INTO THE HIGH MEMORY AREA

To load DOS into the high memory area, you simply need to place the following two entries in your CONFIG.SYS file:

```
DEVICE=C:\DOS\HIMEM.SYS
DOS=HIGH
```

To begin, select the root directory and then use the EDIT command to edit the CONFIG.SYS file, as shown here:

```
C:\> EDIT  CONFIG.SYS   <ENTER>
```

Examine your CONFIG.SYS entries closely to ensure that the file does not already contain these entries or a similar entry, as shown here:

```
DEVICE=C:\DOS\HIMEM.SYS
DOS=HIGH,UMB
```

If your CONFIG.SYS file does not contain the entry previously shown, add the entries to the file. Next, use the ALT-F keyboard combination to select EDIT's File menu. Select the Save option. Select the File menu a second time and choose Exit. Next, use the CTRL-ALT-DEL keyboard combination to restart your system.

LOADING DOS INTO HIGH MEMORY

By loading DOS into your PC's high memory area, you free conventional memory for your program use. To load DOS into the high memory area, your CONFIG.SYS file must contain the following entries:

```
DEVICE=C:\DOS\HIMEM.SYS
DOS=HIGH
```

After you place these entries in your CONFIG.SYS file, use the CTRL-ALT-DEL keyboard combination to restart your system.

160

36: Using the High Memory Area

Determining if DOS is Loaded High

As you have learned, the DOS MEM command lets you display your PC's memory use. Using MEM you can determine if DOS is loaded into high or conventional memory, as shown:

```
C:\> MEM    <ENTER>
```

After MEM displays its summary of your memory use, MEM may dsiplay a message that tells you if DOS is loaded in the high memory area as shown here:

```
Largest executable program size     580K (593,440 bytes)
Largest free upper memory block      0K       (0 bytes)
MS-DOS is resident in the high memory area.
```

If DOS is not loaded into the high memory area, MEM will display the following message instead:

```
The high memory area is available.
```

When you move DOS into the high memory area, the amount of available conventional memory MEM displays will increase, making more memory available for your program use.

What You Need to Know

In Lesson 37 you will learn how to use your computer's expanded memory. Before you continue with Lesson 37, make sure that you have learned the following:

- ☑ If you are using a 286 or higher-based computer that contains extended memory, you can load DOS into the a special memory region called the high memory area. By placing DOS into the high memory area, you free up conventional memory for your program use.
- ☑ The high memory area is the first 64Kb region of extended memory.
- ☑ To load DOS into the high memory area, you must place the following entries in your CONFIG.SYS file:
    ```
    DEVICE=C:\DOS\HIMEM.SYS
    DOS=HIGH
    ```

Lesson 37

Using Expanded Memory

When the IBM PC was first released in 1981, the PC could only support 1Mb of memory. If you placed more than 1Mb of memory into your computer, the 8088 processor simply could not use it. The PC could not address (access) memory locations whose addresses were beyond 1Mb. Unfortunately, spreadsheet programs such as Lotus 1-2-3 quickly consumed the PC's available memory. To provide the PC with more memory, hardware developers came up with *expanded memory*, a way to trick the PC into using memory beyond 1Mb. This lesson examines expanded memory in detail. If you are not using a 8088-based computer or very old programs that require expanded memory, continue your reading with Lesson 38. By the time you finish this lesson you will understand how to

- Use expanded memory to trick the PC into using memory beyond 1Mb
- Trick the PC into using extended memory as expanded to support older programs

UNDERSTANDING EXPANDED MEMORY

The only PC that requires expanded memory is the original 8088-based PC, which was released in 1981. If you are using a 286-based PC or higher, your computer should use extended memory discussed in Lesson 35. The original IBM PC could only access memory whose address was below 1Mb. Before the PC can access a memory location, the PC must have enough wires (called a *memory bus*) with which it can select a memory location. The memory bus on the original IBM PC only had 20 wires which restricted it to 1Mb. The 286, on the other hand has 24 wires which lets it address 16Mb, while the 386 has 32 wires and can access 4Gb!

For the original IBM PC to access memory beyond 1Mb, developers had to trick the PC into thinking it was really accessing valid memory locations. Expanded memory combines a special hardware board (called an expanded memory board) and software to trick the PC into accessing memory beyond 1Mb. Using expanded memory, the PC could use as much as 32Mb of memory! As you have learned, DOS-based programs run in the first 640Kb of conventional memory. The remaining 384Kb is reserved for use by the video display and other hardware devices. When the PC uses expanded memory, a 64Kb region of the reserved memory is allocated by the expanded memory software. As shown in Figure 37.1, the 64Kb region is then divided into four 16Kb *pages*.

37: Using Expanded Memory

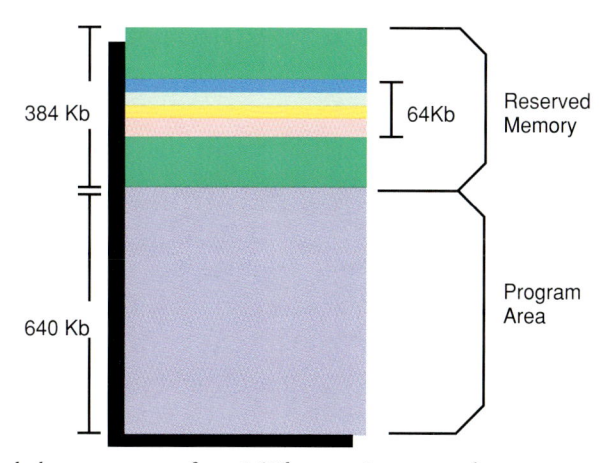

Figure 37.1 Expanded memory uses four 16Kb pages in reserved memory.

Next, programs that support expanded memory use these pages to access locations on the expanded memory board. For example, assume the expanded memory board can hold 4Mb. The expanded memory software divides the 4Mb into 16Kb pages. Next, programs that use the expanded memory map the four pages that reside in the PC's reserved memory to pages on the expanded memory board. Figure 37.2, for example, illustrates how a program might map expanded memory pages.

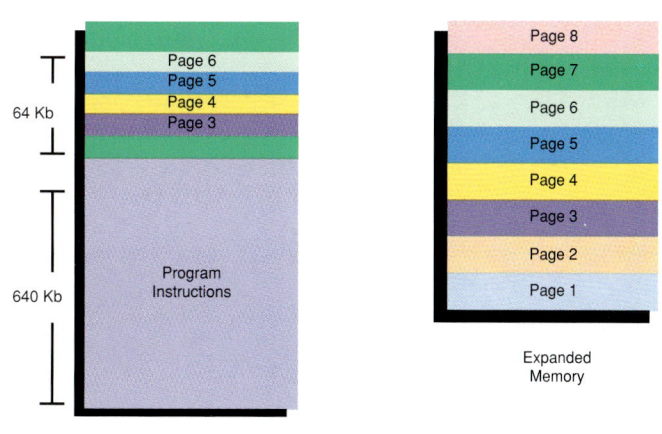

Figure 37.2 Mapping expanded memory pages.

In this case, the program is using the expanded pages 3, 4, 5, and 6. If the program later needed to use a different page, such as page 1, the program would map the page into the reserved area. Because the reserved memory area is within the PC's 1Mb address space, the PC has no problem accessing the pages. The user is unaware that the mapping occurs. The program does all the mapping behind the scenes. It is important to note that while expanded memory lets the PC access

163

memory beyond 1Mb, the continual mapping of pages that is required to access the memory is a slow process, so expanded memory is much slower than the extended memory discussed in Lesson 35. If your PC can support extended memory, use it.

SUPPORTING OLDER PROGRAMS THAT REQUIRE EXPANDED MEMORY

If you are running a 386-based PC (or higher) and you are still using a very old software program that uses expanded memory (and does not support extended memory), you can trick the PC into treating a portion of your PC's extended memory as expanded so the program will run. To do so, you must install the EMM386.EXE device driver into your CONFIG.SYS file:

```
DEVICE=C:\DOS\EMM386.EXE   1024
```

In this case, the DEVICE entry directs the PC to treat 1Mb of extended memory as expanded. The only time you would need to use the EMM386.EXE device driver in this way is if you are using a very old program on 386-based machine or higher. Expanded memory is much slower than extended memory, and you should avoid using it whenever possible.

HOW DOS USES EXPANDED MEMORY

Programs can only use expanded memory to hold data in DOS. Program instructions must reside in the 640Kb program area. If you are using an older PC that contains expanded memory, you can use the expanded memory to hold a RAM drive (as discussed in Lesson 35) with the RAMDRIVE.SYS device driver. In this case, DOS will create a 1Mb RAM drive. In addition, you can use expanded memory to hold a SMARTDRV disk cache, as discussed in Lesson 54.

```
DEVICE=C:\DOS\RAMDRIVE.SYS   1024   /A
```

WHAT YOU NEED TO KNOW

In Lesson 38 you will learn how to use upper memory on a 386-based computer (or higher) to free up more of the 640Kb program area for use by your programs. Before you continue with Lesson 38, however, make sure that you have learned the following:

- ☑ The original 8088-based PC released in 1981 could only access 1Mb of memory. Expanded memory is a technique that combines hardware and software to trick the PC into using memory beyond its 1Mb limits. Expanded memory can only store program data.

- ☑ If you are using a 286-based PC (or higher), you should use extended memory, which is much faster than expanded.

- ☑ If you are running an old program on a 386-based PC (or higher), you can use the EMM386.EXE device driver to trick the PC into treating a section of extended memory as expanded.

38: Using Upper Memory

Lesson 38

Using Upper Memory

As you have learned, conventional memory is the PC's first 1Mb of RAM. Normally, your programs run in the first 640Kb of conventional memory. The remaining 384Kb, called *upper memory*, is reserved for use by the PC's video display and other hardware. As you will learn in this lesson, much of the 384Kb reserved memory is unused. If you are using a 386-based computer (or higher) DOS lets you allocate regions of this upper memory to hold memory-resident programs and device drivers. In this lesson you will learn the steps you must perform to use the upper memory region. By the time you finish this lesson you will understand how to

- Direct DOS to let your programs and device drivers use the upper memory area
- Load device drivers into the upper memory area
- Load memory-resident programs into the upper memory area

UNDERSTANDING THE UPPER MEMORY AREA

The upper memory area is the 384Kb block of memory between 640Kb and 1Mb, as shown in Figure 38.1.

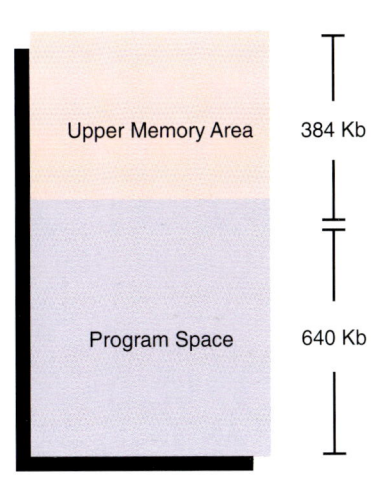

Figure 38.1 The upper memory area resides between 640Kb and 1Mb.

Rescued by DOS

Much of the upper memory area is reserved for the PC's video display. When the PC displays letters on the screen, the letters are first placed in the video memory. The video memory, however, only consumes part of the upper memory area, leaving memory available for your program use. A *memory-resident program* is a program that remains in your computer's memory after you run it. The DOS PRINT command, for examples, remains in memory to print files while you issue other commands from the DOS prompt. Likewise, some device drivers such as MOUSE.COM, remain in memory to let DOS access a specific device. Memory-resident programs and device drivers normally reside within the 640Kb program space, as shown in Figure 38.2.

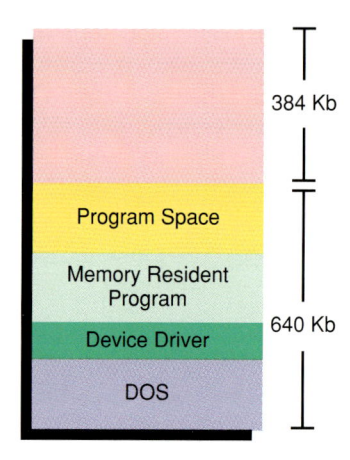

Figure 38.2 *Memory-resident programs and device drivers normally reside in the program area.*

However, you can load memory-resident programs and device drivers into the upper memory area, freeing up more of the 640Kb region for your program use, as shown in Figure 38.3.

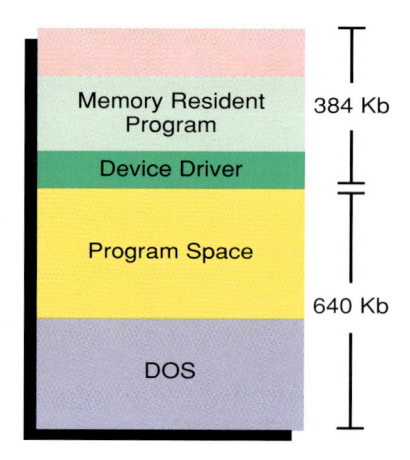

Figure 38.3 Loading memory-resident programs and device drivers into upper memory.

38: Using Upper Memory

DIRECTING DOS TO SUPPORT THE UPPER MEMORY AREA

Before you can use the upper memory area, you must tell DOS to support it. To begin, place the EMM386.EXE device driver in your CONFIG.SYS file, as shown here:

```
DEVICE=C:\DOS\EMM386.EXE    NOEMS
```

In Lesson 37 you learned that the EMM386.EXE device driver lets you allocate extended memory for use as expanded memory. In this case, the NOEMS parameter tells DOS that you do not want to use expanded memory. Instead, you are simply using the device driver to provide support for the upper memory area. Next, you must place a DOS entry similar to the following in your CONFIG.SYS file:

```
DOS=UMB
```

If you are loading DOS into the high memory area as discussed in Lesson 36, your DOS entry might appear as follows:

```
DOS=HIGH,UMB
```

The letters UMB are an abbreviation for upper memory block. An upper memory block is a section of memory within the upper memory area. When you load a device driver or memory-resident program into the upper memory area, DOS will allocate an upper memory block to hold the program.

After you place these entries in your CONFIG.SYS file, you must restart your system for the changes to take effect.

PROVIDING UPPER MEMORY SUPPORT

Before you can place a program or device driver into the upper memory area, you must direct DOS to provide upper memory support. To do so, place the following entries in your CONFIG.SYS file:

```
DEVICE=C:\DOS\EMM386.EXE    NOEMS
DOS=UMB
```

If you are loading DOS into the high memory area, your CONFIG.SYS file will appear as follows:

```
DEVICE=C:\DOS\HIMEM.SYS
DEVICE=C:\DOS\EMM386.EXE    NOEMS
DOS=HIGH,UMB
```

Rescued by DOS

Putting the Upper Memory Region to Use

Once you provide upper memory support, you can direct DOS to load device drivers and memory-resident programs into the upper memory area. In Lesson 31 you learned that to install a device driver you place a DEVICE entry in your CONFIG.SYS file. For example, the following DEVICE entry installs the ANSI.SYS device driver:

```
DEVICE=C:\DOS\ANSI.SYS
```

To install a device driver into the upper memory area, use the DEVICEHIGH entry, as shown here:

```
DEVICEHIGH=C:\DOS\ANSI.SYS
```

When DOS encounters a DEVICEHIGH entry in your CONFIG.SYS file, it first tries to load the device driver into the upper memory area. If there is not enough memory in the upper memory area to hold the driver, DOS will load the driver into the 640Kb memory region, just as if you had used the DEVICE entry. You cannot use the DEVICEHIGH entry until you have installed upper memory support. Thus you cannot use DEVICEHIGH for the HIMEM.SYS or EMM386.EXE device drivers. The following entries illustrate how you might use DEVICEHIGH within your CONFIG.SYS file:

```
DEVICE=C:\DOS\HIMEM.SYS
DEVICE=C:\DOS\EMM386.EXE   NOEMS
DOS=HIGH,UMB
DEVICEHIGH=C:\DOS\ANSI.SYS
```

Installing a Device Driver into Upper Memory

By default, DOS installs device drivers into the 640Kb program region. Using the DEVICEHIGH entry, however, you can direct DOS to place the driver into the upper memory area. For example, the following entry directs DOS to load the RAMDRIVE.SYS device driver into upper memory:

```
DEVICEHIGH=C:\DOS\RAMDRIVE.SYS
```

When DOS encounters the DEVICEHIGH entry, it will try to load the driver into the upper memory area. If there is not enough memory in the upper memory area to hold the driver, DOS will load the driver into the 640Kb memory region.

By default, when you load a memory-resident program such as PRINT, DOS will place the program in the 640Kb program area. If you have provided support for the upper memory area, however, you can use the LOADHIGH command to place the memory-resident program into the upper memory area.

38: Using Upper Memory

For example, the following LOADHIGH loads the PRINT command into upper memory:

```
LOADHIGH C:\DOS\PRINT
```

Note that LOADHIGH is a command, not a CONFIG.SYS entry. Thus, you can use LOADHIGH within your AUTOEXEC.BAT file. Because of its frequency of use, DOS lets you abbreviate LOADHIGH as simply LH.

> ### Loading a Memory-Resident Program into Upper Memory
>
> By default, DOS installs memory-resident programs into the 640Kb program area. Using the LOADHIGH command, you can direct DOS to load a command into the upper memory area. For example, the following LOADHIGH command directs DOS to install the PRINT command into the upper memory area:
>
> ```
> LOADHIGH  C:\DOS\PRINT
> ```
>
> When DOS encounters the LOADHIGH command, it tries to place the command into the upper memory area. If there is not enough memory to hold the command, DOS will place the command into the 640Kb program area.

What You Need to Know

In Lesson 39 you will learn how to configure your PC's memory using the MEMMAKER command. Before you continue with Lesson 39, make sure that you have learned the following:

- ☑ The upper memory area is the 384Kb region between 640Kb and 1Mb. Much of the upper memory area is reserved for use by the PC's video. However, part of the memory region is available for use by DOS. To use the upper memory area, you must have a 386-based computer or higher.

- ☑ By placing memory-resident programs and device drivers in the upper memory area, you free up the 640Kb program area for use by programs.

- ☑ Before you can use upper memory, you must install the EMM386.EXE device driver and place a DOS=UMB entry in your CONFIG.SYS file.

- ☑ To load a device driver in the upper memory area, use the DEVICEHIGH entry. If DOS is unable to fit the device driver into the available upper memory, it will load the driver into the 640Kb program area.

- ☑ To load a memory-resident program into the upper memory area, use the LOADHIGH command. If DOS is unable to fit the command into the available upper memory, it will load the program into the 640Kb program area.

Lesson 39

Configuring Your Memory Use with MemMaker

As you have learned, DOS provides many different ways for you to configure your computer's memory. Unfortunately, most new users consider memory management as one of the most confusing aspects of DOS. To simplify your memory management, DOS provides a program named MemMaker, which examines your CONFIG.SYS and AUTOEXEC.BAT files to determine how you are currently using memory and then makes adjustments. In this way, MemMaker automates the process of getting the most from your available memory. This lesson examines the MemMaker command.

By running MemMaker, you don't have to worry about fully understanding the upper memory area, the high memory area, and the required device drivers. By the time you finish this lesson you will understand how to

- Run MemMaker to configure your system's memory use
- Determine the changes MemMaker has made to your CONFIG.SYS and AUTOEXEC.BAT files
- Know when you should run MemMaker in the future

RUNNING MEMMAKER

You can run the MemMaker command at any time. If you have never run MemMaker or if you have made changes to your CONFIG.SYS or AUTOEXEC.BAT files or added memory to your computer, you should run MemMaker from the DOS prompt as shown here:

```
C:\> MemMaker    <ENTER>
```

MemMaker will display an opening screen similar to that shown in Figure 39.1.

39: Configuring Your Memory Use with MemMaker

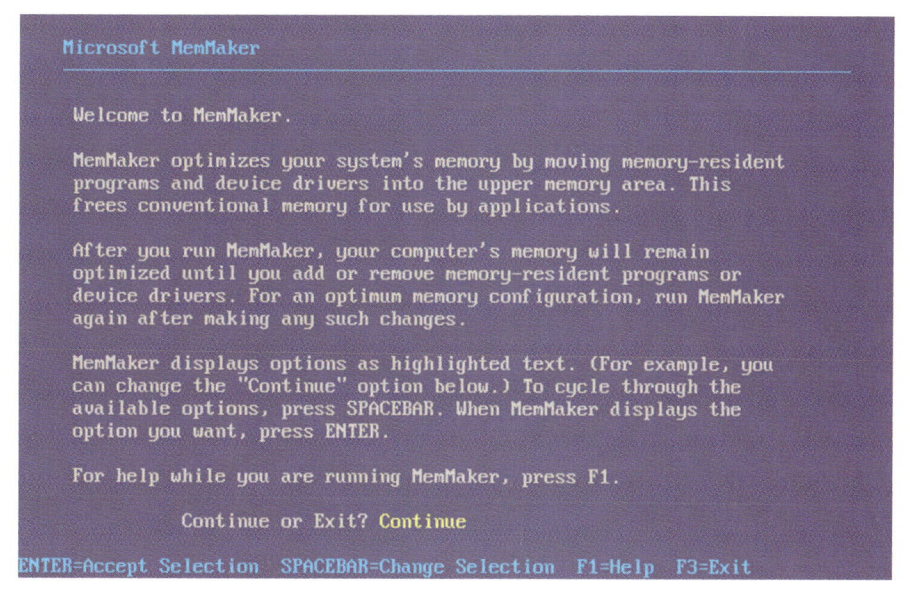

```
Microsoft MemMaker

Welcome to MemMaker.

MemMaker optimizes your system's memory by moving memory-resident
programs and device drivers into the upper memory area. This
frees conventional memory for use by applications.

After you run MemMaker, your computer's memory will remain
optimized until you add or remove memory-resident programs or
device drivers. For an optimum memory configuration, run MemMaker
again after making any such changes.

MemMaker displays options as highlighted text. (For example, you
can change the "Continue" option below.) To cycle through the
available options, press SPACEBAR. When MemMaker displays the
option you want, press ENTER.

For help while you are running MemMaker, press F1.

                    Continue or Exit? Continue

ENTER=Accept Selection   SPACEBAR=Change Selection   F1=Help   F3=Exit
```

Figure 39.1 *MemMaker's opening screen.*

Press ENTER to continue MemMaker's processing. MemMaker will display a series of messages on your screen. Read each message closely, pressing ENTER to continue. Next, MemMaker will restart your system to determine your system's current memory use. When your system restarts, MemMaker will automatically run, displaying a message telling you to press ENTER to restart your system. Press ENTER, and MemMaker will restart your system, using its changes to your CONFIG.SYS and AUTOEXEC.BAT files. When your system restarts, MemMaker will again be active. MemMaker will display a message asking you if your system appears to be running. Press ENTER to select Yes. MemMaker will display a message box similar to that shown in Figure 39.2 that shows your "Before and After MemMaker" memory use. Press ENTER to exit MemMaker.

DETERMINING MEMMAKER'S CHANGES

To improve your system's memory management, MemMaker makes changes to your CONFIG.SYS and AUTOEXEC.BAT files. Using the DOS PRINT command, print the files, as shown here:

```
C:\> PRINT \CONFIG.SYS  \AUTOEXEC.BAT  <ENTER>
```

MemMaker stores the original contents of your CONFIG.SYS and AUTOEXEC.BAT files in the DOS directory, using the UMB extension. Compare the files to determine the changes MemMaker has made. To print a copy of those two files, use the following command:

```
C:\> PRINT C:\DOS\CONFIG.UMB  C:\DOS\AUTOEXEC.UMB  <ENTER>
```

Rescued by DOS

```
Microsoft MemMaker

MemMaker has finished optimizing your system's memory. The following
table summarizes the memory use (in bytes) on your system:

                              Before      After
Memory Type                   MemMaker    MemMaker    Change

Free conventional memory:     549,376     624,208     74,832

Upper memory:
    Used by programs                0      77,968     77,968
    Reserved for Windows            0           0          0
    Reserved for EMS                0           0          0
    Free                            0      72,304

Expanded memory:              Disabled    Disabled

Your original CONFIG.SYS and AUTOEXEC.BAT files have been saved
as CONFIG.UMB and AUTOEXEC.UMB.  If MemMaker changed your Windows
SYSTEM.INI file, the original file was saved as SYSTEM.UMB.

ENTER=Exit    ESC=Undo changes
```

Figure 39.2 Viewing MemMaker's memory-management improvements.

WHEN TO RUN MEMMAKER IN THE FUTURE

You should run the MemMaker command if you add more memory to your computer, install new device drivers in your CONFIG.SYS file, or invoke new memory-resident programs from within your AUTOEXEC.BAT file. MemMaker will examine your CONFIG.SYS and AUTOEXEC.BAT files and make any changes you require.

WHAT YOU NEED TO KNOW

In Lesson 40 you will learn how to use the DOS Shell to simplify running programs, copying files, and many other daily operations. Before you continue with Lesson 40, make sure that you have learned the following:

- ☑ To simplify memory management operations, DOS provides the MemMaker command.

- ☑ When you run the MemMaker command, MemMaker will examine your CONFIG.SYS and AUTOEXEC.BAT files and make changes to improve your current memory use.

- ☑ If you add memory to your computer or make changes to your CONFIG.SYS or AUTOEXEC.BAT files, you should run the MemMaker command.

Section Eight

Using the DOS Shell

Throughout this book, you have executed different commands and run different programs by typing the command name at the DOS prompt and pressing ENTER. To make executing commands easier, DOS provides a special program called the DOS shell. The shell lets you perform the same operations that once required you to memorize difficult commands with easy-to-use menu options. As you will learn, using the shell's menu options, you can quickly copy, rename, delete, and print files. Likewise, you can create and select directories within the shell. Finally, as you will learn, the DOS shell lets you start two or more programs at the same time. In this way, you can quickly switch between running programs without having to end one program in order to start another. When you run two or more programs within the shell, only one program actually runs at any given time. However, quickly switching between programs using the shell can be very convenient.

Lesson 40 Getting Started with the DOS Shell

Lesson 41 Working with Files and Directories

Lesson 42 Running Programs Within the Shell

Lesson 43 Using the Task List

Lesson 40

Getting Started with the DOS Shell

Throughout this book you have issued your commands and run your programs from the DOS prompt. As you have learned, to run a program, you simply type the program name at the prompt and press ENTER. To make DOS even easier to use, DOS provides a special program called the DOS Shell. When the shell is running, you can run programs by selecting menu options and you can quickly copy, print, and delete files by selecting files from within a directory tree. This lesson introduces the DOS Shell. By the time you finish this lesson, you will understand how to

- Run the DOS Shell from the DOS prompt or from within your AUTOEXEC.BAT file
- Recognize the different parts of the shell
- Use the shell menus
- Exit the shell when you want to work from the DOS prompt

STARTING THE DOS SHELL

In the simplest the sense, the shell is a program that hides many of the complexities of DOS. When you work within the shell, you replace once difficult commands with menu options. Using the shell menus you can create directories, copy, rename, and delete files, and even run programs such as your word processor.

To start the shell, issue the DOSSHELL command:

```
C:\> DOSSHELL <ENTER>
```

DOS, in turn, will start the shell, displaying a screen similar to the one shown in Figure 40.1.

40: Getting Started with the DOS Shell

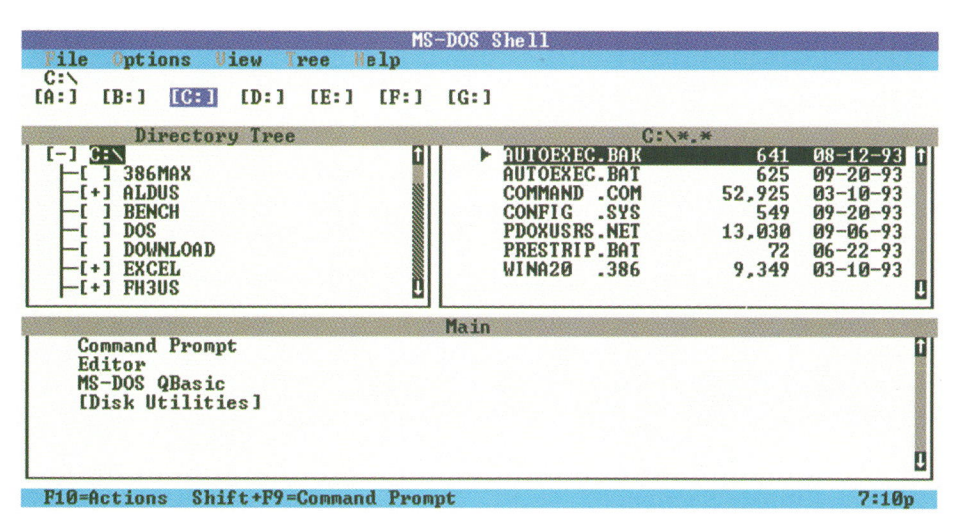

Figure 40.1 The DOS Shell interface.

As you can see, the shell actually consists of several different sections. Each time you press the TAB key, the shell advances the highlight from one section to the next. For example, if the disk drive icons are highlighted, pressing the TAB key directs the shell to highlight the directory tree. Likewise, pressing the TAB key again directs the shell to highlight the file list. If you hold down the SHIFT key and press the TAB, the shell highlights the previous section.

TRAVERSING SHELL MENUS

To begin, the File bar contains menus that let you perform common DOS operations. To select a specific menu, hold down the ALT key and press the first letter of the desired menu name. For example, to select the File menu you would press ALT-F. Likewise, to select the Options menu you would press ALT-O. When you select a menu, the shell will display one or more options. Figure 40.2, for example, shows the shell's File menu.

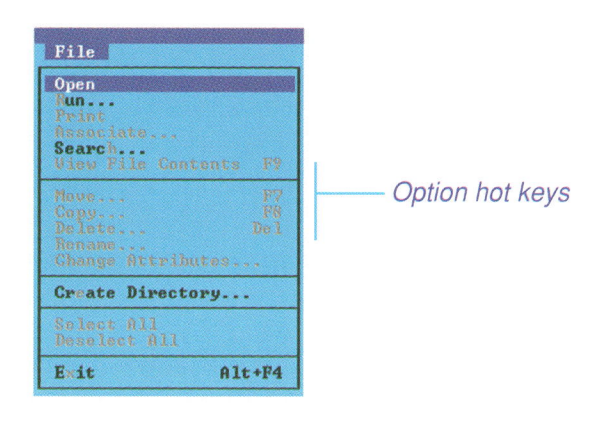

Figure 40.2 The File menu.

When you examine a menu, some of the options may appear dimly lit. Such options are not currently available. For example, before you can select the Print or Copy option, you must first select the file with which you want to work. To select an option, you have several choices. First, using your keyboard arrow keys, you can highlight the option and then press ENTER. Second, you can type the letter that appears highlighted within the desired option's name. Finally, many commonly used menu options are followed by a hot-key combination. If, at any time while you are using the shell, you type the corresponding hot key combination, the shell will immediately perform the operation without requiring you to use the menu. For example, you can press the ALT-F4 keyboard combination at any time to end the shell program. Should you select a menu and later decide you don't want to perform a menu operation, you can cancel the menu by pressing the ESC key.

WORKING WITH A MOUSE

If you have installed a mouse device driver, such as MOUSE.COM, the shell will let you use a mouse. As shown here, the shell displays the mouse pointer as small rectangle:

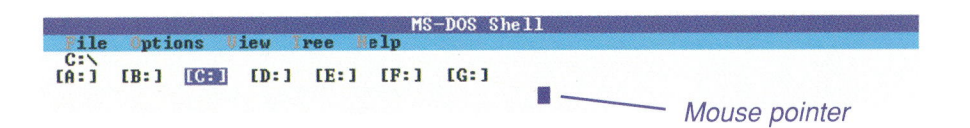

As you mouse the mouse across your desk, the shell will move the mouse pointer across your screen. To select an option using the mouse, aim the mouse pointer at the object and click the left mouse button. Using the mouse, you can quickly click on menus or different menu options.

CHANGING DISK DRIVES

As you can see in Figure 40.1, the shell displays *icons* (small graphics) for each available disk drive. In addition the shell highlights the current drive. Just as you can change the current drive from the DOS prompt, you can change the current drive from within the shell. The fastest way to change disk drives is to hold down the CTRL key and press the desired drive letter. For example, to select drive A, press CTRL-A. Likewise to select drive C, press CTRL-C. Second, you can press the TAB key until the shell highlights the disk drive icons. Next, using your keyboard arrow keys, highlight the desired drive and press ENTER. Finally, if you are using a mouse, click on the desired drive.

SELECTING A DIRECTORY

The shell displays a directory tree and highlights the current directory. Just as you can select the current directory from the DOS prompt using the CHDIR command, the shell lets you select the current directory. To begin, press the TAB key until the shell highlights the directory tree. Next, use

40: Getting Started with the DOS Shell

your keyboard arrow keys to highlight the desired directory. As you highlight a directory, the shell will display the files the directory contains. If you are using a mouse, simply click on the desired directory name with your mouse. Lesson 41 examines shell directory and file operations in detail.

Using the Shell Main Menu

Near the bottom of your screen, the shell displays a list of menu options:

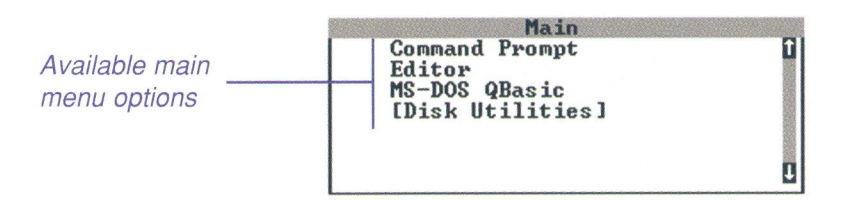

```
                    Main
         Command Prompt
         Editor
         MS-DOS QBasic
         [Disk Utilities]
```

Available main menu options

By selecting these menu options, you can quickly run EDIT, the DOS editor, run QuickBasic which lets you create your own programs, select a second level of menu options, and even temporarily exit the shell to the DOS prompt. Lesson 42 covers running programs and commands from within the shell. At that time, you will learn to use the shell's main menu options.

Exiting the Shell

When you no longer want to use the shell, or if you are ready to turn off your computer, you can exit the shell by selecting the File menu's Exit option or pressing the ALT-F4 keyboard combination. Do not turn off your computer while the shell is running. Instead, exit the shell to the DOS prompt, just as you would exit any other program, before you turn off your computer's power.

What You Need to Know

In Lesson 41 you will learn how to perform file and directory operations from within the shell. Before you continue with Lesson 41, however, make sure you have learned the following:

- ☑ The DOS Shell is a program that lets you replace commands with menu options. To run the DOS Shell, type **DOSSHELL** from the DOS prompt.

- ☑ The DOS Shell consists of several different sections. To advance from one section to the next, press the TAB key. To move the highlight back one section, press the SHIFT-TAB keyboard combination.

- ☑ Within the shell, you can perform all the same operations you can from the DOS prompt, such as printing, copying, and renaming files.

- ☑ When you have finished using the shell select the File menu's Exit option or pressing the ALT-F4 keyboard combination.

177

Lesson 41

Working with Files and Directories

As you have learned, the DOS Shell exists to make your computer and DOS itself easier to use. Within the DOS shell, you can perform the same operations you can perform from the DOS prompt. In this lesson you will learn how to perform file and directory operations within the shell. By the time you finish this lesson you will understand how to

- Copy, rename, print, move, view, and delete a file
- Work with two or more files
- Create, expand, and collapse directories within the directory tree
- Change the information and format the shell displays on your screen

PERFORMING FILE OPERATIONS

Within the shell you can quickly copy, rename, move, print, delete, or view a file's contents. The steps you must follow to perform each of these operations is very similar. To begin, press the TAB key to highlight the file list. Next, using your keyboard arrow keys, highlight the desired file. Press the ALT-F keyboard combination to select the shell's File menu. The File menu contains options for each of the common file operations. When you select a specific option, the shell will display a message box asking you to type in more information or to confirm the specified operation. For example, if you select the Copy option, the shell will display the Copy File message box, as shown in Figure 41.1, asking you to type in the pathname to which you want the file's contents copied.

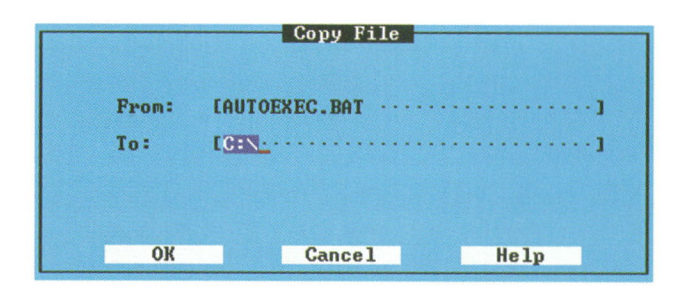

Figure 41.1 The Copy File message box.

41: Working with Files and Directories

Type in the desired filename and press ENTER. Assume for example, you need to copy a file named BUDGET.RPT to the floppy disk in drive A. To perform the file copy operation, you would first highlight the file within the file list and then select the File menu's Copy option. When the shell displays the Copy File message box, type the filename **A:BUDGET.RPT** in the To: field and press ENTER. To print, delete, rename, or move a file you first highlight the file within the file list and then select the corresponding File menu option. If you have highlighted an ASCII file, you can display the file's contents with the File menu's View option.

WORKING WITH TWO OR MORE FILES

As you have learned, there are many times when you need to work with a group of files. For example, you might need to copy several related files to a floppy disk or delete two or more files you no longer need. When you issue commands from the DOS prompt, you can use wildcards to work with two or more files. When you work within the DOS shell, however, you simply select the files for which you want an operation to apply.

To select a file for a file operation, use your keyboard arrow keys to highlight the file within the file list and then press your keyboard's SPACEBAR. If you are using a mouse, you can hold down a CTRL key as you click your mouse on the filename. As you select a file, the shell will place a small highlight next to the file to indicate the file has been selected, as shown in Figure 41.2.

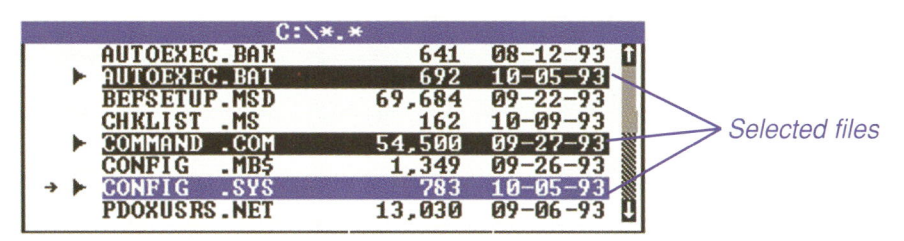

```
                C:\*.*
    AUTOEXEC.BAK        641   08-12-93
  ▶ AUTOEXEC.BAT        692   10-05-93
    BEFSETUP.MSD     69,684   09-22-93
    CHKLIST  .MS        162   10-09-93
  ▶ COMMAND  .COM    54,500   09-27-93
    CONFIG   .MB$     1,349   09-26-93
→ ▶ CONFIG   .SYS       783   10-05-93
    PDOXUSRS.NET     13,030   09-06-93
```
→ Selected files

Figure 41.2 Selected files within the file list.

Should you accidentally select a wrong file, simply highlight the file and press the SPACEBAR a second time. After you select the desired files, you can use the File menu options to copy, move, delete, rename, or print the selected files.

There may be times when you want to perform an operation on all the files in a directory. Using the File menu's Select All option, you can quickly select all the files a directory contains. Likewise, should you select several files and then decide you don't want to perform a specific operation, you can use the File menu's Deselect All option to deselect the files quickly.

Rescued by DOS

Performing Directory Operations Within the Shell

You have learned that, by highlighting a specific directory within the directory tree, you direct the shell to display the names of the files the directory contains. As you traverse the directory tree, there may be times when you encounter a directory folder that contains a plus sign (+), as shown here:

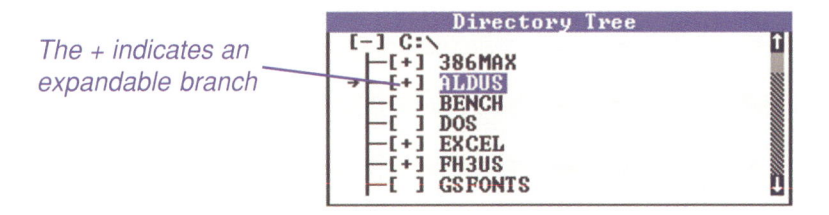

The + indicates an expandable branch

```
        Directory Tree
[-] C:\
 ├─[+] 386MAX
→├─[+] ALDUS
 ├─[ ] BENCH
 ├─[ ] DOS
 ├─[+] EXCEL
 ├─[+] FH3US
 ├─[ ] GSFONTS
```

The plus sign indicates that the directory contains additional levels of subdirectories not currently shown in the directory tree. To display the next level of directory branches, highlight the directory name and press the plus key (+) or click on the plus key within the folder using your mouse. The shell will display the next level of directories, changing the plus sign to a minus sign (–), as shown:

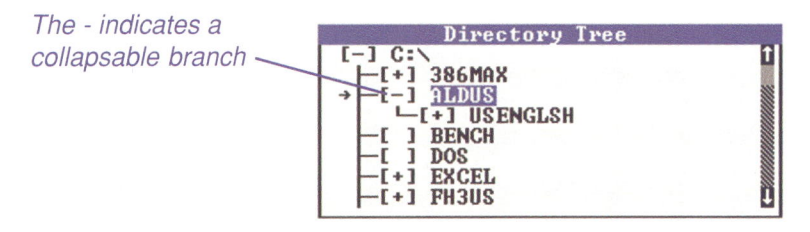

The - indicates a collapsable branch

```
        Directory Tree
[-] C:\
 ├─[+] 386MAX
→├─[-] ALDUS
 │    └─[+] USENGLSH
 ├─[ ] BENCH
 ├─[ ] DOS
 ├─[+] EXCEL
 ├─[+] FH3US
```

To collapse the branch, suppressing the display of the lower level directories, press the minus sign (–) or click on the folder's minus sign with your mouse.

When you expand a directory branch by pressing the a plus sign, the shell will display only the next level of the directory tree. If the next level contains expandable branches, those directory names will appear with plus signs in the directory folder. If you highlight an expandable branch and type an asterisk (*), however, the shell will expand the entire directory branch, including all lower-level directories. In addition to clicking on a folder's plus and minus signs to expand and collapse directories, you can highlight the directory and then use the Tree menu, shown in Figure 43.4.

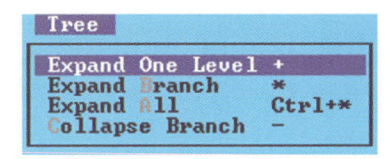

```
Tree
┌─────────────────────────────┐
│ Expand One Level    +       │
│ Expand Branch       *       │
│ Expand All          Ctrl+*  │
│ Collapse Branch     -       │
└─────────────────────────────┘
```

Figure 43.4 *The shell's Tree menu.*

41: Working with Files and Directories

CREATING OR REMOVING A DIRECTORY

When you work within the shell, there may be times when you need to create one or more directories to organize your files. To create a directory, highlight the directory within the directory tree within which you want the new directory created. Next, select the File menu and choose the Create Directory option. The shell will display the Create Directory message box asking you for the desired directory name. Type in the desired directory name and press ENTER. The shell will add the directory to the directory tree. To remove a directory you no longer require, you must first delete the files the directory contains. Next, highlight the directory within the directory tree and press the DEL key. The shell will display a message box, asking you to confirm the deletion. Select Yes.

CHANGING THE SHELL DISPLAY

By default, the shell displays the directory tree, file list, and the main menu of program entries. Depending on how you use the shell, you might want to display only a directory or file list, display only the program menu options, or you might want to display a directory and file list for two different disks at the same time. For example, Figure 43.6 illustrates a directory and file list for drive C and the floppy disk contained in drive A.

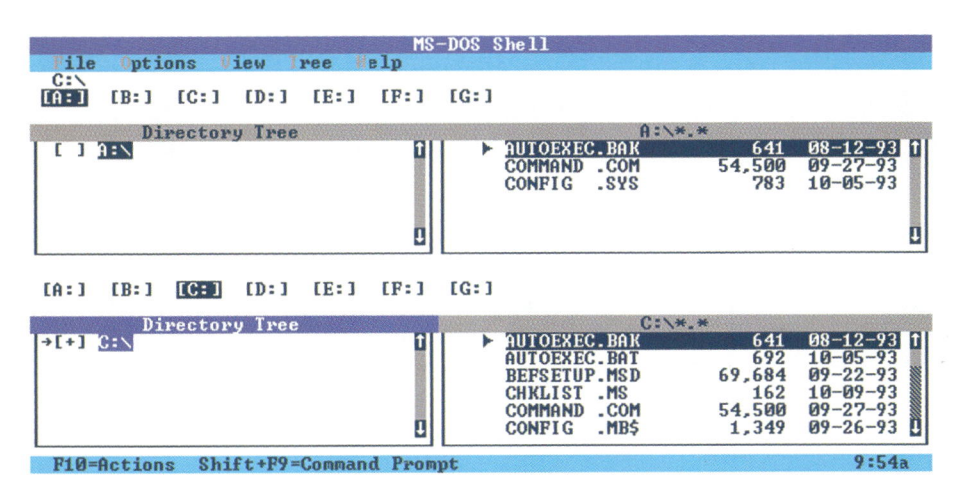

Figure 43.6 Displaying a directory tree and file list for two different drives.

To control the shell's appearance, select the View menu, shown in Figure 43.7. Experiment with the View menu options until the shell displays the information you desire.

181

Rescued by DOS

What You Need to Know

In Lesson 42 you will learn different ways to run programs within the shell. Before you continue with Lesson 42, however, make sure that you have learned the following:

- ☑ Within the DOS shell you can quickly perform file copy, move, view, rename, print, and delete operations. To perform these operations, highlight the desired file within the file list. Next, select the File menu and choose the option that corresponds to the operation you desire. Depending on the option you select, the shell might display a message box, requesting additional information or requesting you to confirm the operation.

- ☑ To perform file operations on two or more files, individually highlight each file within the file list and press the SPACEBAR or hold down a CTRL key and click on the filename using your mouse. After you select the files you desire, select the corresponding File menu option you require.

- ☑ As you traverse the shell's directory tree, you might encounter directory folders that contain a plus or minus sign. The plus sign indicates that the directory branch can be expanded to reveal additional levels of directories. To expand the branch press the plus sign or click on the folder's plus sign with your mouse. The minus sign indicates that the directory has been expanded, to collapse the directory, press the minus sign or click on the folder's minus sign using your mouse.

- ☑ To create a directory within the shell, highlight the directory within the directory tree within which you want the new directory created. Next, select the File menu's Create directory option. The shell will display a message box asking you type in the desired directory name.

- ☑ To delete a directory within the shell you must first delete the files the directory contains. Next, highlight the directory and press the DEL key. The shell will display a message box asking you to confirm the operation. Select Yes.

- ☑ Finally, the shell's View menu lets you control the items that appear on the shell screen. Using the View menu you can direct the shell to display only a file or directory list, only the program menu, or even a file and directory list for two different disks.

Lesson 42

Running Programs Within the Shell

The DOS Shell exists to make using your computer and running programs easier. In this lesson you will learn several different ways to run programs within the DOS Shell. By the time you finish this lesson you will understand how to

- Run a program using the File menu's Run option
- Run a program by selecting the program from the file list
- Run programs from the shell's main menu

USING THE FILE MENU'S RUN OPTION

Throughout this book you have run programs and DOS commands by typing the command's name at the DOS prompt and pressing ENTER. Using the File menu's Run option, you can run your programs from within the shell in a similar way. To begin, press the ALT-F keyboard combination. The shell will display the File menu. Select the Run option. The shell will display the Run message box, as shown in Figure 42.1.

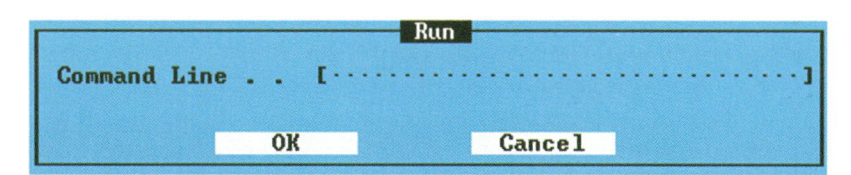

Figure 42.1 The Run message box.

Within the dialog box, type in your program name and optional command-line parameters, pressing ENTER to execute the command. When you have finished using the program, end the program as you normally would from the DOS prompt. The shell will display a message asking you to press any key to continue. When you press a key, the shell will reappear on your screen.

Using the Run message box, you can issue any DOS command, including such commands as COPY, RENAME, MKDIR, and so on.

Rescued by DOS

RUNNING PROGRAMS USING THE FILE LIST

As you learned in Lesson 41, when you highlight a directory in the directory tree, the shell will display the names of files the directory contains. If you highlight a file with the EXE, COM, or BAT extension within the file list and press ENTER, the shell will run the corresponding command. If you are using a mouse, double-click your mouse on the file to run the corresponding program. Assuming, for example, that you wanted to run the WordPerfect word processor, which resides in the directory WP60, you would first highlight the WP60 directory and then highlight the WP.EXE file in the file list, pressing ENTER to run the program.

RUNNING PROGRAMS FROM THE SHELL'S MAIN MENU

As you have learned, the shell contains a menu of commands similar to those shown in Figure 42.2.

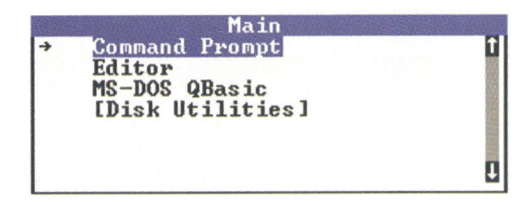

```
              Main
→  Command Prompt
   Editor
   MS-DOS QBasic
   [Disk Utilities]
```

Figure 42.2 *The shell's main menu of commands.*

To execute a command from the Main menu, first press the TAB key to highlight the menu area. Next, using your keyboard arrow keys, highlight the desired command. The Main menu's Command Prompt option lets you temporarily exit the shell the to the DOS prompt. Select this option when you want to execute one or two commands from the DOS prompt, later returning to the shell. The Command Prompt option does not end the shell program. Instead, the shell continues to run the entire time you work at the DOS prompt. When you are ready to return to the shell, invoke the DOS EXIT command as shown here:

```
C:\> EXIT  <ENTER>
```

Note: *Many DOS-based programs, such as your word processor, let you temporarily exit the program to the DOS shell. You should not turn off your computer while temporarily exited to the DOS prompt because your previous program is still running. If you turn off your computer and the previous program has open files, the information the files contain can be damaged or lost. Instead, use the EXIT command to return to the program and then end the program before turning off your computer.*

The Main menu's Editor option invokes the DOS EDIT command, which you used earlier in this book to create DOS batch files. Likewise, the MS-DOS QBasic option lets you work with Microsoft QuickBasic to create your own programs. If you are interested in learning to program with

42: Running Programs Within the Shell

QuickBasic, there are several very good books available on the subject. If you select the Disk Utilities option, the shell will display a new menu of options, as shown in Figure 42.3.

Figure 42.3 *The shell's Disk Utilities menu options.*

Most of the disk utility programs are discussed in lessons throughout this book. To run a disk utility program, use your arrow keys to highlight the option and press ENTER. To return to the shell's main menu, select the [Main] option.

CREATING YOUR OWN MENU OPTIONS

If you work with the shell on a regular basis, you might want to add your own programs, such as your word processor to the shell's main menu. When you add a menu option, you can place a program entry within the menu or you can add a program group, such as [Disk Utilities], which will hold several programs.

ADDING A PROGRAM ENTRY

To add a program entry to a menu, press the TAB key to highlight the menu area. Next, select the File menu and choose New. The shell will display the New Program Object message box, as shown in Figure 42.4.

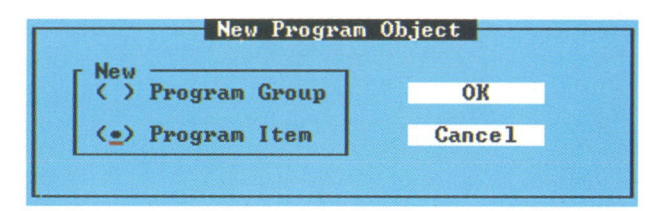

Figure 42.4 *The New Program Object message box.*

Select the Program Item option. The shell will display the Add Program message box, as shown in Figure 42.5.

185

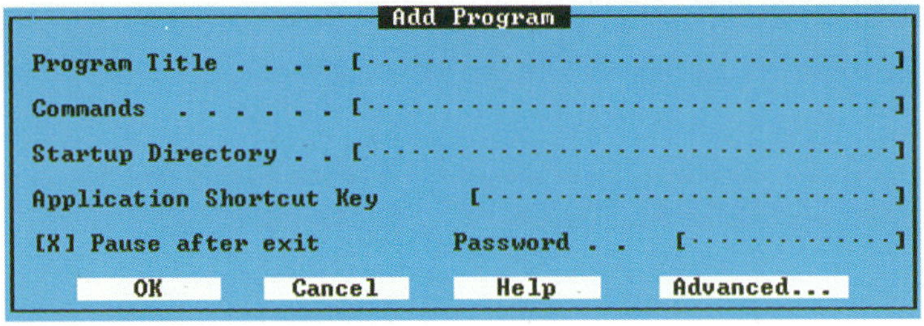

Rescued by DOS

```
            ┌─────── Add Program ───────┐
Program Title  . . . .  [······························]
Commands    . . . . .   [······························]
Startup Directory . .   [······························]
Application Shortcut Key   [··························]
[X] Pause after exit      Password . .  [··············]
        OK        Cancel         Help         Advanced...
```

Figure 42.5 *The Add Program message box.*

Within the Program Title field, type in the option name you want to appear in the menu and press the TAB key. Within the Commands field, type in the command you would normally type at the DOS prompt to run the program. You can normally leave the remaining entries unused. Select the OK option to save your menu entry. Should you later want to remove a menu entry, highlight the entry and press DEL. The shell will display a message box asking you to verify that you want to delete the entry. Select OK.

ADDING A PROGRAM GROUP

If you have a group of related programs, such as those you use for work or those you use for school, you may want to place the programs within a program group. To create a program group, highlight the desired menu and choose the File menu New option. The shell will display the New Program Object message box previously shown in Figure 42.5. Select the Program Group option. The shell will display the Add Group message box. Type in the name of the program group, such as Work or School and press ENTER. Next to add programs to group, select the group and follow the steps previously discussed in the "Adding a Program Entry" section of this lesson.

WHAT YOU NEED TO KNOW

In Lesson 43 you will learn how to load two or more programs into memory at the same time using the shell's task list. Before you continue with Lesson 43, make sure you have learned the following:

- ☑ The shell provides you with three different ways to run programs.

- ☑ To run programs by typing in the command name, selecting the File menu and choosing Run. The shell will display a message box prompting you for the desired command.

- ☑ To run a program using the file list, first highlight the directory containing the program you want to run. Next, highlight the program name and press ENTER or double-click on the program name with your mouse.

- ☑ The shell provides a menu of program names you can run by highlighting and pressing ENTER. In addition, the shell lets you add your own program entries to the menu, making your commonly used programs easy to run.

Lesson 43

Using the Task List

In Lesson 42 you learned several different ways to run programs within the DOS Shell. As you have learned, DOS only lets you run one program at any given time. When you want to run a second program, you must end the first program before you can start the second. The DOS shell, however, is a special program. Using the shell's *task list*, the shell lets you start several different programs at the same time. When you want to run a specific program, you select the desired program, and the shell immediately displays the program. Although only one program is running at any given time, the other programs are loaded into memory so you can quickly switch between them. When you select a program, the program immediately starts to run. This lesson examines the DOS shell task list in detail. By the time you finish this lesson, you will understand how to

- Turn the task list on and off
- Use the task list to start multiple programs at the same time
- Use the task list to switch between programs

ENABLING AND DISABLING THE SHELL'S TASK LIST

Before you can start two or more programs at the same time, you must turn on the shell's task list. To do so, select the Options menu. When you select the Enable Task Swapper option, the shell will add a Active Task List box, as shown in Figure 43.1.

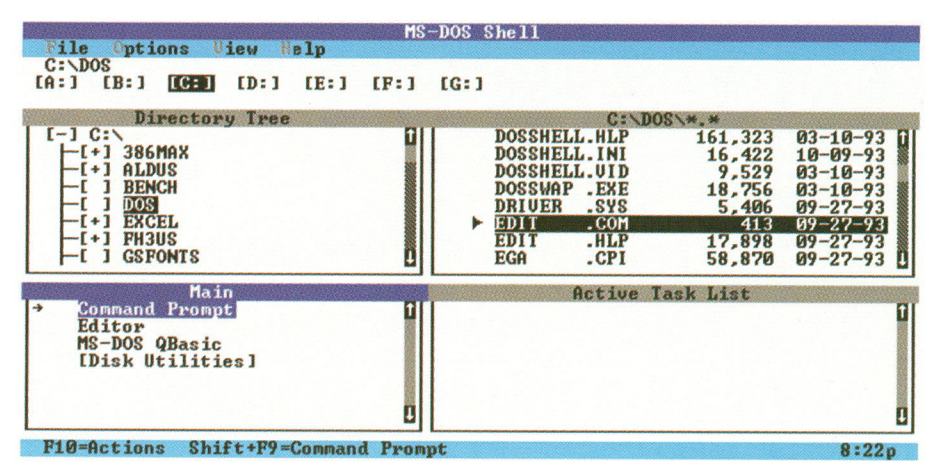

Figure 43.1 The Active Task List.

Rescued by DOS

Should you later decide that you don't want to use the task list, select the Options menu Enable Task Swapper a second time. The shell will remove the Active Task List box.

Taking the Task List for a Test Drive

The best way to understand how the task list works, is to put it to use. To begin, press the Tab key to highlight the Editor option in the main menu. Press Enter to run the program. The shell will display a message box asking you for command-line parameters. Press Enter to run the program. When DOS displays the Edit window, press the Ctrl-Esc keyboard combination. The shell will reappear. The task list will display the Editor name within the Active Task List.

Next, press the Tab key to highlight the MS-DOS option and press Enter. As before, the shell will display a message box asking you for command line parameters. Press Enter to run the program. When the program appears, press the Ctrl-Esc keyboard combination to return the shell. The task list will display the MS-DOS QBasic program name within the Active Task List.

To switch between active programs, use Ctrl-Esc to select the shell. Next, highlight the name of the program you desire within the Active Task List and press Enter. To end a program, select the program from the Active Task List and then perform the same steps you would normally use to end the program. The shell will remove the program from the Active Task List. In the case of the Edit and QBasic programs, select each program one at a time. Next, use the File menu's Exit option to end the program.

What You Need to Know

In Lesson 44 you will learn the importance of backing up the files on your hard disk to floppies. Before you continue with Lesson 44, however, make sure that you learned the following:

- ☑ When you use the DOS Shell, you can take advantage of the task list to load multiple programs into memory at the same time. Although the shell will only run one program at any given time, you can use the task list to switch quickly between programs without the overhead of stopping and starting programs.

- ☑ To return to the shell from an active program, press the Ctrl-Esc keyboard combination. The shell will display the program name within the Active Task List.

- ☑ To run an active program, press the Tab key to highlight the Active Task List. Next, use the keyboard arrow keys to highlight the desired program name and press Enter.

- ☑ To end an active program, select the program from the Active Task List. Next, perform the same steps you normally perform to end the program.

Section Nine

BACKING UP YOUR FILES

When you store information on a disk, the information is at risk from several different sources. For example, disks fail over time. Likewise, an errant command can quickly delete or overwrite needed files, or a disk can be lost or stolen. To reduce your risk of lost data, you need to make backup copies of your files. To help you create backups quickly, DOS provides the MSBACKUP command. As you will learn, you can quickly backup all the files on your disk or only those files you have created or changed since the last backup operation with the MSBACKUP command.

Lesson 44 Understanding Disk Backups

Lesson 45 Performing Full Disk Backup

Lesson 46 Performing an Incremental Backup

Lesson 47 Restoring Files from Your Backup Disks

Lesson 48 Creating a Backup Policy

Lesson 44

Understanding Disk Backups

When you store information on your computer's hard disk, make sure that you regularly make backup copies of your files, placing the files on a floppy disk or tape and then storing your backups in a safe location. This lesson examines disk backup operations. By the time you finish this lesson you will understand how to

- Determine when you need to backup your files
- Place your backup files in a safe location
- Track your hardware and software for insurance purposes

As more users travel with PCs and work with a PC at home, their PCs tend to hold more and more key information. To prevent a disk failure or errant command from destroying the information on your disk, you need to make backup copies of your files.

BACKING UP YOUR FILES

When you store information on your disks, you need to remember that disks do not last forever, they can be damaged by smoke, files can be erased by an errant command, and your computer can be lost or even stolen. In other words, the information you store on your disk is not safe. If you cannot afford to replace all the files on your disk, retyping reports, memos, and so on, you need to make backup copies of your files. Ideally, you will back up the files you store on your disk each day. In that way, the most work you can ever lose due to a disk failure is one day's work.

To backup your hard disk, you will copy files to floppy disks. After you copy your files to floppies, you must then store your floppies in a safe location. To help you organize your floppy disks, you should place them in a disk storage container similar to the one shown in Figure 44.1.

Next, you should keep your disk storage container in a safe location. Keep in mind that, if you keep your container in the same room as your computer, the container can be destroyed or stolen with your computer. Ideally, therefore, you should store your backup disks at a remote location, such as your home or even in a safe deposit box.

44: Understanding Disk Backups

Figure 44.1 Place your floppy disks in a disk storage container.

PERFORMING A BACKUP OPERATION

If you create or change one or two key files each day, you can quickly copy the files to a floppy disk using the DOS COPY command. However, if you change a large number of files, you should use MSBACKUP to back up your files. To begin, invoke MSBACKUP from the DOS prompt:

```
C:\> MSBACKUP    <ENTER>
```

If you have not used MSBACKUP before, MSBACKUP will display a message box, as shown in Figure 44.2, telling you that you must configure MSBACKUP for your system.

Rescued by DOS

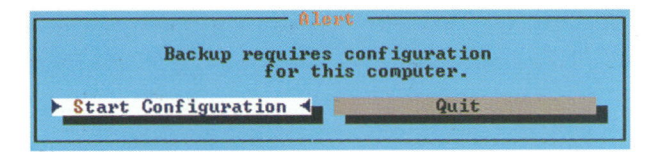

Figure 44.2 MSBACKUP's configuration prompt.

If this message box appears, press ENTER to select the Start Configuration option. MSBACKUP will display a screen allowing you to customize your hardware settings. If you need to change one of the hardware settings, press the corresponding highlighted letter. MSBACKUP will display a box asking you to select the desired setting. After you select the setting, choose OK. If your hardware settings are correct, select the OK option. MSBACKUP will display the message box shown in Figure 44.3 telling you that it will perform a floppy disk change-line test.

Figure 44.3 MSBACKUP's hardware customization screen.

The change-line test determines if your PC can detect when you remove one floppy disk and insert another. To perform the change-line test, remove the floppy disks from your computer and press ENTER. MSBACKUP will perform the test for each floppy drive on your computer. When the test completes, select the OK option. MSBACKUP will then test your processor and hard disk speed, briefly displaying a performance index. Next, MSBACKUP will display a message box telling you that it will perform a compatibility test.

44: Understanding Disk Backups

The compatibility test lets you verify that the MSBACKUP settings you have selected are correct. To perform the compatibility test, you will need two unused floppy disks of the same size. Press ENTER to begin the test. MSBACKUP will ask you to select the disk drive into which you will place the backup floppy disk. Next, MSBACKUP will back up several files to the disk, later prompting you to insert the second floppy. When the backup operation completes, MSBACKUP will then compare the contents of the files backed up to the original files. To perform the compatibility test, simply follow the message boxes that appear on your screen. After the test completes, MSBACKUP will display the Configuration.

Select the Save option. MSBACKUP will display its Backup message box, shown in Figure 44.4. In Lesson 45 you will learn how to perform a complete disk backup using the Backup message box. For now, however, select the Quit option to return to DOS.

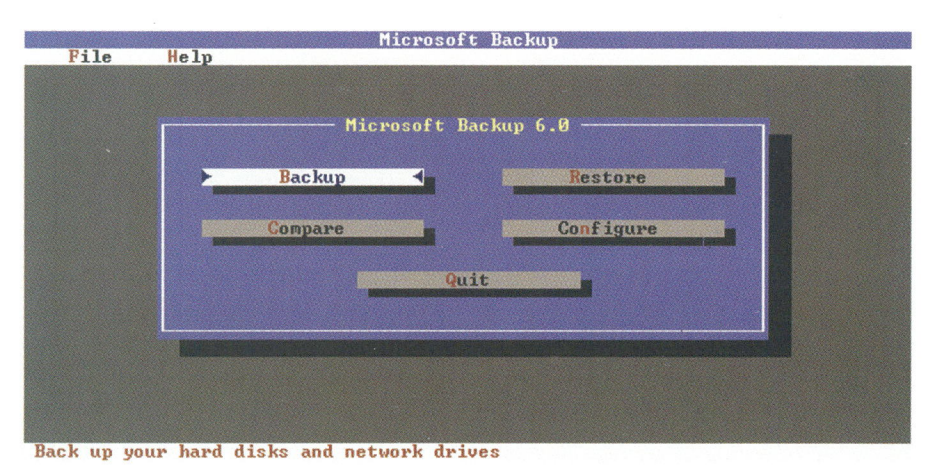

Figure 44.4 The Backup message box.

WHAT YOU NEED TO KNOW

In Lesson 45 you will learn how to back up all the files on your disk to floppies. Before you continue with Lesson 45, however, make sure that you have learned the following:

- ☑ The files you store on your hard disk are not safe. Your disk can fail, an errant command can erase or overwrite the files, or your computer can be stolen. Thus, you need to back up your files to floppy disks on a regular basis.

- ☑ Store your backup floppy disks in a disk storage container. In addition, you should store the disk container at a location away from your computer.

- ☑ The MSBACKUP command lets you backup the files on your disk to floppies.

Rescued by DOS

Lesson 45

Performing Full Disk Backup

As you learned in Lesson 44, the MSBACKUP command makes it easy for you to back up the files on your disk. In this lesson you will learn how to perform a full disk backup operation using MSBACKUP. By the time you finish this lesson you will understand how to

- Select the files you want to back up
- Specify the location to which you want the file backed up
- Select a full backup operation
- Save your backup configuration to a setup file
- Perform the actual backup operation

PREPARING FOR A FULL-DISK BACKUP

Before you can perform a full-disk backup operation, you need to select the files you want to back up, the location to which you want the files written, and the backup type. Once you assign these values, you can save them in a setup file that you can later use each time you need to perform a full-disk backup operation. To begin, invoke the MSBACKUP command from the DOS. MSBACKUP, in turn, will display its main menu. Select the Backup option. MSBACKUP will display the Microsoft Backup screen as shown in Figure 45.1.

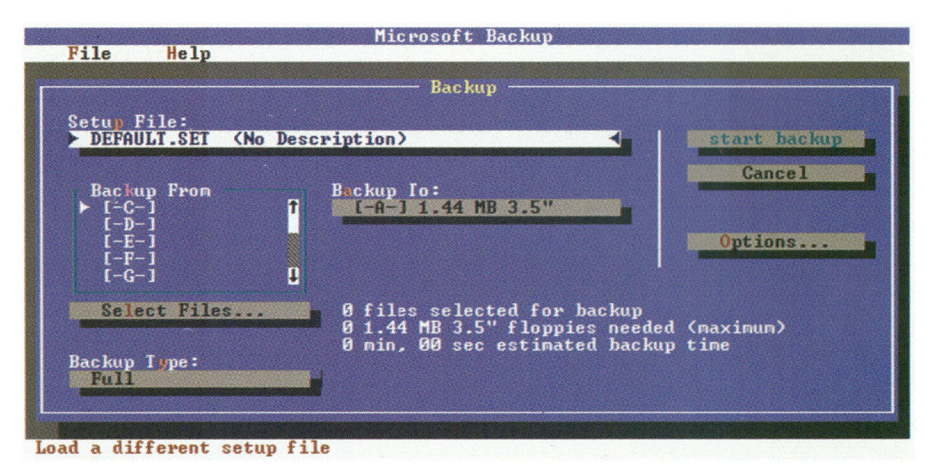

Figure 45.1 The Microsoft Backup screen.

45: Performing Full Disk Backup

You will first select the files you want to back up, the backup type, and the location to which you want the backup files written. Press the TAB key to highlight the **Backup from** field. Next, highlight the letter of the drive you want to back up. When you perform backups, you can back up every file on your disk, or you can back up selected files. If you want to back up every file on the disk, press the SPACEBAR. MSBACKUP will display the message **All files** next to the disk drive letter:

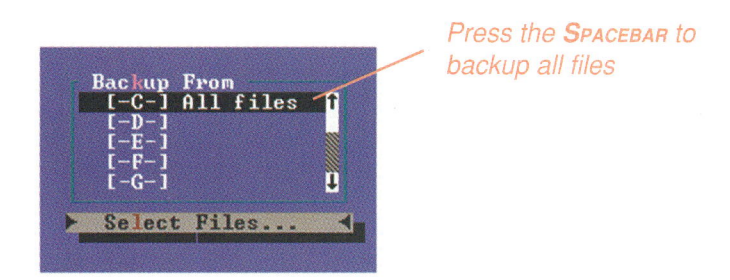

Press the SPACEBAR to backup all files

As a general rule, however, you probably don't need to back up of every file on your disk. Programs such as Microsoft Windows consume tremendous amounts of disk space. You might find it preferable to reinstall such programs in the event of a disk error, rather than continually backing the files up to floppy. If you are using a program such as Word or Excel, you would normally only back up the files you create with the programs, as opposed to the program files themselves. To select specific files for backing up, highlight the drive and press ENTER. MSBACKUP will display a Select Backup Files screen, similar to the one shown in Figure 45.2.

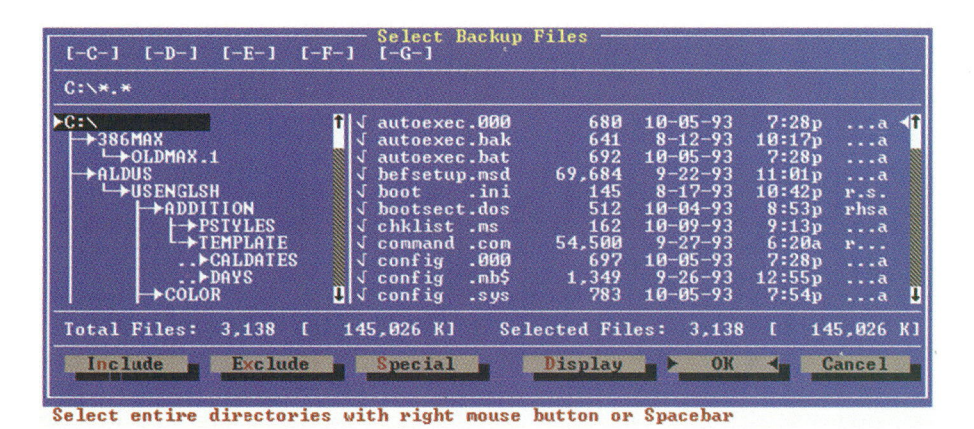

Figure 45.2 The Select Backup Files screen.

Normally, you will select an entire directory of files for backing up. To select a directory's files, highlight the directory name within the directory tree and press the SPACEBAR. MSBACKUP will immediately place check marks next to the files that appear in the file list. To deselect a directory's files, simply press the SPACEBAR a second time.

Rescued by DOS

After you select each of the directories you want to backup, press ENTER to select the OK option. MSBACKUP will redisplay the Microsoft Backup screen. Should you later need to change the selected files, highlight the Selected Files option and press ENTER. Next, if the Backup Type displayed does not say Full, highlight the option and press ENTER. Next, use your keyboard arrow keys to highlight the Full option and press the SPACEBAR followed by ENTER:

Select a Full backup

```
Backup Type:
  Full
```

Next, press the TAB key to highlight the Backup To option and press ENTER. MSBACKUP will display the Backup To dialog box Highlight the MS-DOS Drive and Path option and press the SPACEBAR followed by ENTER. MSBACKUP will display a box prompting you for the desired path. Type in the pathname A:\ as shown here:

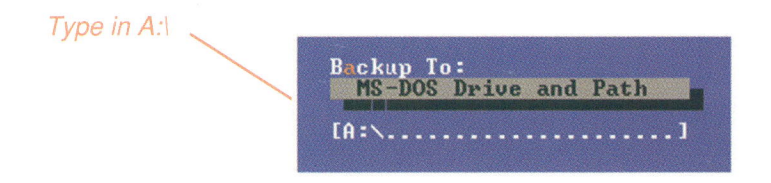

Type in A:

```
Backup To:
  MS-DOS Drive and Path
[A:\....................]
```

Next, save your settings to a setup file by selecting the File menu's Save Setup As option. MSBACKUP will display Save Setup File dialog box. Type in the filename **FULLDISK.SET** and press ENTER. You are now ready to perform you backup operation.

PERFORMING A FULL-DISK BACKUP

To perform a full-disk backup, start MSBACKUP and choose the Backup option (if you have not already done so). Next, if the Setup File is not FULLDISK.SET, highlight the option, press ENTER. When MSBACKUP displays the available setup files, highlight the FULLDISK.SET setup file and press the SPACEBAR, followed by ENTER. Next, highlight the Selected Files option and review the directories selected for backing up. If you have created new directories since the last full-disk backup operation, you might want to select the directory for backing up at this time. If you make changes to the selected files, use the File menu's Save option to save your changes to the setup file.

Press the TAB key to highlight the Start Backup option and press ENTER. MSBACKUP will display a message, prompting you to insert a floppy disk into drive A, as in Figure 45.4.

45: Performing Full Disk Backup

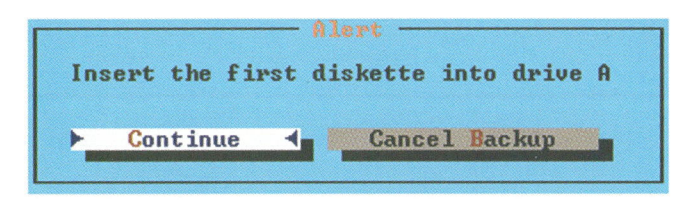

Figure 45.4 MSBACKUP's prompt to insert a floppy disk in drive A.

Place the floppy disk in drive A and press ENTER. MSBACKUP will begin the backup operation, copying files to the floppy disk. Eventually, the disk will fill, and MSBACKUP will prompt you to insert a new disk. Remove the floppy disk from drive A and insert a new disk, pressing ENTER to continue the backup operation. Assign a label to the disk you have just removed from the drive that contains the backup type, disk number, and date, similar to those shown here:

> Full Disk Backup
>
> Disk 1
>
> Date: 12-08-93

Repeat this process for each floppy disk until the backup operation completes. Place your backup floppies in a disk storage container.

What You Need to Know

In Lesson 46 you will learn how to perform an incremental backup operation, backing up only those files that you have created or changed since the last backup operation. Because incremental backups do not back up every file on your disk, you can perform an incremental backup very quickly. Before you continue with Lesson 46, however, make sure that you have learned the following:

- ☑ When you perform backup operations, you might not want to back up every file on your disk. For example, if you can install program files using your original floppies, you might not want to spend time backing up the files. The MSBACKUP command lets you select specific files and directories for backing up.

- ☑ Because you will perform full-disk backups on a regular basis in the future, you should take time to create a setup file that contains your desired backup options. Name that file FULLDISK.SET. When you later need to perform the full-disk backup, you can quickly select the setup file.

- ☑ Before you begin the full-disk backup, double-check the selected directories to ensure that you are backing up all the files and directories you need. If you make changes to the selected files, use the File menu's Save option to save your changes to the setup file.

Rescued by DOS

Lesson 46

Performing an Incremental Backup

In Lesson 45 you learned how to perform a full backup of all the files on your disk. When you perform a full disk backup, MSBACKUP will back up every file you have selected. Because full backup operations can become quite time consuming, most users only perform full-disk backups once in a while. The rest of the time, the users perform *incremental backups*. An incremental backup operation backs up the files on your disk that have been changed or created since your last backup operation. Assuming you perform an incremental backup operation every day, your backups only have to backup that day's files. As a result, incremental backups normally complete very quickly. This lesson examines the steps you must follow to perform an incremental backup operation. By the time you finish this lesson you will understand how to

- Select the files you want to back up
- Specify the location to which you want the file backed up
- Select an incremental backup operation
- Save your backup configuration to a setup file
- Perform the actual backup operation

PREPARING FOR AN INCREMENTAL BACKUP OPERATION

In Lesson 45 you created the setup file FULLDISK.SET, which contains the options you want MSBACKUP to perform for a full-disk backup. Using the FULLDISK.SET setup file, you can quickly specify the options for your incremental backup. To begin, start MSBACKUP, if it is not already running, and select the BACKUP option. Within the Setup File option, select the FULLDISK.SET setup file. Next, press the TAB key to highlight the Backup Type option and press ENTER. MSBACKUP will display a Backup Type dialog box, as shown in Figure 46.1.

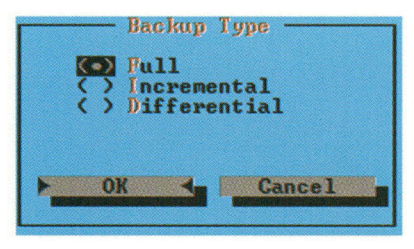

Figure 46.1 The Backup Type dialog box.

46: Performing an Incremental Backup

Using your keyboard arrow keys, highlight the Incremental option and press the SPACEBAR followed by ENTER. Use the ALT-F keyboard combination to select the File menu and choose Save Setup As option. MSBACKUP will display the Save Setup File dialog box. Type in the filename **INCREMEN.SET** and press ENTER. You are now ready to use the setup file to perform an incremental backup.

PERFORMING THE INCREMENTAL BACKUP OPERATION

To perform an incremental backup, start MSBACKUP and choose the Backup option (if you have not already done so). Next, if the Setup File is not INCREMEN.SET, highlight the option, press ENTER. When MSBACKUP displays the available setup files, highlight the INCREMEN.SET setup file and press the SPACEBAR followed by ENTER.

Next, highlight the Selected Files option and review the directories selected for backing up. If you have created new directories since the backup operation, you might want to select the directory for backing up at this time. If you make changes to the selected files, use the File menu's Save option to save your changes to the setup file.

Press the TAB key to highlight the Start Backup option and press ENTER. MSBACKUP will display a message prompting you to insert a floppy into drive A.nto drive A. If you have recently performed an incremental backup, you can append today's backup files to your previous backup disk. In this way, you can reduce the number of backup floppy disks you need to manage. If you don't have an incremental backup floppy to append to, start the backup with an unused disk. If you are appending your backup to a disk that contained other backup files, MSBACKUP will display an Alert dialog box similar to the one shown in Figure 46.2.

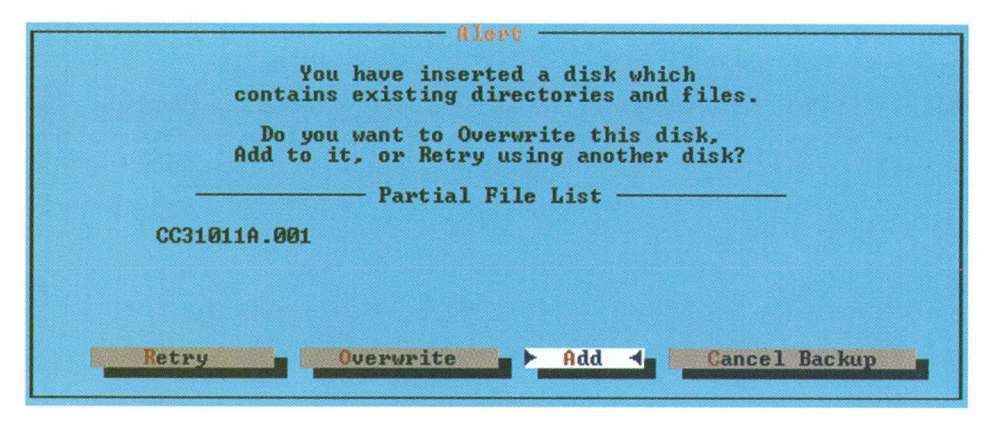

F*igure 46.2 MSBACKUP's Alert dialog box.*

Rescued by DOS

To add today's backup files to the disk, select the Add button. MSBACKUP will begin the backup operation, copying files to the floppy disk. Eventually, the disk will fill, and MSBACKUP will prompt you to insert a new disk as shown in Figure 46.3.

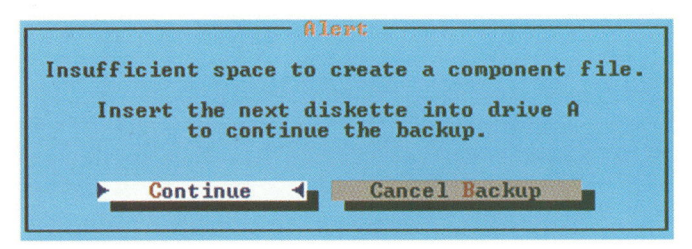

Figure 46.3 MSBACKUP's prompt to insert a new floppy disk.

Remove the floppy disk from drive A and insert a new disk, pressing ENTER to continue the backup operation. Assign a label that contains the backup type, disk number, and date to the disk you have just removed from the drive, as shown here:

> Incremental Disk Backup
>
> Disk 1
>
> Date: 12-09-93

Repeat this process for each floppy disk until the backup operation completes. Place your backup floppies in a disk storage container.

WHAT YOU NEED TO KNOW

In Lesson 47 you will learn how to restore one or more files from your backup disks with MSBACKUP. Before you continue with Lesson 47, make sure that you have learned the following:

- ☑ An incremental backup operation backs up only those files that have been created or changed since the previous backup. If you perform backups on a regular basis, your incremental backups should complete very quickly.

- ☑ Because you will perform incremental backups on a regular basis in the future, you should take time to create a setup file that contains your desired backup options. Name that file INCREMEN.SET.

- ☑ Before you begin an incremental backup, double-check the selected directories to ensure that you are backing up all the files and directories you need. If you make changes to the selected files, use the File menu's Save option to save your changes to the setup file.

Lesson 47

Restoring Files from Your Backup Disks

Hopefully, you will never have to rely on your backup disks to recover key files. If you should, however, you will very thankful you have performed backups on a regular basis. This lesson examines the steps you must perform to restore files from your backup disks. By the time you finish this lesson you will understand how to

- Use a backup catalog to locate your file
- How to restore files from a specific backup operation
- How to restore files from several backup operations

UNDERSTANDING BACKUP CATALOG FILES

Each time you perform a backup operation, MSBACKUP creates a *catalog file* in the DOS directory. The catalog file contains information MSBACKUP uses to determine the number of files backed up, specifics about each file, and the backup date and type. If you only perform full-disk and incremental backups, your catalog files will use the FUL and INC extensions. Using the following DIR commands, you can display the catalog files your DOS directory may contain:

```
C:\> DIR   *.FUL   <ENTER>
```

```
C:\> DIR   *.INC   <ENTER>
```

Don't worry about the number of catalog files your DOS directory contains. Each time you perform a full-disk backup operation, MSBACKUP deletes the previous catalog files.

Catalog files use an eight-character basename, whose character positions can provide you with specifics about the file's contents. Table 47.1 briefly describes each character's meaning. If you know that you backed up a needed file on a specific day, you can determine the corresponding catalog filename using the character position values listed in Table 47.1.

Rescued by DOS

Position	Meaning
1	Specifies the first drive that was backed up, such as drive C.
2	Specifies the last drive that was backed up. Normally the same as the first drive.
3	Specifies the last digit of the backup year. 1994 would use the digit 4.
4,5	Specifies the two digits of the backup month. January would use 01.
6,7	Specifies the two digits of the backup day.
8	Specifies the backup count for a specific day, where A is the first backup, B is the second, and so on.

Table 47.1 The meaning of character positions in a catalog filename.

RESTORING A SPECIFIC FILE FROM A BACKUP DISK

To restore specific files from a backup disk, you should first try to determine the catalog file that corresponds to the last backup operation you performed that would have backed up the desired files. For example, if you need to restore document files that you created yesterday, and you performed an incremental backup yesterday, you can easily determine the name of the catalog file.

Next, invoke MSBACKUP from the DOS prompt. When MSBACKUP displays its main menu, select Restore. MSBACKUP will display the Restore screen, as shown in Figure 47.1.

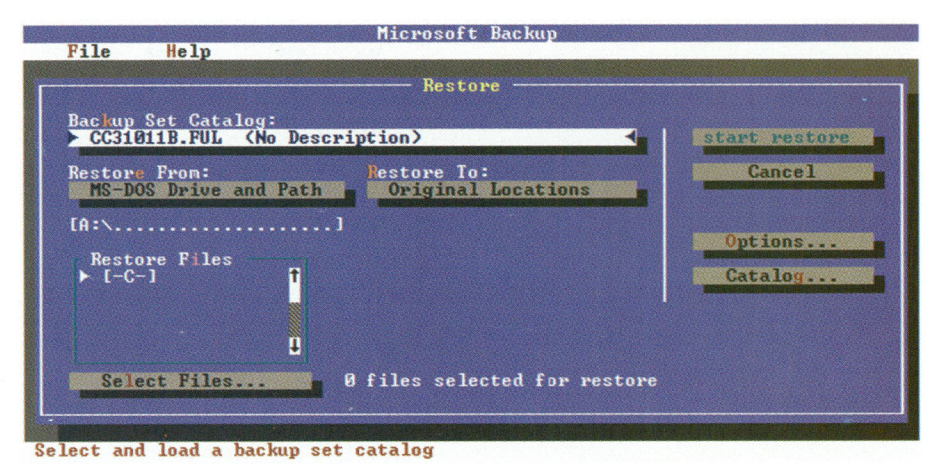

Figure 47.1 The MSBACKUP Restore screen.

47: Restoring Files from Your Backup Disks

Highlight the Backup Set Catalog option and press ENTER. MSBACKUP will display a dialog box that contains the available catalog files. Highlight the corresponding catalog file and press the SPACEBAR followed by ENTER. Next, highlight the Restore From option and press ENTER. MSBACKUP will display the Restore From dialog box. Highlight the MS-DOS Drive and Path option and press the SPACEBAR followed by ENTER. Within the path box, type in **A:** as shown here:

Restore from A:

```
Restore From:
 MS-DOS Drive and Path
[A:\.....................]
```

Make sure the Restore To option specifies the original locations. Next, to choose specific files to be restored, highlight the Select Files option and press ENTER. MSBACKUP will display the Select Restore Files screen, as shown in Figure 47.2.

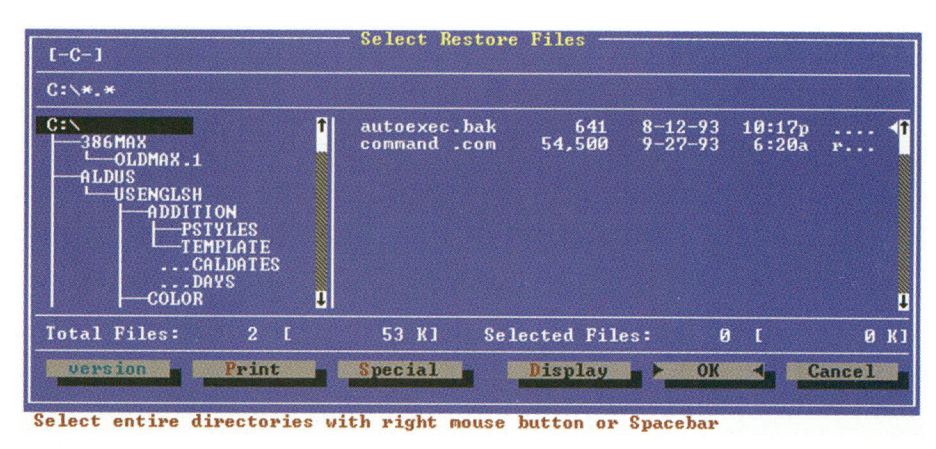

Figure 47.2 The Select Restore Files screen.

Highlight each directory you want to restore and press the spacebar or highlight specific files within a directory and press the SPACEBAR. After you have selected the desired files, press ENTER.

Within the Restore screen, select the Start Restore option. MSBACKUP will display an Alert dialog box, asking you to place the disk containing the backup files into drive A, as shown in Figure 47.3.

203

Rescued by DOS

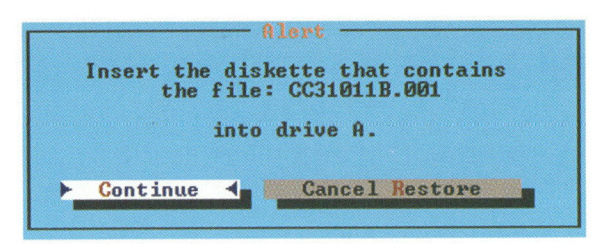

```
┌──────────── Alert ────────────┐
│                                │
│  Insert the diskette that contains │
│        the file: CC31011B.001  │
│                                │
│           into drive A.        │
│                                │
│  ► Continue ◄    Cancel Restore │
└────────────────────────────────┘
```

Figure 47.3 *The Alert dialog box.*

Place the disk in drive A and press ENTER. MSBACKUP will begin the restore operation. If the files require a second disk, MSBACKUP will display a dialog box, asking you to insert the disk in drive A. Do so and press ENTER.

RESTORING FILES FROM TWO OR MORE BACKUPS

If you need to restore files from several different backups, the steps you must perform are very similar to those just discussed. To begin, select the first catalog file you require. As before, make sure the Restore From option is set to MS-DOS Drive and Path and that the path is A:\ (or the drive into which you will place floppy disks). Next, use the Select Files option to select specific files to be restored, or you can highlight the drive the within the Restore Files option and press the SPACEBAR to restore all the files. Next, select the Start Restore option, and MSBACKUP will prompt you to insert the correct backup disk in drive A. Do so and press ENTER. If MSBACKUP requires a second disk, it will prompt you to insert one. Repeat these steps for each catalog of files you need to restore.

WHAT YOU NEED TO KNOW

In Lesson 48 you will learn how to create a backup policy to help ensure that you perform the correct backup operations as needed. Before you continue with Lesson 48, however, make sure that you have learned the following:

- ☑ If you ever need to restore one or more files from your backup disk, use the MSBACKUP command's Restore option.

- ☑ Each time you perform a backup operation, MSBACKUP creates a catalog file that lists the files you backed up. MSBACKUP places the catalog files in the DOS directory. By examining the catalog filename, you can determine the backup operation that corresponds to the catalog.

- ☑ To restore files from a specific backup, locate the disk that contains the backup files and place the disk in drive. Next, invoke MSBACKUP and select the corresponding catalog file. Make sure you are restoring files to their original locations from the MS-DOS Drive and Path A:\. Select the files you want to restore and begin the operation. Repeat these steps for each catalog of files you need to restore.

Lesson 48

Creating a Backup Policy

In the previous lessons you have learned how to back up your entire disk, as well as how to back up specific files. In order for your backup operations to be effective, you need to perform your backups on a regular basis. The best way to ensure that backups are done as needed is to establish a backup policy. This lesson examines the steps you should perform to establish a backup policy. By the time you finish this lesson you will understand how to

- Perform a complete backup of your disk either monthly or at other regular intervals
- Perform an incremental backup, backing up only those files you have created or changed since the last backup operation.
- Store your backup floppy disks in a safe location.

UNDERSTANDING THE BACKUP POLICY

Depending on the number and size of files on your disk, performing a full disk backup can be a time-consuming task. Thus, most users will not back up their entire disk on a regular basis. That's OK. As you will learn, you don't have to back up every file on your disk every day, every week, or even monthly for that matter. However, if you get into the habit of performing a full disk backup operation monthly, managing your backup disks will become an easier task.

The first time you back up your disk, you should perform a full-disk backup operation, as discussed in Lesson 45. If you created the setup file FULLDISK.SET, as discussed in Lesson 45, you should use the file to perform a full-disk backup operation at the beginning of every month. To do so, invoke MSBACKUP from the DOS prompt as follows:

```
C:\> MSBACKUP <ENTER>
```

When MSBACKUP displays its main menu, select the Backup option. Next, type **P** to select the Setup File. MSBACKUP will display the available setup files, as shown in Figure 48.1.

Rescued by DOS

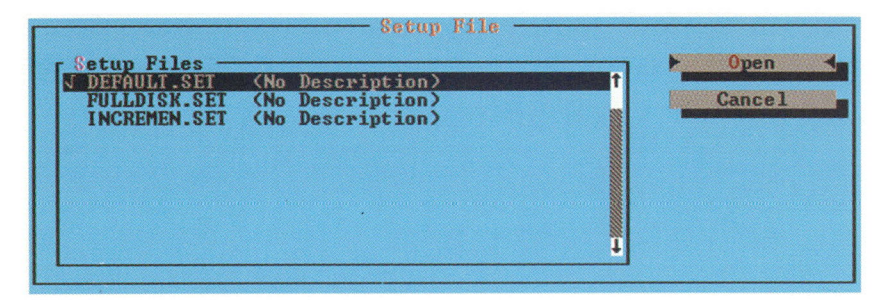

Figure 48.1 MSBACKUP's available setup files.

Select the full-disk setup file. Before you begin the backup operation, highlight the Selected Files option and press ENTER. Double-check the files and directories you have selected for backing up. If you have created directories since the last backup operation, you might need to select the directories for backing up. Should you make changes to your selected files, use the File menu's Save option to save your changes to the setup file.

Perform the backup operation. Next, place your backup disks in a disk storage container similar to the one shown in Figure 48.2.

Figure 48.2 Store your backup disks in a disk storage container.

48: Creating a Backup Policy

On the days that follow, you will perform an incremental backup operation, backing up only those files you have created or changed since the last backup operation. If, for example, you perform the full-disk backup operation yesterday, today's incremental backup will only back up those files you created or changed today. In this way, the backup operation will complete very quickly.

If you created the INCREMEN.SET setup file, as discussed in Lesson 46, select the setup file, as just discussed. Using this setup file, you will perform an incremental backup every day for the rest of the month. Should you miss a day, don't panic. The next incremental backup you perform will back up all the files you have created or changed since the previous backup. However, keep in mind that if you don't perform backup operations for several days, you might lose several days work should your disk fail. Before you begin the incremental backup operation, highlight the Selected Files option and press ENTER. Double-check the files and directories you have selected for backing up. If you have created directories since the last backup operation, you might need to select the directories for backing up. Should you make changes to your selected files, use the File menu's Save option to save your changes to the setup file. At the start of the next month, use the FULLDISK.SET setup file to backup your entire disk. If the backup operation is successful, you can replace all of your previous month's backup floppies with those containing your full disk backup. For the remainder of the month, perform an incremental backup using the setup file INCREMEN.SET.

RESTORING FILES FROM YOUR FLOPPY DISK

Lesson 47 discussed the steps you must perform to restore files from your backup disks. Should you need to restore specific files, use the catalog files FULLDISK.CAT and INCREMEN.CAT to determine the disk that contains the required files.

WHAT YOU NEED TO KNOW

In Lesson 49 you will learn how to reduce the possibility of a virus damaging your disk and the files the disk contains. Before you continue with Lesson 49, make sure you have learned the following:

- ☑ For your backup operations to be effective, you must perform backups on a regular basis.

- ☑ Because a full-disk backup is a time-consuming operation, most users will not perform full-disk operations on a regular basis. That's OK. Ideally, however, you should perform a full-disk backup once a month.

- ☑ After you perform a full-disk backup, you can then perform incremental backups each day to back up only those files you created or changed that day. Because incremental backups normally do not back up every file on your disk, you can perform them very quickly.

- ☑ Make sure you store your backup floppy disks in a disk container and that you place the disk container in a safe location. Each time you successfully perform a full-disk backup operation, you can replace the previous month's backup floppies with those from the full-disk backup.

Section Ten

PREVENTING DISASTER AND IMPROVING SYSTEM PERFORMANCE

As you work with your computer, an errant command can accidentally delete one or more needed files, or you might format a disk that contains information you still need. In addition, a floppy disk given to you by another user could contain a computer virus. Likewise, your disk can begin to fail, over time. To help you prevent data loss from such occurrences, DOS provides commands that let you undelete files, unformat disks, check your disk for computer viruses, and even check the health of your disk. This section examines each of these commands. In addition, you will learn how to defragment your files and use a disk buffer to improve your system performance. The commands presented in this section are very powerful. Take time to learn their capabilities.

Lesson 49 Detecting Computer Viruses

Lesson 50 Undeleting a Deleted File

Lesson 51 Unformatting a Disk

Lesson 52 Using SCANDISK to Examine Your Disk's Health

Lesson 53 Correcting Fragmented Files

Lesson 54 Improving Performance with SMARTDRV

49: Detecting Computer Viruses

Lesson 49

Detecting Computer Viruses

A *virus* is a computer program written specifically to destroy the information contained on your computer. Depending on the virus type, the virus might delete one or more files or render your entire disk unusable. The thing that makes viruses most dangerous is that they disguise themselves as other programs. For example, a virus might attach itself to the program WORDPROC.COM that you invoke to start your word processor. When you issue the WORDPROC command to run your word processor, you also load the virus into your computer's memory. The virus may immediately destroy your files, or it may attach itself to other files. Some viruses remain inactive for months until a specific date occurs, such as Friday the 13th. On the specific day, the virus will awaken and destroy your files. Your computer might already have a virus and you don't know it! This lesson examines how you can use the DOS MSAV and VSAFE commands to detect and eliminate viruses. By the time you finish this lesson you will understand how to

- Examine your disk and files for known viruses using MSAV
- Use MSAV to examine floppy disks given to you for use by other users

UNDERSTANDING VIRUSES

For your computer to have a virus, your disks must have been exposed to a virus. If you purchase and use only packaged software from reputable software manufacturers, your chances of encountering a virus are very small. However, if you exchange floppy disks with other users or download files from a computer bulletin board, you greatly increase your risk of encountering a virus. To determine if the files on your disk contain a virus, you can use the DOS MSAV command. When you invoke MSAV, your screen will display MSAV's main menu, as shown in Figure 49.1.

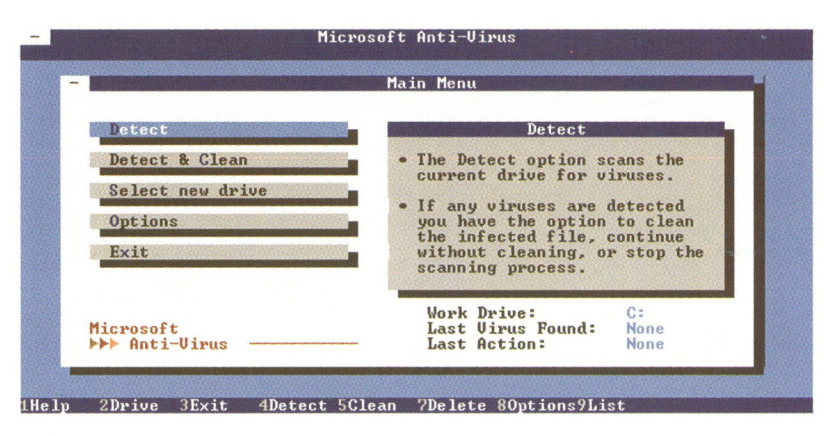

Figure 49.1 The MSAV main menu.

Rescued by DOS

Using MSAV, you can examine your hard disk for viruses. If MSAV encounters a known virus, MSAV can erase the virus from your disk. If you exchange floppy disks with other users, use MSAV to examine each floppy disk before you use the files the disk contains.

Detecting and Erasing Viruses

To examine your disk for viruses, select the Detect and Clean option from MSAV's main menu. MSAV will begin examining the files on your disk, displaying a screen, similar to that shown in Figure 49.2, that shows MSAV's progress.

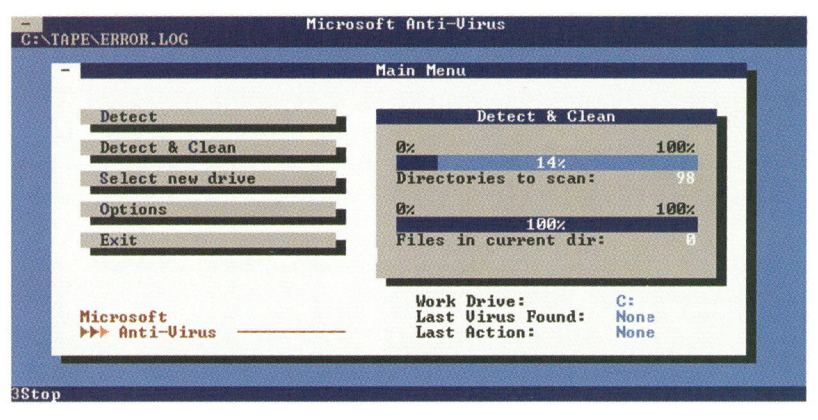

Figure 49.2 Scanning a disk for viruses.

If MSAV encounters a virus, MSAV will remove the virus from your disk. When the virus-scan operation ends, MSAV will display a summary screen, similar to the one shown in Figure 49.3, that displays the number of files searched and the number of viruses found.

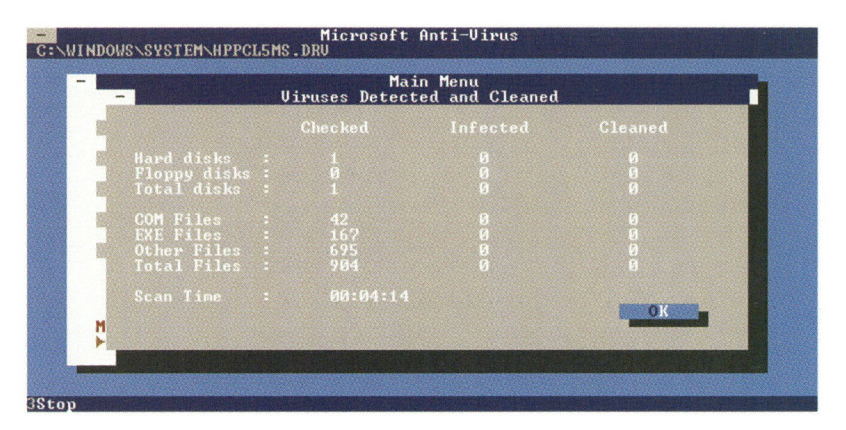

Figure 49.3 MSAV's summary screen.

49: Detecting Computer Viruses

Most users will never encounter a computer virus. However, using MSAV, you can find out if your computer has a virus, and you can remove the virus before it damages your files. Before you copy files from a floppy disk provided to you by another user, you should use MSAV to examine the files the floppy disk contains. In this way, you reduce the possibility of exposing your files to a virus.

EXAMINING A FLOPPY DISK FOR A VIRUS

Sharing floppy disks with other users is a common way computers are exposed to viruses. Before you use the files on a floppy disk given to you by another user, start MSAV and examine the floppy disk for viruses. To begin, select MSAV's *Select new drive* option. MSAV will display a list of the available drives near the top of its screen:

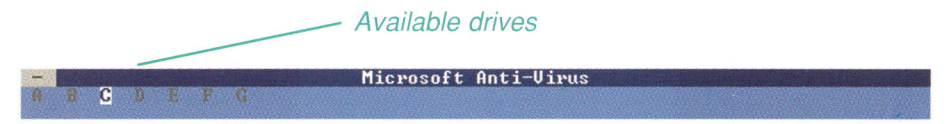

Available drives — Microsoft Anti-Virus
A B C D E F G

Using your keyboard arrow keys, highlight the desired disk drive and press ENTER. Next, select the Detect and Clean option. MSAV will examine the floppy disk's contents for a virus. When the examination completes, MSAV will display a summary screen similar to the one previously shown in Figure 49.3. If no viruses are found, you can use the files the disk contains. If a virus was found, do not use the disk. To exit MSAV, use the Exit menu option.

MSAV CANNOT DETECT ALL VIRUSES

Using MSAV, you greatly reduce the risk of a virus damaging your files. Unfortunately, MSAV can only detect those viruses it is aware of. The number of viruses grows each day. To protect your computer better, you need to keep you file of MSAV viruses up to date. The Microsoft documentation that accompanied your computer or DOS 6 upgrade should include a phone number you can call to get updates to the known virus file.

DETECTING VIRUSES WITH VSAFE

Before a virus can damage your computer, the virus must be loaded into your computer's memory. Normally, a virus will attach itself to another program. When you execute the program, the virus gets a free ride into memory from DOS. To help DOS detect viruses in memory, you can use the VSAFE command. VSAFE first searches your computer's memory for viruses. Next, VSAFE remains in your computer's memory to monitor your system use.

Viruses normally destroy your system by deleting files or by overwriting important information. The VSAFE command waits for these operations to occur and then displays a message notifying you of their use. VSAFE is a very powerful command that supports several different command-line options. Depending on how you use VSAFE, you might need to change many of its option settings. Such a discussion of VSAFE is beyond this book's scope. For specifics on VSAFE, use the HELP command discussed in Lesson 4 or turn to the book, *DOS the Complete Reference,* Fourth Edition, Osborne/McGraw-Hill, 1993.

WHAT YOU NEED TO KNOW

In Lesson 50 you will learn how to undelete a previously deleted file. Before you continue with Lesson 50, make sure that you have learned the following:

- ☑ A virus is a computer program maliciously written to destroy your disk and the files it contains.

- ☑ For a virus to damage your computer, you must expose your computer to the virus. The two most common ways viruses reach a computer is by sharing floppy disks with another user or by downloading files from a computer bulletin board.

- ☑ To help you detect and eliminate viruses from your disk, you can use the DOS MSAV command. When you invoke MSAV, the program will examine every file on your disk in search of viruses. Before you use the files given to you by another user on floppy, examine the floppy disk using the MSAV command.

- ☑ The MSAV command can only detect known viruses. The number of viruses grows each day. To improve your likelihood of detecting a virus, you must keep the file of known viruses up to date. You should be able to get updates to MSAV's virus file from Microsoft.

Lesson 50

Undeleting a Deleted File

As you have learned, the DEL command lets you erase files from your disk when the files are no longer needed. Should you accidentally delete one or more files you need using DEL, don't panic. You may be able to recover the files with the UNDELETE command. This lesson examines the UNDELETE command. By the time you finish this lesson you will understand how to

- Undelete a specific file or a group of files using wildcards
- Use UNDELETE's file tracking and data sentry to improve your chances of a successful recovery

PUTTING *UNDELETE* TO WORK

The best way to understand the UNDELETE command is to try it out. To begin, place an unused floppy disk in drive A. Next, use the following COPY command to copy several files from the DOS directory to the floppy:

```
C:\> COPY   \DOS\*.SYS   A:   <ENTER>
```

Use the DIR command to display the files the floppy disk contains:

```
C:\> DIR   A:   <ENTER>
```

Next, issue the following DEL command to delete the file ANSI.SYS from drive A:

```
C:\> DEL   A:ANSI.SYS   <ENTER>
```

Use the DIR command to verify the ANSI.SYS file has been deleted:

```
C:\> DIR   A:   <ENTER>
```

Assuming that immediately after deleting the ANSI.SYS file you realize that you still need it, you can use the following UNDELETE command to recover the file:

```
C:\> UNDELETE   A:ANSI.SYS   <ENTER>
```

Rescued by DOS

UNDELETE will examine the floppy disk's contents in search of the file. If UNDELETE successfully locates the file, it may ask you if you want to undelete the file, as shown here:

```
UNDELETE - A delete protection facility
Copyright (C) 1987-1993 Central Point Software, Inc.
All rights reserved.

Directory: A:\
File Specifications: ANSI.SYS
    Delete Sentry control file not found.

    Deletion-tracking file not found.

    MS-DOS directory contains     1 deleted files.
    Of those,    1 files may be recovered.

Using the MS-DOS directory method.

     ?NSI     SYS      9065   9-27-93   3:59p   ...A
Undelete (Y/N)?Y
```

If you type **Y**, UNDELETE will prompt you to type in the first letter of the file's name:

```
Please type the first character for ?NSI    .SYS:
```

In this case, type **A**. UNDELETE will display a message telling you the file has been undeleted:

```
File successfully undeleted.
```

Use the DIR command to verify the file exists:

```
C:\> DIR   A:    <ENTER>
```

UNDELETING A SPECIFIC FILE

Should you accidentally delete a needed file using the DEL command or from within the DOS Shell, you may be able to recover the file with the UNDELETE command. For example, assuming you accidentally deleted a file named FILENAME.EXT, you would use the following UNDELETE command to recover the file:

```
C:\> UNDELETE   FILENAME.EXT    <ENTER>
```

50: Undeleting a Deleted File

UNDELETING A GROUP OF FILES

Undeleting a group of files is very similar to the steps you just performed, except that you now need to remember the starting letter for several different filenames. To begin, use the following command to delete all the files you just copied to the floppy disk in drive A:

```
C:\> DEL   A:*.SYS   <ENTER>
```

Use the following DIR command to verify the files have been deleted:

```
C:\> DIR   A:   <ENTER>
```

Next, issue the following UNDELETE command to recover the files:

```
C:\> UNDELETE   *.SYS   <ENTER>
```

The UNDELETE command will prompt you for each file to determine if you want to undelete the file. If type **Y**, UNDELETE will ask you to type the first letter of each file's name. You must repeat this process for each file you want to undelete.

Note: *Should you ever accidentally delete one or more files from your disk, do not copy any files to the disk or create any files on the disk until you successfully undelete the needed files. If you copy or create a new file on the disk, you risk overwriting the deleted file's contents, which will prevent the file's recovery.*

INCREASING YOUR CHANCE OF A SUCCESSFUL UNDELETION

If you examine the previous undelete commands closely, you will encounter the following messages:

```
Delete Sentry control file not found.
Deletion-tracking file not found.
```

To increase you likelihood of successfully recovering a deleted file, UNDELETE lets you install data sentry or file-tracking protection. When you use data sentry protection, the DEL command will place a copy of every file you delete in a special directory named SENTRY (for data sentry). When you later need to undelete a file, UNDELETE can use the file copy. In this way, you greatly increase your likelihood of successfully recovering the file. In addition, because UNDELETE has a copy of the file information, UNDELETE does not require you to type in the first letter of the filename!

Unfortunately, keeping copies of each file you delete can quickly consume a considerable amount of disk space. If you have plenty of disk space, you might want to place the following UNDELETE command in your AUTOEXEC.BAT file:

```
UNDELETE   /LOAD
```

When you use UNDELETE's data sentry protection, UNDELETE will not use more than eight percent of your disk space. Should you delete several files, UNDELETE may purge (discard) some older files from the SENTRY directory. In addition, if you are sure you will not need to undelete files in the future, you can purge the files yourself using the following UNDELETE command:

```
C:\> UNDELETE   /PURGE   <ENTER>
```

If you don't have enough disk space to support UNDELETE's data sentry protection, you can use file tracking to increase your chance of successfully recovering deleted files. To use file tracking for drive C, for example, place the following command in your AUTOEXEC.BAT file:

```
UNDELETE  /TC
```

Each time you delete a file, DEL will record specifics about the file such as the filename, size and disk locations in a special file on your disk. Should you later need to undelete one or files, UNDELETE will use the file's contents to help recover your file. In this way, UNDELETE will not have to prompt you for the first letter of each filename. To prevent the undelete file from becoming too large, UNDELETE periodically discards old file entries.

What You Need to Know

In Lesson 51 you will learn how to recover your disk in the event of an accidental format operation. Before you continue with Lesson 51, however, make sure that you have learned the following:

- ☑ Should you accidentally delete one or more files you still need, you might be able to recover the files with UNDELETE

- ☑ The best protection you can provide your files against accidental deletion is UNDELETE's data sentry protection. When you enable data sentry protection, DEL will make a copy of each file you delete, placing the file copy in a directory named SENTRY on your disk.

- ☑ The second best protection you can provide your files is UNDELETE's file tracking protection. When you enable file tracking, UNDELETE will record information about each file you delete, such as the file's name, size, and locations on disk.

Lesson 51

Unformatting a Disk

You have learned that, before you can use a disk, the disk must be formatted for use by DOS. Thus, DOS provides the FORMAT command. Every once in a while, users accidentally format a disk that contains needed information. In such cases, you can recover the disk's previous contents using the UNFORMAT command. This lesson teaches you the basics of the UNFORMAT command. By the time you finish this lesson you will understand how to

- Unformat a disk to recover the disk's previous contents
- Create a bootable floppy disk that contains the UNFORMAT command

USING THE UNFORMAT COMMAND

When you format a disk, the FORMAT command overwrites the disk's existing contents. Should you accidentally format the wrong disk, you might be able to recover the disk's previous contents using the UNFORMAT command. The best way to understand how UNFORMAT works is to put the command to use. To begin, place newly formatted disk in drive A. Next, issue the following COPY command to copy files to the disk:

```
C:\> COPY  \DOS\*.SYS   A:   <ENTER>
```

Use DIR to display the disk's contents as shown here:

```
C:\> DIR  A:   <ENTER>
```

DIR should display the names of several files with the SYS extension. Next, use the FORMAT command to format the floppy disk in drive A, overwriting the disk's current contents:

```
C:\> FORMAT   A:   <ENTER>
```

When the format command completes, perform a directory listing of the disk, as shown here:

```
C:\> DIR  A:   <ENTER>

 Volume in drive A has no label
 Volume Serial Number is 4053-13D8
 Directory of A:\

File not found
```

As you can see, FORMAT has overwritten the disk's contents. To recover the disk's contents, issue the UNFORMAT command, as shown here:

```
C:\> UNFORMAT   A:   <ENTER>
```

UNFORMAT will prompt you to place the formatted disk in drive A. Do so and press ENTER:

```
Insert disk to rebuild in drive A:
and press ENTER when ready.
```

Next, UNFORMAT will display a message telling you that you should only use the command in the case of an accidental format. In addition, UNFORMAT will display information telling you when the disk was formatted. UNFORMAT will then ask you if you want to unformat the disk:

```
Restores the system area of your disk by using the im-
age file created by the MIRROR command.

     WARNING !!        WARNING !!

This command should be used only to recover from the
inadvertent use of the FORMAT command or the RECOVER
command.  Any other use of the UNFORMAT command may
cause you to lose data!  Files modified since the MIR-
ROR image file was created may be lost.

Searching disk for MIRROR image.

The last time the MIRROR or FORMAT command was used was
at 12:14 on 10-07-93.

The MIRROR image file has been validated.

Are you sure you want to update the system area of your
drive A (Y/N)?
```

51: Unformatting a Disk

If you type **Y**, UNFORMAT will rebuild your disk, as shown here:

```
The system area of drive A has been rebuilt.

You may need to restart the system.
```

When UNFORMAT completes, perform a directory listing of the floppy to reveal that your files have been successfully recovered!

```
C:\> DIR  A:   <ENTER>
```

UNFORMATTING A DISK

Should you accidentally format a disk that contains files you still need, you might be able to recover the disk's previous contents using the UNFORMAT command. Assuming that you accidentally formatted the floppy disk in drive A, you would invoke UNFORMAT as follows to recover the disk's files:

```
C:\> UNFORMAT  A:   <ENTER>
```

PROTECTING YOUR HARD DISK

In the previous example, recovering the floppy disk's contents was easy because you could quickly invoke the UNFORMAT command, which resides in the DOS directory on your hard disk. Should you accidentally format your hard disk, however, unformatting the disk is harder because the format operation has overwritten the UNFORMAT command. To simplify the process of recovering your hard disk in the event of an accidental format operation, you should create a bootable floppy disk onto which you copy the UNFORMAT command. In this way, should you every accidentally format your hard disk, you can start your system using the floppy disk and then invoke UNFORMAT from the floppy disk as follows to recover your hard disk:

```
A> UNFORMAT  C:   <ENTER>
```

To create a bootable floppy disk, place an unused floppy disk in drive A and issue the following FORMAT command:

```
C:\> FORMAT  A: /S  <ENTER>
```

219

Rescued by DOS

When the format command completes, copy UNFORMAT to floppy, as shown here:

```
C:\> COPY   \DOS\UNFORMAT.*   A:   <ENTER>
```

Next, label the floppy disk as UNFORMAT and place the floppy in a safe location. Should you ever need to unformat your hard disk, you will be thankful you have the floppy.

UNFORMAT Is Not Always Successful

Depending on the contents of your disk, UNFORMAT might not always be able to recover your disk's contents. Here's why. When you format a disk, the FORMAT command makes a copy of key disk information and stores the information in an unused portion of your disk. Should you later need to unformat the disk, the UNFORMAT reads and uses the disk information to rebuild your disk. Unfortunately, when your disk is full, FORMAT cannot place the information on your disk which will prevent a future unformat operation. When FORMAT is unable to place the key disk information on your disk, FORMAT will display the following message:

```
Drive A error. Insufficient space for MIRROR image file

There was an error creating the format recovery file.
This disk cannot be unformatted.
Proceed with Format (Y/N)?
```

If you type Y to format the disk, you will be unable to recover the disk's contents at a later time using UNFORMAT. Also, the FORMAT command supports the /U switch, which directs FORMAT not to save the disk information required by UNFORMAT. If you format a disk using the /U switch, you will not be able to unformat the disk at a later time.

What You Need to Know

In Lesson 52 you will learn how to use the SCANDISK command to check your disk's health. Before you continue with Lesson 52, make sure you have learned the following:

- ☑ Should you accidentally format a disk that contains files you need, you might be able to recover the disk using the UNFORMAT command.

- ☑ To help you recover your hard disk in the event of an accidental format operation, you should create a bootable floppy disk that contains the UNFORMAT command. Place the floppy disk in a safe location.

- ☑ Depending on the disk's contents prior to the format operation, the UNFORMAT command might not be able to recover your disk.

Lesson 52

Using SCANDISK to Examine Your Disk's Health

Over time, because your disk is a mechanical device, it is possible for your disk to begin to fail. In most cases, however, your disk will show symptoms of failing before it finally quits. To help you examine your disk's health, DOS 6.2 provides the SCANDISK command. In the past, users used the CHKDSK command to examine their disks. Like CHKDSK, the SCANDISK command examines the files on your disk to ensure that they are stored correctly. In addition, SCANDISK actually examines your disk's magnetic surface to ensure it can still correctly record information. Should it encounter problems, SCANDISK will notify you and try to correct the error. This lesson examines the steps you should perform to run SCANDISK. By the time you finish this lesson you will understand

- How to run SCANDISK to examine your disk's health
- How to correct errors detected by SCANDISK
- When you should use the SCANDISK command

In Lesson 55 you will learn how to use the DBLSPACE command to double the storage capacity of your hard disk. As you will learn, DBLSPACE uses the SCANDISK command to ensure that it is safe to compress the files on your disk.

CHECKING YOUR DISK'S HEALTH

To examine your disk's health, you simply invoke SCANDISK from the DOS prompt, as shown here:

```
C:\> SCANDISK  <ENTER>
```

SCANDISK will display its opening screen which shows the parts of your disk SCANDISK will examine. SCANDISK will automatically begin its evaluation. As SCANDISK successfully tests each part of your disk, SCANDISK will place a check mark next to the component name. Next, SCANDISK will begin a surface analysis of your disk, ensuring that your disk's magnetic surface is still capable of recording information. As SCANDISK analyzes your disk's surface, SCANDISK will display a status screen, as shown in Figure 55.1.

Rescued by DOS

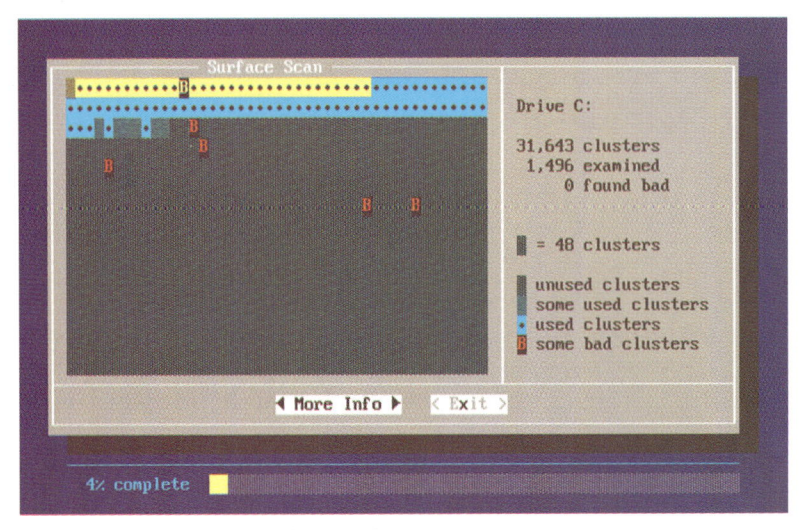

Figure 52.1 The SCANDISK disk surface analysis.

In most cases, SCANDISK will not find any errors and will display a message screen so stating. If you select the Exit option when this message screen appears, you have finished. Should SCANDISK encounter an error, however, you can direct SCANDISK to correct the error, as discussed next.

CORRECTING SCANDISK ERRORS

If, SCANDISK encounters an error when it examines your disk, it will display a Problem Found message box similar to that shown in Figure 52.2.

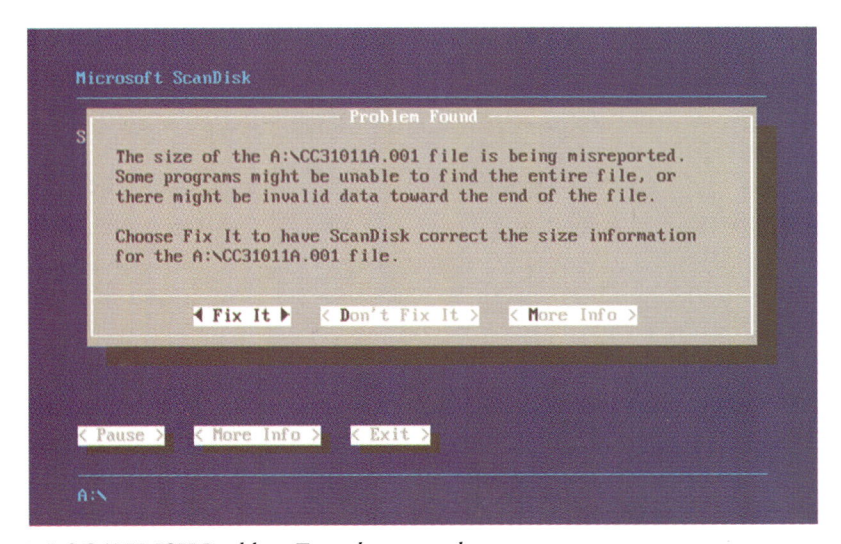

Figure 52.2 A SCANDISK Problem Found message box.

52: Using SCANDISK to Examine Your Disk's Health

As you can see, SCANDISK describes the problem it has encountered and the steps it will perform to fix the problem. If the message box provides you with instructions you must perform after the error is corrected, write down the instructions on a piece of paper. Next, direct SCANDISK to fix the error by selecting the Fix It option. When SCANDISK completes, perform the steps you previously wrote down.

To use SCANDISK to examine a drive other than the current drive, place the drive letter in the SCANDISK command line. For example, the following command uses SCANDISK to examine the floppy disk in drive A:

```
C:\> SCANDISK   A:    <ENTER>
```

When You Should Use SCANDISK

SCANDISK is a very powerful utility program that can correct minor errors on your disk before the errors become serious. You should get into the habit of running the SCANDISK command at least once a week. If SCANDISK repeatedly finds errors when it examines your disk, consider the errors as an indicator of your disk's impending doom and immediately back up your disk. Next, have your disk examined by a technician at your local computer store. If SCANDISK repeatedly encounters lost or damaged clusters, someone is very likely turning off your computer with programs other than DOS still running. As have read, you should only turn off your computer from the DOS prompt after you have ended your other programs.

What You Need to Know

In Lesson 53 you will learn how to improve your disk's performance by consolidating files whose contents have been fragmented about your disk. Before you continue with Lesson 53, however, make sure that you have learned the following:

- ☑ Beginning with DOS 6.2, the SCANDISK command examines your disk's health, correcting and reporting on errors it encounters.

- ☑ In most cases, SCANDISK will not encounter any errors, and the steps you must perform are few. Should SCANDISK encounter an error, SCANDISK will display a message box describing the error and the steps required to correct it. Select the Fix It option to direct SCANDISK to correct the error.

- ☑ As a rule, you should run SCANDISK once a week to examine your disk's health. If SCANDISK repeatedly finds errors when it examines your disk, your disk might have serious problems, and you should consider the errors a sign of the disk's impending demise. You should immediately back up all the files on the disk to floppies.

Lesson 53

Correcting Fragmented Files

As you store, delete, and change the size of the files stored on your disk, the information the file contains might eventually be dispersed in many different storage locations across your disk. When your file becomes *fragmented* in this way, it takes DOS longer to read the file's contents. As a result, your system performance decreases. To correct fragmented files, DOS provides the DEFRAG command. In this lesson you will learn how to use DEFRAG to improve the performance of disk operations. By the time you finish this lesson you will understand how to

- Determine if your disk is fragmented and understand why fragmentation occurs
- Correct fragmentation using DEFRAG

WHY FRAGMENTATION OCCURS

When you store a file on disk, DOS allocates a group of disk sectors called a *cluster* within which DOS places the information. As Figure 53.1 shows, depending on the file's size, the number of clusters DOS uses to store the file may differ. In this case, the disk holds three files, SMALL.DAT, MEDIUM.DAT, and LARGE.DAT, which require one, two, and three clusters, respectively.

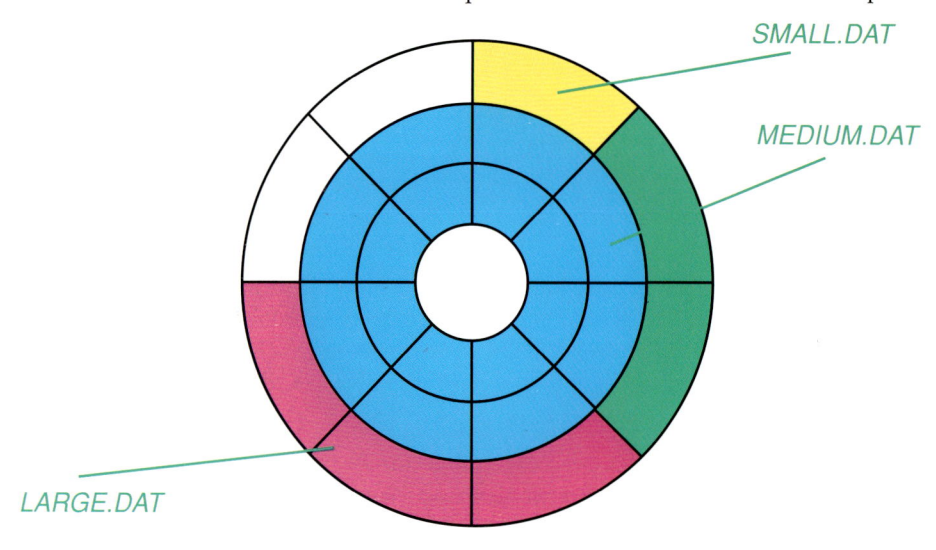

Figure 53.1 Storing files in disk clusters.

53: Correcting Fragmented Files

When you store a file on disk, DOS allocates only the number of clusters for the file required to hold the file's information. Assume, for example, that after creating the file SMALL.DAT, you later edit the file, appending more information. Depending on the amount of information, DOS might need to allocate an additional cluster, as Figure 53.2 shows.

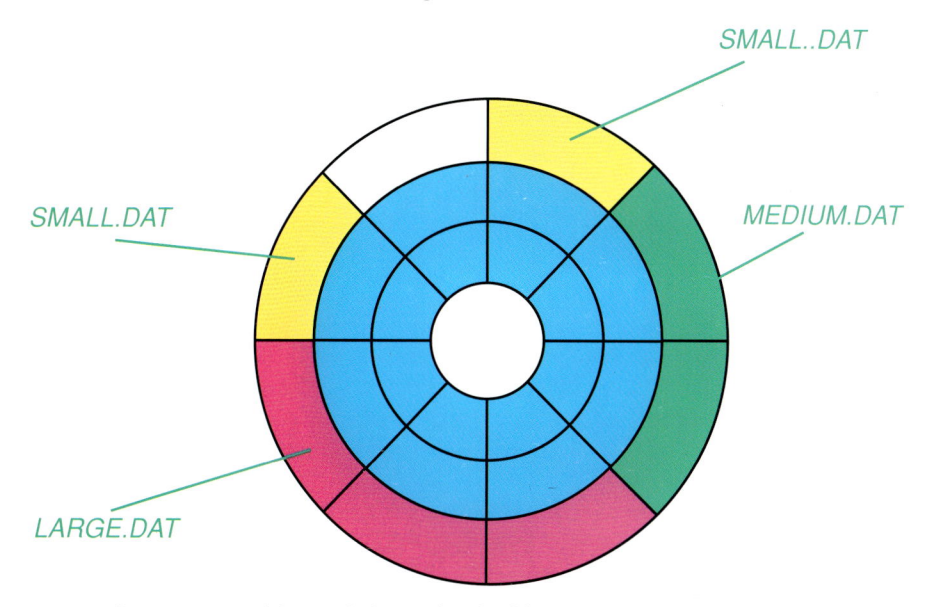

Figure 53.2 Allocating an additional cluster for the file SMALL.DAT.

Likewise, if you add information to the file MEDIUM.DAT, the file might grow, as shown in Figure 53.3.

As you can see, the clusters for the files SMALL.DAT and MEDIUM.DAT are now spread out across the disk. In other words, the files are *fragmented*. Because the clusters for the file LARGE.DAT reside in consecutive clusters, the file is said to be *contiguous*. Fragmented files slow down your system performance by causing disk read and write operations to take more time. As you know, to read or write a file, your disk drive spins a the disk's surface past the drive's read and write heads. When the file resides in consecutive storage locations, the disk drive can read the file's clusters one right after another—a very fast operation. However, when a file is fragmented, the disk drive has to wait for different parts of the file to spin past the read and write heads. Depending on the number of fragmented clusters, several disk rotations may be required to read a file's contents.

Rescued by DOS

Fragmented files occur naturally as you use your computer. As a user, there really isn't anything you can do to prevent fragmented files. Instead, you should periodically test if your disk is fragmented and if so, you should correct the fragmentation. To detect and correct fragmentation, use the DOS DEFRAG command.

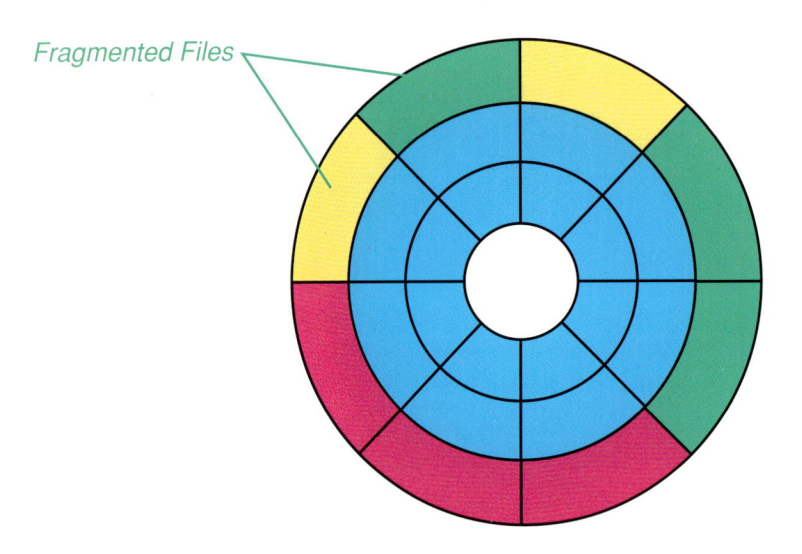

Figure 53.3 Allocating an additional cluster for the file MEDIUM.DAT.

DETECTING AND CORRECTING FRAGMENTED FILES

As you store, delete, and change files, the files on your disk will eventually become fragmented. When fragmentation occurs, you might start to notice that a program takes longer to run or a program's data takes longer to load. To determine if your disk is fragmented, invoke the DEFRAG command, as shown here:

```
C:\> DEFRAG <ENTER>
```

DEFRAG, in turn, will display a small box asking you select the desired disk drive. Using your keyboard arrow keys, highlight the desired drive and press ENTER. DEFRAG will begin analyzing the files on your disk to locate fragmented files. Next, DEFRAG will display a small box, similar to that shown in Figure 53.4, stating the percentage of fragmented files and a recommended action.

53: Correcting Fragmented Files

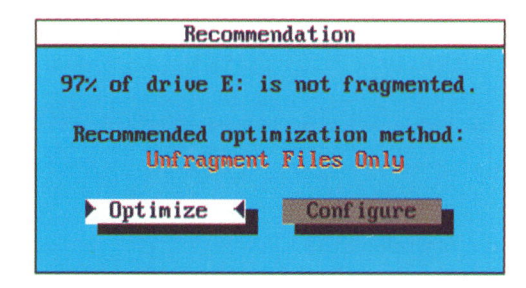

Figure 53.4 Defragmenting your disk using DEFRAG.

Press ENTER to select the Optimize option. DEFRAG will start correcting the fragmented files on your disk. Depending on the number of fragmented files, the amount of time DEFRAG requires will differ. When the operation is complete, DEFRAG will display a small box so stating. Press ENTER. DEFRAG will display a box, as shown in Figure 53.6, asking you if you want to optimize another disk, change one or more DEFRAG settings, or exit. Using your keyboard arrow keys, highlight the Exit option and press ENTER.

WHAT YOU NEED TO KNOW

In Lesson 54 you will learn to improve your disk performance using the SMARTDRV disk cache. Before you continue with Lesson 54, make sure that you have learned the following:

- ☑ DOS stores a file's contents in storage locations on your disk called clusters. Depending on the file's size, DOS may use several clusters to store a file.
- ☑ As you store, delete, and change the size of files stored on your disk, the file's clusters can become dispersed across your disk or fragmented.
- ☑ Fragmented files decrease your system performance because they take longer to read or write.
- ☑ To correct fragmented files, use the DOS DEFRAG command.

Lesson 54

Improving System Performance with SMARTDRV

Floppy and hard disk drives are mechanical devices with moving parts. Thus, disk drives are much slower than your computer's electronic components. One of the best ways to improve your system performance, therefore, is to reduce the number of slow read and write operations your disk drive must perform. To reduce disk I/O (input/output) operations, you can use the SMARTDRV disk buffer. This lesson examines SMARTDRV in detail. By the time you finish this lesson you will understand how

- SMARTDRV reduces disk read and write operations
- To install a SMARTDRV disk buffer
- To view SMARTDRV's status information
- To perform a few simple commands to reduce your chance of losing data

UNDERSTANDING THE SMARTDRV BUFFER

SMARTDRV is often called a disk cache. A *cache* is a fancy name for a storage location. Before winter, for example, squirrels store their nuts in a cache. Likewise, to reduce slow disk read and write operations, DOS can store the information read from or written to disk in a large cache in your computer's fast electronic memory. SMARTDRV's disk buffer normally resides in your PC's extended memory, as shown in Figure 54.1.

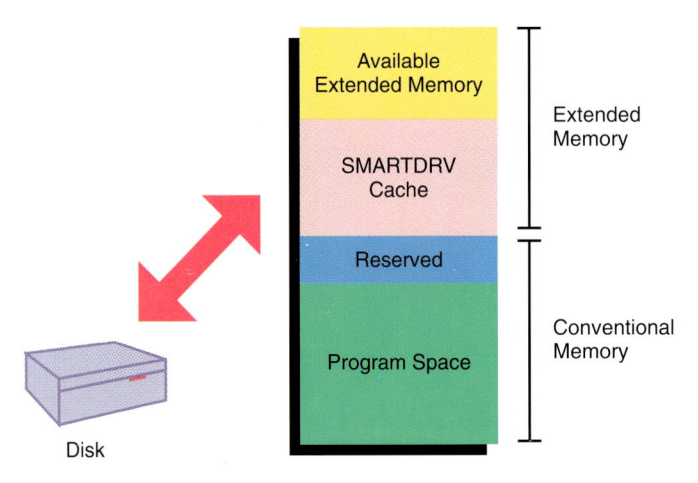

Figure 54.1 SMARTDRV's disk cache resides in the PC's extended memory.

54: Improving System Performance with SMARTDRV

Each time DOS reads information from disk, DOS places the information into the SMARTDRV cache. When a program later asks DOS to read information from disk a second time, DOS first checks the SMARTDRV cache to see if the desired information already resides in the computer's fast electronic memory. If the desired information is already in memory, DOS can provide the information to the program without having to perform a slow disk read operation. Thus, the program can receive the information must faster, improving your system performance. If the size of your SMARTDRV disk cache is very large (about 2Mb), DOS will often find the desired information in SMARTDRV's cache.

Why the SMARTDRV Buffer Normally Contains the Desired Information

To help improve its chance of finding the information your request next in its disk cache, SMARTDRV actually cheats a little bit. Assume, for example, that a program asks DOS to read 2000 bytes from a file. When SMARTDRV reads the requested information, SMARTDRV will also read information that follows, normally 16Kb worth. Thus, if the program requests the next 3000 bytes in the file, SMARTDRV already has the requested information in its buffer.

SMARTDRV Reduces Disk Read and Write Operations

The SMARTDRV command allocates a portion of your extended memory for use as a large disk buffer. Each time DOS reads information from disk, it reads the information into the SMARTDRV disk cache. When a program later asks DOS to read additional information from disk, DOS will first check the SMARTDRV buffer to see if it has already read the desired information. If so, DOS can provide the information to the program without having to perform a slow disk read operation.

Invoking the SMARTDRV Command

Most users will invoke the SMARTDRV command from within their AUTOEXEC.BAT file ensuring that SMARTDRV is active each time their system starts. To invoke SMARTDRV from within your AUTOEXEC.BAT file, place a command similar to the following within the file:

```
C:\DOS\SMARTDRV
```

If you are using the upper memory area, as discussed in Lesson 38, DOS will automatically try to LOADHIGH the SMARTDRV command.

Note: Some disk controllers do not support SMARTDRV when you run Windows in 386 Enhanced mode unless you install SMARTDRV as a device driver using the CONFIG.SYS DEVICE entry:

```
DEVICE=C:\DOS\SMARTDRV.EXE   /DOUBLE_BUFFER
```

Rescued by DOS

If you are using a SCSI disk drive, check the documentation that accompanied your disk to determine if you must install the device driver. After you install the device driver, you can invoke SMARTDRV from within your AUTOEXEC.BAT file as previously discussed.

Specifying the Desired Buffer Sizes

When you invoke the SMARTDRV command for the first time (which normally occurs within your AUTOEXEC.BAT file), you can specify the desired buffer size. For example, the following command directs SMARTDRV to use a 4Mb cache:

```
C:\DOS\SMARTDRV   4096
```

If you don't use extended memory for a RAM drive, you might want to allocate most of your memory for SMARTDRV's use. When you do so, however, you might want to provide programs that use extended memory, such as Microsoft Windows, a chance to reduce the size of SMARTDRV's buffer so they can use more extended memory for their own use. The following command, for example, initially allocates a 4Mb disk cache. However, should a program such as Windows need to use extended memory, the program can reduce the size of the SMARTDRV buffer to 2Mb:

```
C:\DOS\SMARTDRV   4096   2048
```

If you do not specify sizes for the SMARTDRV buffer, SMARTDRV chooses its own sizes based on your computer's available memory. Table 54.1 lists SMARTDRV's default buffer sizes.

Available Extended Memory	Initial Buffer Size	Reduced Size
1Mb	1Mb	0Mb
2Mb	1Mb	256Kb
4Mb	1Mb	512Kb
6Mb	2Mb	1Mb
> 6Mb	2Mb	2Mb

Table 54.1 SMARTDRV's default buffer sizes.

How SMARTDRV Reduces Disk Write Operations

When a program directs DOS to write information to disk, DOS first writes the data to the SMARTDRV buffer and then to disk. In this way, should the program later want to read the information, the buffer already contains it. In addition, SMARTDRV supports a technique called *write-behind caching*. When you let SMARTDRV perform write-behind caching, DOS will write the disk information into the disk cache. SMARTDRV, in turn, will wait for the system to become

54: Improving System Performance with SMARTDRV

idle before it writes the information to disk. In this way, your program does not have to wait for the slow disk write operation to complete. Normally, SMARTDRV will write the information to disk as soon as the PC is not doing anything or when the program ends.

Unfortunately, many users, thinking the information has been recorded to disk, turn off their computers with the program still running. Thus, the information that was never written from the SMARTDRV buffer to disk was lost. Worse yet, some programs do not tell SMARTDRV to write its buffer to disk when they end. Thus, users who wait for the DOS prompt to appear briefly before turning off their computer lose data because the system has not been idle long enough for SMARTDRV to write information.

To prevent such errors from occurring, you have two choices. First, you can direct SMARTDRV not to perform write-behind caching by invoking SMARTDRV (for the first time) using the /X switch, as shown here:

```
C:\DOS\SMARTDRV  4096  2048  /X
```

Unfortunately, disabling write-behind caching will slightly decrease SMARTDRV's performance. As a solution, many users allow write-behind caching, but they always invoke SMARTDRV using the /C switch before they turn off their computer:

```
C:\> SMARTDRV  /C  <ENTER>
```

The /C switch directs SMARTDRV to writes its buffered output to disk.

Determining How Much SMARTDRV Helps Your Performance

Most users experience improved system performance the moment they start using SMARTDRV. To appreciate better how often SMARTDRV successfully locates data in its cache, invoke SMARTDRV from the DOS prompt as shown here:

```
C:\> SMARTDRV  /S  <ENTER>
Microsoft SMARTDrive Disk Cache version 5.0
Copyright 1991,1993 Microsoft Corp.

Room for     256 elements of   8,192 bytes each
There have been   21,805 cache hits
    and    3,503 cache misses

Cache size:  2,097,152 bytes
Cache size while running Windows:  2,097,152 bytes
```

Rescued by DOS

```
              Disk Caching Status
drive     read cache    write cache    buffering

  A:          yes            no            no
  B:          yes            no            no
  C:          yes            yes           no
Write behind data will be committed before command
prompt returns.

For help, type "Smartdrv /?".
```

In this case, in the past 25,308 disk read operations, SMARTDRV successfully found the desired information within its cache on 21,805 tries. Each time SMARTDRV experienced a *cache hit*, SMARTDRV eliminated a slow disk read operation.

What You Need to Know

In Lesson 55 you will learn how to double your disk's storage capacity using the DBLSPACE command. Before you continue with Lesson 55, however, make sure that you have learned the following:

- ☑ A cache is a storage location. A disk cache is a storage location in your computer's memory used to store information read from or written to disk.

- ☑ The SMARTDRV command lets you install a disk cache in your computer's extended memory. Most users invoke SMARTDRV from within their AUTOEXEC.BAT file.

- ☑ SMARTDRV lets you specify an initial buffer size, as well as a second size to which programs such as Windows can reduce the buffer size when they need to use extended memory.

- ☑ In addition to buffering data read from disk, SMARTDRV can buffer data being written to disk. When you let SMARTDRV perform write-behind caching, there will be a brief period of time when DOS thinks that it has successfully recorded information on disk, while the information still resides in your computer's memory. If you turn off the PC during this window of time, the information in memory will be lost.

- ☑ To reduce the possibility of lost data due to write-behind caching, you can turn off write-behind caching by invoking SMARTDRV using the /X switch, or you can direct SMARTDRV to write buffered information to disk by invoking SMARTDRV with the /C switch.

Section Eleven

Increasing Your Disk Capacity

There is a hitherto unwritten law that states:

Users will find a way to use up all of the available disk space.

With that law in mind, DOS 6 provided the DBLSPACE command, which lets you double the storage capacity of your disk by storing your files in a compressed format. When DOS 6 was first released, some users experienced problems with DBLSPACE that caused the users to lose the information stored on their disks! Thus, the original DBLSPACE command received a lot of negative publicity. In fairness to Microsoft, however, it is important to note that millions of users successfully used DBLSPACE to double the storage capacities of their disk. With the release of DOS 6.2, Microsoft has addressed the problems that caused the errors. However, as you read in Section 9, if you don't back up your files on a regular basis, the information you store on your disk is always at risk. If you perform backups on a regular basis, you should feel comfortable using DBLSPACE to increase your disk's storage capacity.

Lesson 55 Understanding DBLSPACE

Lesson 56 Installing DBLSPACE

Lesson 57 Removing DBLSPACE

Lesson 58 DBLSPACE and Floppies

Rescued by DOS

Lesson 55

Understanding the DBLSPACE Command

As programs become more powerful, they also grow in size. Likewise, the files the programs create are becoming larger as they integrate text, graphics, and even multimedia sound clips. To help users keep up with never-ending disk space demands, DOS has provided the DBLSPACE command, which lets you double a disk's storage capacity. For example, if you are using a 30Mb hard disk, DBLSPACE will create a 60Mb disk. Likewise, using DBLSPACE, a 100Mb hard disk becomes 200Mb. The DBLSPACE command doubles the size of your hard disk by storing the files on your disk in a compressed format. This lesson introduces the DBLSPACE command. By the time you finish this lesson you will understand

- How DBLSPACE doubles your disk capacity
- How you can use compressed disks

The DBLSPACE command was originally introduced with DOS 6.0. Before you compress your disk, you should first upgrade to DOS 6.2. Microsoft has made several key enhancements to DBLSPACE since DOS 6.0 that will protect the files you store on your disk. If you are currently using DBLSPACE with DOS 6.0, you should immediately upgrade to DOS 6.2.

UNDERSTANDING DISK COMPRESSION

The DBLSPACE command doubles the storage capacity of your disk by storing your files in a compressed format. When DOS stores information on your disk, the disk actually records a series of 1s and 0s. Assume, for example, your disk has recorded these 15 1s and 0s: 111110000011111. To compress the information on your disk, DBLSPACE looks for repeated patterns such as this. In this case, DBLSPACE could record the numbers using a code that states: five 1s, followed by five 0s, followed by five 1s. Using such a code, DBLSPACE can reduce the amount of information that must be recorded for each file. In this way, each file consumes less disk space, creating the illusion that your disk's capacity has actually doubled. Depending on the information stored on your disk, you might find that DBLSPACE cannot quite double your disk's storage capacity, or you might find that DBLSPACE has more than doubled the amount of information your disk can store.

HOW DBLSPACE WORKS

When you use DBLSPACE to compress a disk, DBLSPACE actually divides your disk into two parts, a compressed drive and an uncompressed drive, as shown in Figure 55.1.

55: Understanding the DBLSPACE Command

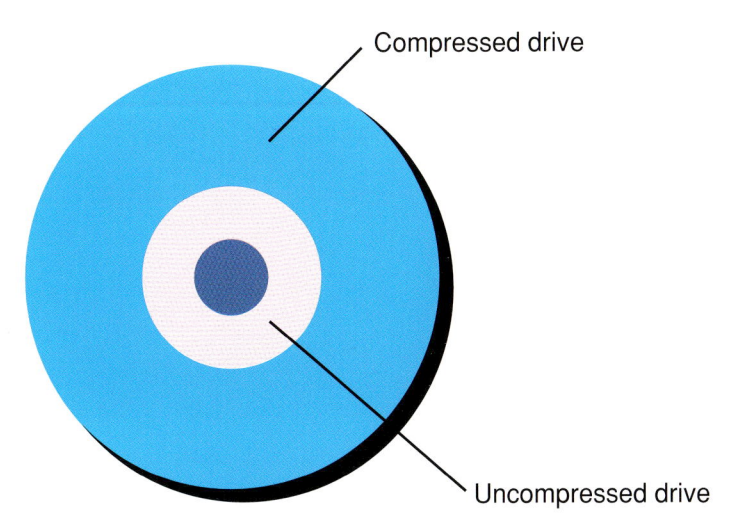

Figure 55.1 DBLSPACE divides a disk into a compressed and uncompressed drive.

The compressed drive is the drive that contains your files in the compressed format. If you compress drive C, for example, you will use the drive letter C to access your compressed files. After you compress a drive, you will use the drive just as you always, have, with the exception that the drive can now hold much more information. Most users do not need to worry about the uncompressed drive. Normally, DBLSPACE will assign an unused drive letter such as G or H to the uncompressed drive (don't worry about updating LASTDRIVE—DBLSPACE does it automatically). The uncompressed drive stores information about the files on the compressed drive. In general, you can use your disks without every worrying about the uncompressed drive. However, should you encounter the strange drive letter within the shell or Microsoft Windows, you will know why the drive exists.

UNDERSTANDING COMPRESSED AND UNCOMPRESSED DRIVES

When you use DBLSPACE to compress a drive, DBLSPACE actually divides your disk into two parts: a compressed drive and an uncompressed drive. The compressed drive contains your files in the compressed format. You will use the same drive letter that you have used in the past to access the compressed drive. For example, if you compress the files on drive C, you will the drive letter C to access the files in future. The uncompressed drive stores information about the compressed files. You will normally never use the uncompressed drive. DBLSPACE will assign an unused drive letter such as G or H to the uncompressed drive. If you work with the DOS Shell or Microsoft Windows, you might encounter an uncompressed drive letter. The uncompressed drive contains files that lets DOS access your compressed files. Never delete a file from the uncompressed drive whose purpose you do not fully understand. If you delete the wrong file, you might lose all the information stored on your compressed drive!

235

Determining Your Disk Use

In Lesson 56 you will learn how to compress a disk using DBLSPACE. After you compress the disk, you can determine the amount of available disk space, the ratio by which DBLSPACE was able to increase your disk capacity, and drive letter assigned to the uncompressed disk by invoking DBLSPACE using the /INFO switch, as shown here:

```
C:\> DBLSPACE   /INFO   <ENTER>
DoubleSpace is examining drive C.

Compressed drive C is stored on uncompressed drive H in
the file H:\DBLSPACE.000.

        Space used:                 96.05 MB
        Compression ratio:          1.8 to 1

        Space free:                 246.41 MB
        Est. compression ratio:     2.0 to 1
        Fragmentation:                    0%

        Total space:                342.45 MB
```

What You Need to Know

In Lesson 56 you will learn how to compress a disk with the DBLSPACE command. Before you continue with Lesson 56, however, make sure that you have learned the following:

- ☑ If you are currently using DOS 6.0 and you want to compress your disk, you should first upgrade to DOS 6.2. Microsoft has added several safety features to the 6.2 DBLSPACE command.

- ☑ After you successfully compress the files on your disk, you should immediately perform a full-disk backup, as discussed in Lesson 45.

- ☑ DBLSPACE creates an illusion that your disk capacity has increased by storing the files on your disk in a more compact form.

- ☑ When you compress a disk, DBLSPACE actually creates two drives on the disk: a compressed drive that contains your compressed files and an uncompressed drive that contains information DBLSPACE later uses to access the compressed files. Your compressed drive will use the drive letter with which you normally work. The uncompressed drive will use a drive letter such as G or H.

- ☑ To determine specifics about a compressed drive, invoke DBLSPACE with the /INFO switch.

Lesson 56

Installing DBLSPACE on Your Hard Disk

Tthe DBLSPACE command lets you double your disk's storage capacity. In this lesson you will learn how to install DBLSPACE. By the time you finish this lesson you will understand

- How to double the storage capacity of your hard disk using DBLSPACE
- The purpose of the DBLSPACE device driver in your CONFIG.SYS file

BEFORE YOU INSTALL DBLSPACE

The DBLSPACE command doubles the storage capacity of your disk by storing your files in a compressed format. Before you install the DBLSPACE command, back up all the files on your disk using the MSBACKUP command, as discussed in Lesson 45. *Do not invoke the DBLSPACE command until you have backed up all the files on your disk.*

PERFORMING THE INSTALLATION

To double the storage capacity of your hard disk, invoke the DBLSPACE command from the DOS prompt as shown here:

```
C:\> DBLSPACE    <ENTER>
```

DBLSPACE will display a screen welcoming you to the installation, as shown in Figure 56.1.

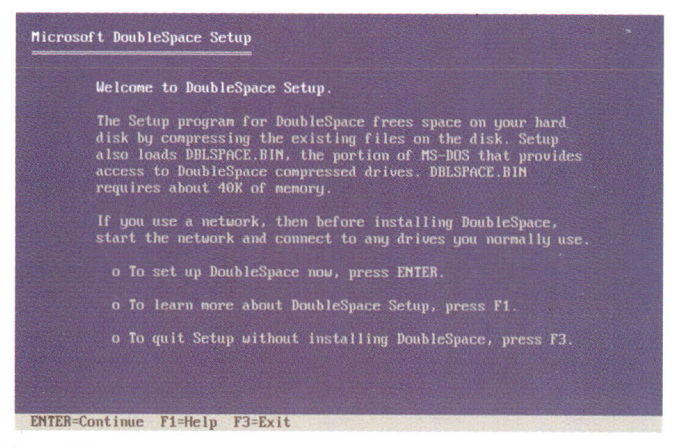

Figure 56.1 DBLSPACE's opening screen.

Rescued by DOS

Press ENTER to continue the installation. DBLSPACE will display a screen, similar to that shown in Figure 56.2, that asks you if you want to perform a custom or express setup.

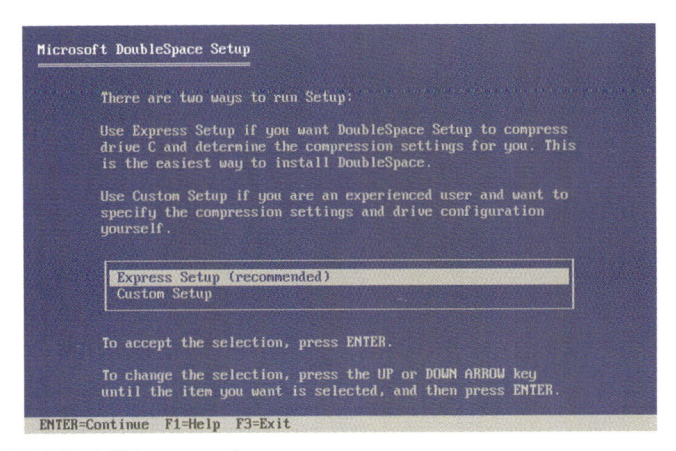

Figure 56.2 The DBLSPACE prompt for an express or custom setup.

Most users will want to perform an express setup. To do so, press ENTER. DBLSPACE will display a message box telling you to perform a backup operation before continuing. If you have performed a backup operation as previously discussed, continue the DBLSPACE setup. DBLSPACE will display a screen, similar to that shown in Figure 56.3, that tells you the amount of time the setup will require.

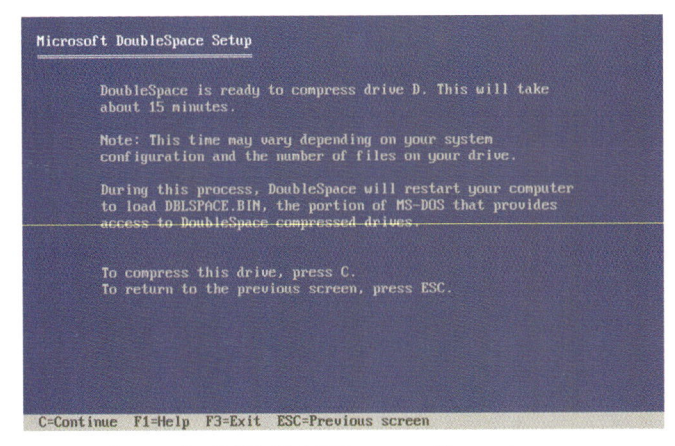

Figure 56.3 The amount of time the DBLSPACE setup will require.

1: What is DOS?

When you press ENTER to continue the installation, DBLSPACE will invoke the SCANDISK command, discussed in Lesson 52 to examine your disk's health before performing the disk compression. After SCANDISK completes, the installation will display a message stating that should your computer lose power during the disk compression, you need only restart your computer, and DBLSPACE will automatically continue the compression. When you press ENTER to continue the installation, DBLSPACE will display a screen that shows the percentage of the disk compressed and the amount of time until the compression is complete. When DBLSPACE has successfully compressed your disk, it will invoke the DEFRAG command, discussed in Lesson 53 to optimize the compressed disk. When the DEFRAG command completes, DBLSPACE will display a summary of the disk compression. Use this screen to determine the amount of disk space you have gained by compressing your files.

Understanding the DBLSPACE Device Driver

If you examine the contents of your CONFIG.SYS after installing DBLSPACE, you might encounter a DEVICEHIGH entry for the DBLSPACE device, as shown here:

```
DEVICEHIGH=C:\DOS\DBLSPACE.SYS /MOVE
```

The DBLSPACE device driver entry does not affect your system's ability to use compressed disk drives. Instead, the device driver entry simply moves the device driver software (installed into memory when your system starts) into the upper memory area, freeing up conventional memory for your program use.

What You Need to Know

In Lesson 57 you will learn how to decompress a disk with DBLSPACE. Before you continue with Lesson 57, however, make sure that you have learned the following:

- ☑ Never use DBLSPACE to compress a disk whose files you have not yet backed up.

- ☑ Compressing your disk with DBLSPACE is time consuming but easy. In general, you simply follow the messages DBLSPACE displays on your screen. DBLSPACE, in turn, will invoke the SCANDISK command to examine your disk's health, will then compress your disk, and will finally optimize the compressed disk with the DEFRAG command.

- ☑ The DBLSPACE installation might place a DEVICEHIGH entry in your CONFIG.SYS for the DBLSPACE.SYS device driver. The DBLSPACE.SYS device driver entry does not control whether or not your system can support compressed disks. Instead, the entry moves the device driver, which is automatically loaded when your system starts, from conventional to upper memory.

Lesson 57

Removing DBLSPACE to Decompress a Drive

When DBLSPACE was first released with DOS 6.0, many users complained because it was difficult to decompress a disk, restoring the disk to its previous disk capacity. With DOS 6.2, you can quickly decompress a disk by invoking DBLSPACE with the /UNCOMPRESS switch. However, before you can decompress a disk, in this way, you must have enough unused disk space to hold the expanded files. If you are currently using more than half of your compressed disk's capacity, you will need to delete compressed files to free up disk space. This lesson examines how to remove DBLSPACE from your disk with the DOS 6.2 DBLSPACE /UNCOMPRESS switch. By the time you finish this lesson you will understand how to

- Determine if your disk can be uncompressed without deleting or removing files
- Decompress a disk with the /UNCOMPRESS switch, available with DBLSPACE in DOS 6.2

DECOMPRESSING A DISK WITH /UNCOMPRESS

Before you can decompress a DBLSPACE disk, you must have enough free space on the disk to hold the expanded files. If you do not have sufficient disk space, DBLSPACE will display an error message similar to the following:

```
DoubleSpace cannot uncompress drive C because there is
not enough space on drive H to hold all of the
uncompressed files.

To uncompress drive C, you must remove at least
1,762,304 bytes of files from either drive.
```

Should an error message similar to this appear on your screen, you must remove the files from the disk before you can perform a decompress option. Examine the disk's contents to determine whether there are files you do not require and that you can simply delete. If you still don't have enough disk space to decompress the disk, copy large files to another disk and then delete them, to free up disk space.

57: Removing DBLSPACE to Decompress a Drive

In Lesson 58 you will learn how to compress floppy disks. Assuming you later want to decompress the floppy disk in drive A, for example, you would invoke DBLSPACE as shown here:

```
C:\> DBLSPACE  /UNCOMPRESS  A:  <ENTER>
```

When you decompress a disk, DBLSPACE performs many of the same operations it performed when you compressed the disk. For example, DBLSPACE will first run the SCANDISK command to examine the disk's health, as shown in Figure 57.1.

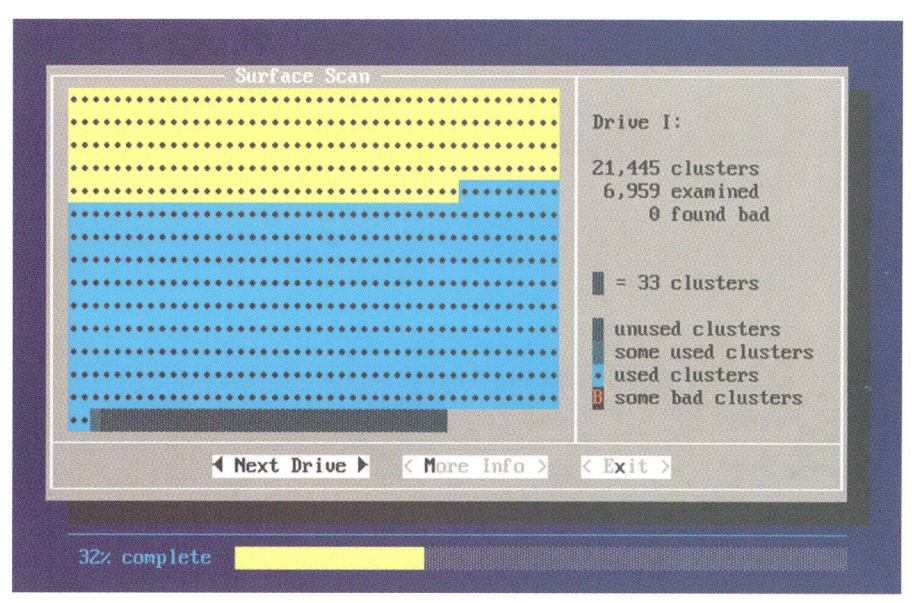

Figure 57.1 Running SCANDISK to verify a disk's health.

If SCANDISK is successful, DBLSPACE will start decompresssing the drive. After the files have been decompressed, DBLSPACE will invoke the DEFRAG command, discussed in Lesson 53 to optimize the disk. After DEFRAG completes, DBLSPACE will automatically display the DOS prompt, and your disk will be decompressed.

DECOMPRESSING YOUR DISK IN DOS 6.0

If you are using DBLSPACE and DOS 6.0, it is possible, but not trivial to decompress your hard disk by performing a series of backup and format operations. However, such operations should only be performed by a very experienced user. If you really want to decompress your hard disk, I strongly recommend that you first upgrade to DOS 6.2 and then use the DBLSPACE /UNCOMPRESS switch. As previously discussed, Microsoft has made many improvements in the new DBLSPACE command. Using the 6.2 /UNCOMPRESS switch, you can easily decompress your disk, assuming that you have sufficient disk space to hold the expanded files.

WHAT YOU NEED TO KNOW

In Lesson 58 you will learn how to compress floppy disks with DBLSPACE. Before you continue with Lesson 58, however, make sure that you have learned the following:

- ☑ If you need to decompress a disk's contents, invoke DBLSPACE (in DOS 6.2) with the /UNCOMPRESS switch.

- ☑ Before you can decompress a disk's contents, the disk must have sufficient space available to hold the expanded files. You might need to move or delete files before you can perform the operation.

- ☑ If you are using DOS 6.0, it is possible, but difficult, to remove DBLSPACE from your hard disk. If you really need to remove DBLSPACE, you should first upgrade to DOS 6.2 and then use the DBLSPACE /UNCOMPRESS switch.

Lesson 58

DBLSPACE and Floppy Disks

After you install DBLSPACE on your hard disk, you can use DBLSPACE to compress 1.2Mb and 1.44Mb floppy disks, doubling each disk's storage capacity. If you need to share the floppy disks with another user, that user must have DBLSPACE installed and running on their disk as well. As you will learn in this lesson, compressing a floppy disk with DBLSPACE is very easy. By the time you finish this lesson you will understand how to

- Compress a floppy disk with DBLSPACE
- Mount and unmount a compressed floppy disk

COMPRESSING A FLOPPY DISK

You must have DBLSPACE installed on your hard disk before you can compress a floppy. In addition, you can only compress 1.2Mb and 1.44Mb floppy disks. Further, before you can compress a floppy, the floppy must have at least 0.5Mb (512Kb) of available disk space. If you try to compress a floppy with insufficient disk space, DBLSPACE will display the error message:

```
Drive A does not have enough free space to allow it to
be compressed.
Compressing a drive requires 0.50 MB of free space.
```

To compress a floppy disk in drive A, issue the following DBLSPACE command:

```
C:\> DBLSPACE  /COMPRESS  A:  <ENTER>
```

Compressing a floppy disk using DBLSPACE is actually very similar to compressing your hard disk. Thus, DBLSPACE will first run the SCANDISK command to examine the health of your floppy disk, as shown in Figure 58.1. If SCANDISK successfully examines your disk, DBLSPACE will immediately start, displaying a screen that tells you how long the compression will require. When the compression is complete, DBLSPACE will automatically return you to the DOS prompt. Your compressed floppy disk is ready for use.

Rescued by DOS

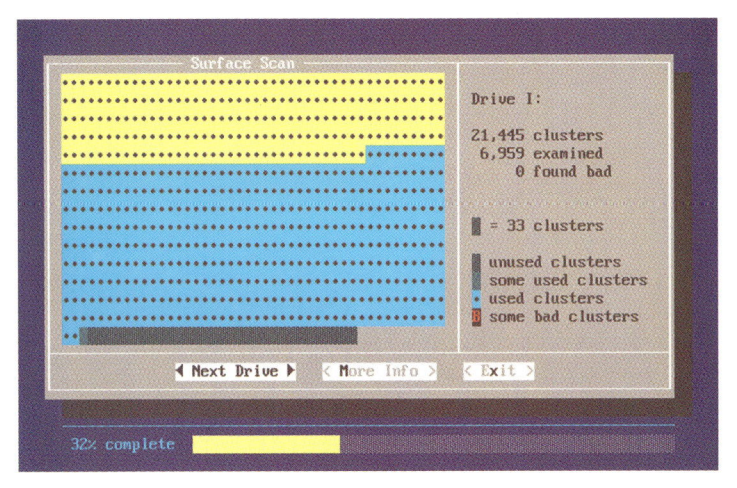

Figure 58.1 Using SCANDISK to verify a floppy disk's health.

Using Compressed Floppy Disks

By default, DBLSPACE (in DOS 6.2) uses the /AUTOMOUNT:1 switch, which directs DBLSPACE to check each floppy disk you insert to determine whether the floppy contains a compressed disk. If the disk is compressed, DBLSPACE will automatically mount the compressed disk so it is ready for use. In this way, you can insert and remove compressed and noncompressed floppy disks in and out of the drive without regard for each floppy disk's contents. In other words, DBLSPACE makes using your compressed floppy disks very easy.

Should you give another user who is not running DBLSPACE a compressed floppy disk, the user will find a file named READTHIS.TXT when he or she performs a directory listing of the floppy, as shown here:

```
C:\> DIR  A:   <ENTER>

 Volume in drive G has no label
 Volume Serial Number is 115E-10D6
 Directory of A:\

READTHIS TXT            441 10-09-93   9:16a
       1 file(s)             441 bytes
                                0 bytes free
```

58: DBLSPACE and Floppy Disks

If the users uses the TYPE command to display the file's contents, the user will learn that the disk is compressed, as shown here:

```
C:\> TYPE  A:READTHIS.TXT  <ENTER>

This disk has been compressed by Microsoft DoubleSpace.
To gain access to the contents of this disk, your com-
puter must be running DoubleSpace.

To make this disk's contents accessible, change to the
drive that contains it, and then type the following at
the command prompt:

   DBLSPACE/MOUNT

(If this file is located on a drive other than the
drive that contains the compressed disk, then the disk
has already been mounted).
```

As you can see, the file informs the users that they must be running DBLSPACE before accessing the compressed files and that they then must mount the floppies as discussed next.

MOUNTING AND UNMOUNTING COMPRESSED DISKS

You have learned that, when you use the /AUTOMOUNT:1 switch, DBLSPACE will automatically check each floppy disk you insert into a drive to determine if the floppy contains compressed files. If the floppy is a compressed disk, DBLSPACE will automatically mount the disk as such. As you learned in Lesson 55, when you compress a disk, DBLSPACE only compresses part of your disk, creating a compressed and uncompressed drive on each disk. In the simplest sense, *mounting* a disk directs DBLSPACE to use the compressed drive. If you are not using the DBLSPACE /AUTOMOUNT switch, you can mount a compressed disk in drive A by invoking DBLSPACE with the /MOUNT switch, as shown here:

```
C:\> DBLSPACE   /MOUNT   A:   <ENTER>
```

When you mount a compressed drive, DBLSPACE assigns the normal drive letter to the compressed drive and a different drive letter to the uncompressed drive (don't worry about updating your LASTDRIVE setting in CONFIG.SYS—DBLSPACE takes care of that automatically). To determine the drive letter assignments, you can invoke DBLSPACE using the /LIST switch, as shown here:

Rescued by DOS

```
C:\> DBLSPACE   /LIST   <ENTER>
Drive   Type                 Total Free   Total Size   CVF Filename

  A     Compressed floppy disk  2.64 MB     2.64 MB    G:\DBLSPACE.000
  C     Compressed hard drive 246.42 MB   342.45 MB    H:\DBLSPACE.000
  D     Available for DoubleSpace
  E     Available for DoubleSpace
  F     Available for DoubleSpace
  G     Floppy drive            0.00 MB     1.39 MB
  H     Local hard drive        2.36 MB   199.24 MB

DoubleGuard safety checking is enabled.
Automounting is enabled for drive(s) A
```

If you no longer want to work with a compressed drive, you can unmount the drive, as shown here:

```
C:\> DBLSPACE   /UNMOUNT   A:   <ENTER>
```

When you unmount a drive, DBLSPACE will resume using the standard drive letter for the uncompressed drive, and your compressed files will be unavailable.

WHAT YOU NEED TO KNOW

Congratulations! You have come a long way since you first turned on your PC in Lesson 1. Before you continue on your DOS journey, make sure that you have learned the following:

- ☑ DBLSPACE lets you compress 1.2Mb and 1.44Mb floppy disks. Before you can compress a floppy disk, you must have DBLSPACE installed on your hard disk.

- ☑ If you need to exchange compressed floppy disks with another user, that user must be running DBLSPACE as well.

- ☑ If try to access a compressed disk that is not yet mounted, you will encounter a file named READTHIS.TXT file that directs you to mount the floppy disk.

- ☑ If you use DBLSPACE with the /AUTOMOUNT:1 switch, DBLSPACE will automatically examine each floppy disk you insert in the drive to determine if the drive is compressed. If so, DBLSPACE will automatically mount the compressed drive.

- ☑ Using the DBLSPACE /MOUNT and /UNMOUNT switches, you can mount and unmount a compressed drive as you require.

Index

$G (metacharacter), 90
$P (metacharacter), 90
* (as wildcard character), 30-32
. (current directory), 49-50
.. (parent directory), 49-50
<DIR>, 52-53
? (as wildcard character), 32-35
@ECHO OFF, 70-72
    problems with, 74-76

A

Abort, Retry, Fail (error message), 37-39
ALT key combinations, 100
ASCII
    files, 30
        printing, 109-10
asterisk (as wildcard character), 30-32
AUTOEXEC.BAT
    adding commands, 90-92
    editing, 89-90
    protecting, 92
    understanding, 89
    viewing, 88-89

B

backups
    catalog files, 201-2
    disk, full, 194-98
        performing, 196-98
        preparing for, 194-96
    file, 190
    incremental, 198-200
        performing, 199-200
        preparing for, 198-99
    MSBACKUP, using, 190-93
    policy for, creating, 205-7
    restoring files from, 201-4
        multiple backups, 204
        specific files, 202-4
basename (of filenames), 22
basic input and output system, *see* BIOS
batch files, 65-69
    blank lines, displaying, 73
    branching to locations in, 86-88
    commands in, 73-77
        @ECHO OFF, 70-72
        ECHO, 72-73
        GOTO, 87-88
        IF, 81-82
        PAUSE, 73-74
        REM, 76-77
    creating, 66-68
    decisions in, making, 81-89
    explaining with remarks, 76-77
    messages in
        controlling, 69-73
        displaying, 72-73, 74
        suppressing, 69-72
    naming, 68
    parameters in
        testing, 83-86
        understanding, 77-80
        using multiple, 80-81
    pausing execution, 73-74
    problems with
        @ECHO OFF, 74-76
        PAUSE, 74-76
    testing
        failed conditions, 86
        parameter values, 83-86
        program success, 82-83
    understanding basics, 65-66
BIOS, 154
booting DOS
    AUTOEXEC.BAT, 89
    cold boot, 132
    CONFIG.SYS
        bypassing, 141-42
        processing specific entries from, 142-44
    description of, 2-4
    warm boot, 132
BREAK, 134
brightness, monitor, 104
BUFFERS, 134
bytes, 117

C

cache, 228
    hit, 234
caching, write-behind, 231
catalog files, backup, 201-2
CGA resolution, 103
CHDIR, 47-49
clear screen command, 15
CLS, 15
CMOS
    battery, 16
    errors, troubleshooting, 16
    memory, 152-54
cold boot, 132
COM1 printer port, 109
command path, 60-64
    defining, 63-64
    directories to include in, 64

using, 62-63
commands, *see DOS command(s)*
compression, disk, 234
computer system
    desktop, 93-94
    hardware, 93-96
        common PC components, 93-94
        disk drives, 115-18
        floppy disks, 118-26
        hard disks, 124-28
        keyboard, 97-101
        monitor, 101-5
        mouse, 104-7
        ports, 111-17
        printers, 107-11
    notebook, 94
    tower, 93-94
    turning
        off, 12-13
        on, 7
CONFIG.SYS
    bypassing (at boot time), 141-42
    creating, 131-32
    editing, 130-31
    entries, 133-37
        assigning values, 133-35
        device drivers, 135
        table of, 135-37
    locating, 129-30
    making changes effective, 132
    processing
        control of, 141-44
        specific entries, 142-44
    understanding, 129-33
contrast, monitor, 104
conventional memory, 149-50
copying files, 26-27
    using pathnames, 55-56
CPU, 94
crash, hard disk, 127-28
CTRL key combinations, 100
current directory, 42-43, 47-49
current drive, 36-37
cursor control keys, 98-99
cylinders, 126

D

DATE, 15-16
DBLSPACE, 234-37
    /INFO switch, 236-37
    /UNCOMPRESS switch, 240-41
    decompressing drives, 240-42
        under DOS 6.0, 241-42
    disk use, determining, 236-37
    how it works, 234-36
    purpose of, 7
DBLSPACE (DOS command)
    device drivers, 239
    floppy disks, use with, 243-47

compressing, 243-44
    mounting, 245-47
    unmounting, 246-47
installation, 237-40
    before performing, 237
    performing, 237-39
    preparation for use, 237
DEFRAG, 224-27
deleting
    directories, 59-60
    files, 28-29
    using pathnames, 57
DELTREE, 59-60
density of floppy disks, 120
desktop computer, 93-94
DEVICE, 134
device drivers, 138-42
    installing, 139-41
    understanding, 138-39
DEVICEHIGH, 134, 168
DIR, 24-26, 44-46
    /p switch, 26-27
    /s switch, 57
    /w switch, 27
    controlling output of, 26-27
directories, 40-46, 45-54
    . (current directory), 49-50
    .. (parent directory), 49-50
    creating, 45-47
    current, 42-43, 47-49
    deleting, 59-60
    displaying files in, 44-46
    names of, 43-44
    organizing files using, 40-42
    parent, 49-50
    pathnames, 44, 54-58
    recognizing (in file listings), 52-53
    relative names, 51-52
    removing, 50-51
    root, 40
    selecting, 47-49
    subdirectories, displaying, 57
    viewing graphically (using TREE), 57-59
disk compression, 234
disk crash, 127-28
disk drive(s)
    capacity, checking, 116-17
    care of, 117-18
    changing between, 36-37
    current drive, 36-37
    decompressing, 240
    identifying, 34-35, 115-16
    letters (as drive names), 35-36
        filenames, using with, 39-40
    names of, using, 35-36
    SCANDISK
        checking with, 221-23
        correcting errors found by, 223-24
    storage of information, 116-17
    unformatting, 217-23

Index

working with files on other, 34-40
disk operating system, 2
DOS
    as entry in CONFIG.SYS, 134
    AUTOEXEC.BAT, use of, 89
    booting, 2-4, 89
        cold boot, 132
        warm boot, 132
    description of, 2-4
    environment, 91-92
    error messages
        Abort, Retry, Fail, 37-39
        troubleshooting, 16-17
    extended memory use, 155
    extended memory, use of, 158
    help on commands, 17-20
    high memory area (loading DOS into), 160
    memory
        expanded, 164
    memory location of, 160-61
    purpose of, 4-5
    recognizing, 7-9
    starting, 2-4, 89
        errors, troubleshooting, 16
    storage of information, 116-17
    switching between programs, 187-88
    versions, 6-7
    wildcard characters in, 30-36
    Windows, relationship to, 5-6
DOS 6.0
    decompressing drives under, 241-42
DOS command(s), 15-17
    @ECHO OFF, 70-72
    CHDIR, 47-49
    CLS, 15
    DATE, 15-16
    DBLSPACE, 234-37, 240, 243-47
    DEFRAG, 224-27
    DELTREE, 59-60
    DIR, 24-26, 44-46, 57
    ECHO, 72-73
    ECHO OFF, 70-72
    HELP, 17-20
    MEM, 147-49, 156, 160-61
    MKDIR, 45-47
    MSAV, 209-12
    MSBACKUP, 190-93
    PATH, 90, *see also* command path
    PRINT, 109-10, *166*
    PROMPT, 5, 8-9, 90
    RMDIR, 50-51
    SCANDISK, 221-24
    SMARTDRV, 90-92, 228-34
    TIME, 16-17
    TREE, 57-59
    TYPE, 30-31
    UNDELETE, 213-16
    UNFORMAT, 217-23
    VSAFE, 211-12

DOS Shell, 174-78
    description of, 5
    directories
        selecting, 176-77
        working with, 180-82
            `creating`, 181-82
            `deleting`, 181-82
    disk drives, changing, 176
    display, changing, 182-83
    DOS comands, running, 12
    exiting, 177
    files
        two or more, 179-80
        working with, 178-79
    menus
        adding your own options, 185-86
        main, 177
        mouse use with, 176
        using, 175-76
    other programs, starting, 9-12
    programs, running, 183-86
        file list, from, 183-84
        Main menu, from, 184-85
        Run Option (File menu), using, 183
    starting, 174-75
    task list, 187-88
        disabling, 187-88
        enabling, 187-88
        example use of, 188
dot matrix printers, 107-8
    compared to laser printers, 108
dot pitch, 104
double density, 120
double-click (mouse), 106
DRIVPARM, 134

E

ECHO, 72-73
ECHO OFF, 70-72
EGA resolution, 103
EMM386.EXE, 164, 167
environment, DOS, 91-92
error messages, DOS
    Abort, Retry, Fail, 37-39
    troubleshooting, 16-17
executable files
    executing, 61-62
    understanding, 60-62
expanded memory, 152, 162-65
    programs using, 164
    understanding, 162-64
extended memory, 150-51, 154-58
    amount in system, determining, 155
    device drivers in, 155-56
    DOS use of, 155, 158
    understanding, 154-55
    usage, displaying, 156
    using, 156-58

extensions of filenames, 21-22

F

FCBS, 134
filenames, 21-24
    basename, 22
    characters allowed in, 22-23
    extensions of, 21-22
files, 21-27
    ASCII, 30
    batch, *see batch files*
    contents of, displaying, 29-31
    copying, 26-27
    deleted, recovering, 213-16
    deleting, 28-29
    executable, understanding, 60-62
    fragmented, correcting, 224-27
    fundamental operations on, 26-31
    groups of, working with, 30-37
    listing, 24-26, *see also DIR*
    names of, 21-24
        wildcards in, 30-36
    on other disk drives, 34-40
    renaming, 27-28
FILES (as entry in CONFIG.SYS), 133-34
floppy disk(s), 118-26
    activation light, 121
    capacities, 120-21
    density of, 120
    description of, 118
    drives
        identifying, 115-16
    formatting, 124-26
    labeling, 122
    sizes of, 118-20
    surfaces, description of, 121-22
    write-protecting, 122-24
floppy disks
    compressing, 243-44
formatting floppy disks, 124-26
fragmented files, 224-27
    correcting, 226-27
    detecting, 226-27
    occurance of, reasons for, 224-26
function keys, 99-100

G

gigabyte, 124
GOTO, 87-88
graphical interface, 9

H

hard copy, 95
hard disk(s), 124-28
    capacity, checking, 124-26
    crash, 127-28
    drive letters, 126-27
    partitions, 126-27
    protecting, 222-23
    SCANDISK
        checking with, 221-23
        correcting errors found by, 223-24
    unformatting, 217-23
hard disks
    decompressing, 240-42
hardware
    common PC components, 93-94
    disk drives, 115-18
    floppy disks, 118-26
    hard disks, 124-28
    keyboard, 97-101
    monitor, 101-5
    mouse, 95, 104-7
    ports, 111-17
    printer, 94-95, 107-11
    system unit , view inside of, 95-96
help on DOS commands, 17-20
high density, 120
high memory area, 151-52, 158-62
    loading DOS into, 160
    understanding, 158-60

I

icons, 6
IF, 81-82
INCLUDE, 134
incremental backups, 198-200
INSTALL, 134
interface, user, *see user interface*
interlacing, 103

K

keyboard
    cursor control keys, 98-99
    function keys, 99-100
    key combinations (CTRL and ALT), 100
    notebook key types, 97-98
    numeric keypad, 99
    QWERTY, 98
    standard keys, 97
        backspace, 98
        capslock, 98
        shift, 98
        using, 98

L

laser printers, 107-8
    compared to dot matrix, 108
LASTDRIVE, 134
LOADHIGH, 168-70
LPT1 (printer port), 108-9

Index

M

megabytes, 117
MEM, 147-49
    /c switch, 147-49
    DOS, determining location of, 160-61
    extended memory, displaying, 156
MemMaker, 170-72
    changes to files, reviewing, 171-72
    running, 170-71
    when to run, 171-72
memory bus, 162
memory, computer
    amount in system, determining, 147
    loading programs into, 146-47
    MemMaker, configuring with, 170-72
    types of, 149-55
        BIOS, 154
        CMOS, 152-54
        conventional, 149-50
        expanded, 152
        extended, 150-51
        high memory area, 151-52
        page, 152, 162
        ROM, 154
        upper, 152
    understanding, 145-49
    usage, displaying, 147-49
memory-resident program, 166
MENUDEFAULT, 134
MENUITEM, 134
metacharacters, 90
Microsoft Windows relationship to DOS, 5-6
MKDIR, 45-47
monitor, 101-5
    brightness, 104
    contrast, 104
    resolution, 101-2
    video card, 102-4
mouse, 104-7
    clicks, 106
    double-clicks, 106
    drivers, 104
    pointer, 95
    ports, 116
    use of, 104-6
MOUSE.COM, 166
MSAV, 209-12
MSBACKUP, 190-93
    full disk backups, 194-98
    incremental backups, 198-200
    restoring files, 201-4
multisynch, 103

N

notebook computer, 94
    keyboard key types, 97-98

    mouse, 106-7
    trackball, 106-7
numeric keypad, 99
NUMLOCK, 134

O

on line button (for printers), 110-11

P

page (of memory), 152, 162
parallel ports, 114-16
partitions, 126-27
PATH, 90, *see also command path*
pathnames, 44, 54-58
    copying or moving files using, 55-56
    deleting files using, 57
    renaming files using, 57
    understanding complete, 54-56
PAUSE, 73-74
    problems with, 74-76
ports, computer, 111-17
    common, 111-12
    mouse, 116
    parallel, 114-16
    serial, 112-14
    video, 112
POST, *see power-on self-test*
power-on self-test, 7
    troubleshooting, 15-16
PRINT, 109-10
    memory-resident, *166*
printer(s), 107-11
    differences between (table of), 108
    on line button, 110-11
    ports, 108-9
    types of, 107-8
    using from applications, 111
PRN (printer port), 108-9
program(s), computer, *see also executable files*
    DOS Shell, running with, 183-86
    executing (or running), 15, 61-62
    expanded memory use, 164
    expanded memory, use of, 164
    loading into memory, 146-47
    location of, 13-15
    memory resident, 166
    names, 13
    switching between, 187-88
PROMPT, 90
    description of, 5
    recognizing, 8-9

Q

quad density, 120
question mark (as wildcard character), 32-35
QWERTY keyboard, 98

251

R

RAM, *see also memory, computer*
    understanding, 145-46
RAM drive, 156-58
RAMDRIVE.SYS, 158, 164
random access memory, *see RAM*
read-only memory, *see ROM*
refresh rate, 103
REM, 134
    remarks in batch files, 76-77
    remarks in CONFIG.SYS, 134-35
renaming files, 27-28
    using pathnames, 57
resolution, 101-2
    video card maximum (table of), 103
RMDIR, 50-51
ROM, 154
root directory, 40

S

SCANDISK, 221-24
    checking disks with, 221-23
    correcting errors found by, 223-24
    when to use, 224
self-test, power-on, 7
serial port(s), 112-14
    as printer ports, 109
    connectors, 109
SET, 134
SHELL, 134
shell program, 12
Shell, DOS, *see DOS Shell*
SMARTDRV, 90-92, 228-34
    buffer, 228-29
        sizes, 231
    determining performance increase, 233-34
    how it works, 231-33
    using, 229-31
software, understanding, 11-13
STACKS, 134
Startup, DOS
    errors, troubleshooting, 16
subdirectories
    displaying with DIR /S, 57
SUBMENU, 134
Super VGA resolution, 103
SWITCHES, 134
system unit
    description of, 94
    view inside of, 95-96
    working inside, 96

T

TIME, 16-17
tower computer, 93-94
trackball, 106-7

TREE, 57-59
troubleshooting techniques, 15-20
    CMOS errors, 16
    DOS
        error messages, 16-17
        Startup errors, 16
    power-on self-test, 15-16
    system configuration, 16
TSR, *see memory-resident programs*
TYPE (DOS command), 30-31

U

UMB (upper memory block), 167
UNDELETE, 213-16
    example use of, 213-15
    groups of files, using for, 214-15
    specific file, using for, 213-14
    success, improving chances for, 215-16
UNFORMAT, 217-23
    failure, reasons for, 223
    using, 217-22
upper memory, 152, 165-71
    device drivers in, 168
    DOS support of, 166-67
    understanding, 165-66
    using, 167-70
upper memory block, *see UMB*
user interface, definition of, 5

V

version number, DOS
    major, 7
    minor, 7
VGA resolution, 103
video card, 102-4
    maximum resolutions, 103
video ports, 112
viruses, computer, 209-12
    detecting with MSAV, 210-11
    erasing with MSAV, 210-11
    testing for, 209-12
        limitations, 211
        on floppy disks, 211
        VSAFE, using, 211-12
    understanding, 209-11
VSAFE, 211-12

W

warm boot, 132
wildcard character(s), 30-36
    *, 30-32
    ?, 32-35
    DEL command, using with, 36
Windows relationship to DOS, 5-6
write-behind caching, 231
write-protecting (floppy disks), 122-24